Starting Over in Eastern Europe

Starting Over in Eastern Europe: Entrepreneurship and Economic Renewal

Simon Johnson

and

Gary Loveman

Foreword by Jeffrey Sachs

Harvard Business School Press

Boston, Massachusetts

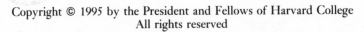

Printed in the United States of America
99 98 97 96 95   5 4 3 2 1

The paper used in this publication meets the requirements of the American National
Standard for Permanence of Paper for Printed Library Materials Z39.49-1984.

LIBRARY OF CONGRESS CATALOGING-IN-PUBLICATION DATA
Johnson, Simon.
   Starting over in Eastern Europe : entrepreneurship and economic
renewal / by Simon Johnson and Gary Loveman.
   p. cm.
   Includes bibliographical references and index.
   ISBN 0-87584-569-X
   1. Poland—Economic policy—1990- 2. Poland—Economic
conditions—1990- 3. Poland—Economic conditions—1981–1990.
4. Capitalism—Poland. 5. Europe, Eastern—Economic policy—1989-
6. Post-communism—Economic aspects—Europe, Eastern. I. Loveman,
G. (Gary) II. Title.
HC340.3.J64 1995
338.9438—dc20   94-43398
                                                            CIP

To my father
and the memory of my mother
Simon Johnson

To my wife, Kathy
Gary Loveman

Contents

Foreword

FIVE years after the start of Poland's radical reforms, Poland has one of the most dynamic market economies in Europe. Though still a poor country with many adverse legacies of forty-five years of communism, Poland has come further and faster than almost anybody imagined possible in 1989, when the first post-communist government took power. Poland's economic renewal is all the more remarkable because the last years of the communist regime were marked by encroaching hyperinflation, intense shortages, and social and political instability. Nonetheless, by 1993 Poland had the fastest growing economy in Europe. In 1994, industrial production increased by around 15 percent over the previous year. Commentators and policymakers in Western Europe now believe that Poland, as well as other dynamic reform countries in Central Europe, may be able to join the European Community by the year 2000.

As Simon Johnson and Gary Loveman describe in *Starting Over in Eastern Europe: Entrepreneurship and Economic Renewal*, Poland's dynamism is rooted in the economic freedom that was unleashed by the fall of communism and by Poland's radical market reforms. Taking us deep into the stories behind many of Poland's new private enterprises, Johnson and Loveman not only provide an engrossing account of Poland's economic rebirth, but also show in detail how economic freedom has translated into a revival of economic growth. Through their extensive surveys and case studies and their judicious marshaling of published data, the authors offer an estimable—and incomparable—record of the early years of Poland's economic reform. This study will prove invaluable on three levels: as a scholarly analysis of the early years of post-communist reforms; as an aid to policymakers in understanding the real sources of economic dynamism in the post-communist countries; and as a window for both corporations and individual business people on the new market economies of Central Europe.

Starting Over in Eastern Europe confirms the essential wisdom of Adam Smith; that economic wealth arises from the complex division of labor made possible by a market economy. Johnson and Loveman demonstrate, in case after case, that Poland's renewal started when energetic and talented individuals, freed from the heavy hand of communist controls, were able to identify and move into specialized niches in the marketplace by reorganizing existing enterprises or setting up new ones. Only profit-seeking entrepreneurs, not central planners, could discover that the future of the garment firm Prochnik lay in high-fashion garments for Poland's domestic market; that the Szczecin Shipyard could prosper in highly competitive world markets by focusing on production of 12,500-ton container ships; or that furniture-maker Styl France would become highly profitable by exporting high-quality, imitation antique wood furniture to France.

To put these entrepreneurial visions into place, Poland's new business managers required close contacts with suppliers and customers, direct access to world markets, freedom to travel, and opportunities to start and own private businesses—all of which had been ruthlessly suppressed under the traditional communist system and only haltingly permitted in the years of communist-led market reforms of the late 1980s. Through fascinating surveys and case studies, Johnson and Loveman demonstrate that Poland's entrepreneurial and managerial class of the early 1990s was initiated into the ways of the marketplace during the chaotic, partial reforms of the late communist period. But while those reforms allowed some space for personal initiative and economic freedom, the protomarkets of the communist era remained too unorganized, fragmented, and restricted to enable a real and sophisticated division of labor to emerge.

The Balcerowicz Plan of 1990 changed all of that, leading to the rapid emergence of Poland's new private sector. Price liberalization ended the crippling shortages of goods that had prevented private firms from getting the inputs they needed for production. Trade liberalization allowed the private firms to get necessary supplies from world markets, as well as to find new customers abroad. Legal reforms ended the restrictions on private ownership—such as prohibitions of joint-stock companies—that had hobbled the start-up of new enterprises. Tight credit policy also encouraged private ownership, ironically enough, by ending the destructive uncertainties of explosive inflation and forcing loss-making state enterprises to sell their equipment, real estate, and other assets, which were eagerly bought up by the new private firms.

The story told by Johnson and Loveman begins after these new policies had been put into place. Economic reforms were the instruments that empowered entrepreneurs and enabled the sophisticated division of labor that underpins economic prosperity. The reforms have not been the sole cause of wealth. As Johnson and Loveman state, Poland's emerging business community had to meet the challenge of capitalizing on the new opportunities—by choosing new product lines, organizing or reorganizing enterprises to face global competition, training new workers, and finding new supply lines and customers.

In addition to providing the freedom for entrepreneurship, the new markets offered high returns to those who could undertake the necessary business activities; they pushed existing enterprises (often with new private owners) to identify new managers who could react to market conditions; and they introduced a harsh struggle for survival among entrepreneurs and managers, leaving the unsuccessful ones with shrinking revenues and, eventually, business failure. Over and over, Johnson and Loveman's case studies reveal why central planners could never substitute for the marketplace in completing these exacting tasks. It is only highly decentralized activity by profit-driven business people, who constantly and aggressively ferret out market information, and who suffer the consequences of poor decisions, that leads to the desired results of growth, efficiency, and sophisticated specialization.

Starting Over in Eastern Europe also emphasizes that much economic renewal springs from the start-up of new firms rather than the reorganization of existing state enterprises through privatization. Poland's post-communist minister of finance, Leszek Balcerowicz, and his advisory team certainly appreciated the imperative of freeing private activity, and stressed early on the huge rewards to the Polish economy that would accrue. Still, the authors' emphasis on new private firms is a welcome balance to the scholarly literature on reform that has focused disproportionately on privatization. Johnson and Loveman's case studies underscore that *both* paths to private markets—startups and privatization—play key roles. Their wonderful case studies of Prochnik and Szczecin Shipyards show that even seemingly moribund or deeply wounded state firms can be revitalized through dynamic entrepreneurship, which conveys the direction and energy for successful restructuring. Private ownership plays an important role in such turnarounds of former state firms, either directly, when new owners of privatized firms choose new managers, or less directly, when the prospect of a future privatization spurs the management of a state-owned firm to initiate a turnaround.

The authors' description of the emergence of Poland's new commercial banking system is particularly significant in this regard. One piece of good, and somewhat surprising, news about the market reforms is that the absence of private capital did not pose a major barrier to entry of new firms. This was clearly true in the service sector, but apparently in much of manufacturing as well. Start-ups began with meager amounts of initial capital—often raised from family and friends—and grew extraordinarily rapidly through retained earnings. The commercial banking system itself was only a minor player in channeling capital to start-ups during the first years of reform, though its role has grown significantly in recent years. Johnson and Loveman provide a particularly interesting discussion of the rise of the new banking system, an area in which they did extensive interviewing and survey analysis.

In their concluding analysis, the authors wholeheartedly endorse the conception and implementation of the Balcerowicz Plan. What looked to some pessimists like wanton destruction of the old system turned out to be the "creative destruction" championed by Joseph Schumpeter. That is, the decline of the old sectors made way for the growth of the new sectors with remarkable speed and depth. Rather than judging the Balcerowicz Plan too harsh, they conclude that, if anything, the actual implementation was too soft, as evidenced by the program's failure to definitively eliminate Poland's inflation and by Poland's continued fiscal difficulties.

These conclusions will likely prove true for other countries in the region. As Johnson and Loveman point out, the fast reformers—countries such as the Czech Republic, Slovenia, and Estonia—emulated Poland's reform strategy and are now experiencing the same kind of economic turnaround and revived growth. We must hope that similar reforms will also be undertaken in the lagging countries, those that have yet to implement necessary economic reforms and therefore remain stuck in a no-man's land between central planning and the market. *Starting Over in Eastern Europe* should be read very widely by everyone—scholars, policymakers, businesspeople, and the public—concerned about the one-third of the world's population in formerly planned economies now attempting to unleash the energies of the market system.

—Jeffrey Sachs
Galen L. Stone Professor of Economics, Harvard University,
and economic advisor to post-communist governments of
Estonia, Kyrgyzstan, Poland, Russia, and Slovenia

Preface

IN January 1990 we asked two questions: How would the newly implemented Polish economic reform affect the private sector? and What role would new private firms play in the process of economic reform? Answers varied widely. Plenty of people—even some in the Ministry of Finance in Warsaw—thought that the policies were "too tough" and would, among other things, strangle private business in its infancy. But no one knew for sure, and there was no received theory or empirical evidence to serve as a guide.

Surely, we thought, it shouldn't be too difficult to find out. We'll collect the existing data, talk to some entrepreneurs, and make comparisons with small business development in the West. This research should lead to an interesting paper.

We quickly discovered government data and secondary sources to be of very limited use. At the same time, several early field trips revealed that entrepreneurs were amazingly willing to meet with us and to discuss all aspects of their businesses. Their stories were absolutely fascinating.

Of course these were only anecdotes, and the official statistics painted a picture of an economy sinking ever deeper into crisis. Our first paper, based on interviews with entrepreneurs, argued that entrepreneurship was bursting forth. Readers suspected that our sampled firms were not representative of the Polish experience in some important ways, and we agreed we had not captured the whole story. We needed to investigate a wider cross section of firms.

In 1990 no survey data existed on Polish private firms. If we wanted data, we had to organize our own surveys. Fortunately, our Polish entrepreneurial friends were willing to help out and obtained unique data from business directories, confirming our initial story; that the Polish private sector was booming.

Yet the macroeconomic reports from Poland continued to show a large fall in output, and in 1990–1991 there was a perception—in both the West and the East—that somehow "too much" reform had been undertaken or that something had been done "too quickly." We and others argued against this view on many grounds, but it persisted among many observers. In particular, however, our position that the private sector would drive a Polish economic recovery continued to meet with skepticism.

The objections have been numerous. "The private sector won't grow further; this is a one-time stock adjustment phenomenon," "It's only a small-scale trade and can't go any further," and "The private sector won't take off in manufacturing" were the three most common.

Attempting to address these points, we expanded our survey work, documented more carefully what had happened in particular firms, and tracked developments in chosen firms over time. We also investigated the transformation of state enterprises in some detail, looking for similarities to and differences from the transformation process clearly underway in the private sector.

As the work grew and as the results became stronger and more interesting, we realized that we would have to write a book. Although our articles (currently five) address various aspects of our work, only a book provides the scope necessary for a full examination of the process of restructuring and renewal at the enterprise level in Poland. Only a book allows us to marshal all the available evidence to show why private sector development is pervasive and has already fundamentally transformed the Polish economy.

Interestingly, by December 1994, as we are submitting our final manuscript, perceptions of Poland (by Poles and others) have begun to shift. The microeconomic transformation processes that we have been studying for the past five years have begun to show in the macroeconomic numbers. Recent Polish economic performance has been remarkable, exhibiting the fastest GDP and industrial production growth of any formerly communist country. Poland already has a strong claim to be the outstanding success story of Eastern Europe.

Yet the reasons for this success are often misunderstood. The most common argument is "the Polish circumstances are different" and, therefore, Poland has done well. They certainly are different, but this very same reason was proferred in the late 1980s to explain why Poland was doing less well than other countries. This book seeks a deeper, economic explanation for what happened in Poland.

Starting Over in Eastern Europe therefore focuses on the reasons for some of Poland's outstanding successes. The book should not, however, be construed as arguing that Poland has no problems. We are quite explicit, by example, about the real constraints on private sector development, particularly the provision of external finance. We also spend a great deal of time explaining why the restructuring of state enterprises is so difficult and has met with such limited success, and we review the disappointing progress achieved in large state enterprise privatization.

There are other important problems that we do not address here, but that we have discussed in other work. The government's budget remains precarious. The current deficit is small, just a few percentage points of GDP, but could destabilize the situation. Politically important lobbies compete for resources or tax breaks. Higher spending without higher revenues would stoke inflation. Higher taxation could choke private sector growth.

It is now apparent that inflation was not reduced to low levels in Poland. Inflation lingers in the 30 percent per year range, lower than in many post-communist countries but higher than in the Czech Republic or Hungary. As we discuss at length, this level is high enough to disrupt the development of financial intermediation—particularly loans from banks—needed to sustain private sector growth in the future.

Higher inflation means that interest rates remain high. The central bank has not been able to lower its refinance rate, a key benchmark rate, as much as it wanted. The interest rate now hovers just above 30 percent per year. Poland faces a tough choice: lower interest rates and risk higher inflation, or maintain high interest rates and risk slowed economic growth. In our analysis, bringing inflation to West European levels has distinct advantages.

The banking sector has been slow to make necessary adjustments. Too many bad loans were made after the reform program began. In particular, far too much was lent to state enterprises that had no prospects of being able to repay.

Unemployment is finally beginning to drop. In 1994 the rate of registered unemployment fell from 16.8 percent in August to 16.5 percent in September. Unemployment in major cities stands at around 8 to 12 percent, though it climbs to over 25 percent in depressed regions. Unemployment remains a serious problem, but it cannot be addressed through simply "raising demand." Rather, policies must be implemented that reduce payroll taxes and lower the costs of employing people, particularly in the private sector. As we also discuss in the book, particular effort must be devoted to high-unemployment regions that lie far from the rapidly growing large cities.

Poland has experienced tremendous success in private sector development, and we believe that the new private sector will remain the central mechanism for economic renewal and growth in Poland. Other aspects of the reform program have not gone so well. But reform is a continuing process and if this book helps academics, businesspeople, journalists, and policymakers better understand the nature of private business, the challenges facing enterprise managers, and the mechanisms for enhancing the role new private businesses can play in post-communist economic reform, then our efforts will have been worthwhile.

Acknowledgments

THE lengthy field work and survey evidence that constitute the core of this book were the result of generous guidance, assistance, and hospitality on the part of many people. Our access to
entrepreneurs and managers was provided by two of Poland's best
and most influential economists, Dr. Jan Szomberg and Dr. Janusz
Lewandowski, and was arranged through their Gdansk Institute for
Economics. Maciej Grabowski, a member of the Institute, served as
interpreter, logistician, and colleague on many of our trips, and his
efforts were instrumental to our ability to assemble a large sample of
field sites.

David Kotchen, who progressed from Harvard Business School
Research Associate to Fulbright Scholar in Poland to Harvard Business School MBA Class of 1995 during the life of this research project,
made invaluable data-collection and case-writing contributions. We
could not have completed this project without his remarkable skills
and his commitment to helping us understand economic reform. We
are also deeply grateful to Marzena Kowalska and Piotr Strzalkowski
for their participation and help in the creative process of developing
this book. Over the past five years we also learned a great deal about
Poland from Jeffrey Sachs and Anthony Levitas.

Material for this book, previous drafts, and papers on which this
book draws have benefited from the thoughtful comments provided

by Olivier Blanchard, Simon Commander, Fabrizio Coricelli, Alexander Dyck, Stephan Haggard, James Heskett, Paul Lawrence, Stan Lultman, Kalman Mizsei, Barry Stein, and Richard Walton.

Our employers have been both patient and generous in their support of our research. The Harvard Business School Division of Research has funded Gary Loveman's research and supported his efforts to introduce new materials from post-communist economies into the Harvard Business School curriculum. Gary is especially grateful to his research directors, Richard Tedlow, Richard Ruback, Jay Lorsch, and Warren McFarlan, for their willingness to provide resources for field research. Simon Johnson gratefully acknowledges financial support from the Fuqua School of Business, Duke University, the National Bureau of Economic Research, the United Nations Development Programme, and the World Bank. He also thanks the Ostekonomiska Institutet for its hospitality during fall 1994, providing the opportunity to reflect carefully on the final manuscript. Simon particularly thanks Bob Winkler and Wesley Magat, associate deans at the Fuqua School, for their continuous support and encouragement.

A number of people have helped us with data analysis and manuscript preparation. In particular, Philip Hamilton and Sarah Woolverton have provided expert computer and statistical assistance, and Donna Teague and Tina Nuñez carefully assembled much of the manuscript and related papers. Diane Brooks and Martha Synnott are always helpful, irrespective of where the call or e-mail originates. Nicholas Philipson has been a supportive and instructive editor throughout the process of completing the book. Despite the valuable efforts of so many talented people, this book undoubtedly contains errors of various kinds, which are the sole responsibility of the authors.

Finally, the researching and writing of this book has required sacrifice from Gary's wife, Kathleen Welsh, and children, Jeremy, Monica, and Kristine. Kathy has done a marvelous job of shielding their children from the disruption associated with his travels and has been a source of inspiration through her dedication to excellence in all she does. Gary hopes that this book comes close to meeting Kathy's high standards and that their children will come to understand and appreciate the historic events that drew their father to such a far away place.

Starting Over in Eastern Europe

CHAPTER 1

Introduction

Overview

On January 1, 1990, the Polish government launched an economic program that permanently altered both the Polish economy and the terms of all subsequent debate about reform in post-communist countries. This program, popularly known as the Balcerowicz Plan (after Leszek Balcerowicz, the country's first post-communist minister of finance), was implemented at a time of economic crisis. The new democratic, Solidarity-backed government faced inflation spiraling out of control, pervasive shortages of basic goods, and declining industrial production.

The Balcerowicz Plan aimed to deal with these problems through a combination of macroeconomic stabilization and liberalization measures known loosely as "shock therapy." Broadly speaking, the new economic policies aimed immediately to stop rapid inflation, eliminate shortages, make the country's currency convertible, and liberalize international trade. Remarkably, all these goals were achieved at the beginning of 1990.

The second, complementary, objective was to change the microeconomic structure of the Polish economy so as to create the basis for sustained growth. Most policymakers and analysts in and outside Poland considered privatization of state enterprises to be the central mechanism for microeconomic reform. Having achieved their macroeconomic stabilization and liberalization objectives, most reformers considered the establishment of private ownership and, consequently, profit-driven incentives to be the process that would ultimately lead to the restructuring of potentially viable enterprises and the liquidation and closure of others.

However, the challenges associated with the restructuring of state enterprises were formidable. The legacy of communism was roughly eight thousand state enterprises that were very large, highly vertically integrated, heavily concentrated in the manufacturing sector, and typically far below Western standards in efficiency, product quality, and production technology. Most large enterprises also operated a variety of social organizations, including schools, apartments, hospitals, and vacation facilities. Workers viewed these perks and their jobs in the same way—as entitlements. Unlike Western countries, Poland had an insignificant small business sector, and a very small percentage of economic activity was involved in services. Thus, as of 1990, Poland was poorly positioned for a market economy.

Because economic reform required a massive redistribution of people and capital, most analysts suggested that the success of reform hinged on whether macroeconomic stability and privatization would be sufficient to revitalize former state enterprises that would, in turn, stimulate economic growth and job creation. Four years of experience, however, have shown that the restructuring, privatization, and revitalization of large Polish state enterprises have not been the central mechanism for reform at the enterprise level. Instead, and much to the surprise of many policymakers, the emergence and growth of small private businesses have played by far the more important role in the necessary reallocation of labor and capital from activities driven by plans to productive employment driven by markets. Some simple figures are illustrative. From the mid-1980s to 1994, the private sector share of nonagricultural GDP rose from less than 10 percent to more than 40 percent, and continues to grow rapidly. The vast majority of this increase came after January 1, 1990, and virtually all of it resulted from the creation of new private firms rather than from the privatization of state firms. The private sector share of urban employment has increased by a similar multiple. This is more rapid growth than has occurred in other post-communist countries—for example, Hungary and the Czech Republic—and private sector growth has taken place amid an overall increase in unemployment fueled by large-scale labor shedding in the state sector (Johnson 1994a and 1994b). One estimate is that since 1988 employment in the state sector has fallen by around 5 million while private sector employment has increased by at least 2.2 million, which does not include the mere 300,000 private sector jobs transferred from the state due to privatization.

An understanding of the fundamental reasons for the crucial role of the private sector in microeconomic reform stems from a reconsideration of the basic task of economic reform. The transition from plans to markets involves massive change in the organization of work, away from practices aligned with the needs of central planning and a lack of competition, and toward a very different organization of work aligned with the fast-changing needs of domestic and international markets. Recent experience in the West suggests that large-scale organizational change within well-endowed corporations is exceptionally difficult, slow, and quite often unsuccessful. The large state enterprises of Central and Eastern Europe faced far more difficult challenges with far fewer resources of all kinds.

Another mechanism for economic renewal is what we call "starting over": the creation of new businesses with new organizational forms and work practices that are free from the accumulated baggage of the communist period. The process of starting over began when the gradual dismantling of Polish communism during the 1980s created an entrepreneur's dreamland with abundant opportunities for profit. Simply put, the communists had mismanaged the economy to such an extent that gradual economic liberalization gave rise to an almost unlimited number of markets in need of new and better products and services. Truly sustainable private sector growth, however, required a stable macroeconomy and a liberalization of trade. The almost overnight achievement of these goals by the Balcerowicz Plan made rapid private sector development possible.

The success of private sector development under the Balcerowicz Plan was not a surprise to all policymakers involved in this new stage of economic reform. For example, Jeffrey Sachs, a Harvard professor and influential government adviser, argued strongly that private business formation would play an important role in improving Polish economic performance once the Balcerowicz Plan was adopted. However, the speed and scale of Polish private sector growth over the past four years have exceeded even the most optimistic projections. What explains the remarkable development of the Polish private sector?

Entrepreneurship is a powerful mechanism for quickly redirecting incentives toward the efficient use of resources in the pursuit of profits, and it is ideally suited to the circumstances of post-communist economies. Entrepreneurial companies in Poland are led by talented and enterprising people seeking to profit from the opportunities created by the dramatic turbulence associated with economic reform. They employ other enterprising and capable people who are prepared to be compensated on the basis of the firm's performance. Built with a highly flexible cost structure and business strategies premised on the exploitation of opportunities created by the reform process itself, small businesses have become the driving force for reform at the enterprise level in Poland. New private businesses range from simple trading firms like Citrus Wholesale, founded in 1990, which imported bananas to a Polish market where fruit had been in very short supply for decades, to complicated manufacturing firms like SeCeS-Pol, which produces industrial heat exchangers for the domestic and international market at quality and price levels that are competitive with others made all over the world.

The new private sector firms create high-wage jobs, develop exports, and continue to grow. At the same time, state sector firms struggle to stay in business. The new private firms can adapt better to the new economic environment; state firms have a hard time adjusting. As a result, "starting over" is the principal mechanism for economic renewal at the enterprise level in Poland. And although Polish circumstances are different from those of other post-communist countries, we believe that "starting over" will nonetheless be the principal mechanism for economic renewal at the enterprise level in all post-communist countries.

Explaining Polish Economic Performance

After the collapse of communism, there was a sharp reduction in Polish industrial production together with a steady increase in unemployment (Table 1-1). Initial performance in 1990 and 1991 was disappointing. However, Poland became the first East European country to return to positive GDP growth, with 1 percent in 1992 and 4 percent in 1993, and it will almost certainly lead the region again with 4–5 percent growth in 1994. It also has the highest rates of industrial growth in the region, registering around 4 percent in 1992 and over 5 percent in 1993. Industrial output growth up to September 1994 (compared with the same months in 1993) has been consistently in the 10–13 percent range. Investment in general and fixed capital investment in particular will probably grow by 5–6 percent in 1994. Taken as a whole, this is an impressive performance by any standard, and it contrasts starkly with recent performance in other post-communist countries. But what explains Poland's advantage?

The answer is surely not privatization of state enterprises, because there has been little of this so far in Poland. It is true that of the 8,441 state enterprises in existence at the end of 1990, 2,813 had begun some form of genuine "privatization process" by August 31, 1994. Closer inspection, however, reveals that only 121 firms had gone through some form of "capital privatization," involving the sale of equity to people who did not work in the firm.

An additional 627 state enterprises have been converted into joint stock companies wholly owned by the Treasury, about half of which may be included in the "mass privatization" program. Sharing some important features with recent programs in the Czech Republic and Russia, this privatization would involve the free transfer of shares to citizens (via intermediary funds). This program was ready to be implemented in 1991 but, due to repeated political problems, it has yet to go into effect.

Some progress has been made with the privatization of smaller enterprises. Through August 1994, 990 small and medium enterprises (with fewer than 700 employees) had been privatized through what has been called "liquidation"; but in more than 70 percent of the cases, this means simply that they are leased to their previous managers and employees.

In a further 1,197 cases, the assets of state enterprises have been sold following bankruptcy (pursuant to article 19 of the State Enterprise Act). These assets are usually sold gradually, with the remaining assets belonging to the State Treasury. Most of the enterprises taking this route have been small.

The clearest indicator that privatization has not had a substantial effect on the overall economy is employment numbers. Through the end of 1993, only some 130,000 jobs had been transferred from the state to the private sector through privatization. If we include the sale of units from state enterprises, this total reaches no more than 300,000 (in an economy with total employment over 15 million). Even within industry, where the state enterprises were concentrated, privatized firms' share of sales and employment is no more than 5 percent.

Historically, relatively few large state enterprises accounted for a large part of production and employment. In 1991, 1,842 state enterprises had more than 500 employees, and only 319 had more than 2,000 employees. Most of these large firms are in industry. There has been almost no privatization of large state industrial enter-

Table 1-1   Macroeconomic Indicators, 1989–1992

	Unemployment Rate	Industrial Production (1989 = 100)
1990		
January	0.3	81
February	0.9	74
March	1.5	74
April	2.0	74
May	2.5	74
June	3.2	74
July	3.9	77
August	4.6	77
September	5.2	77
October	5.7	78
November	6.1	76
December	6.3	75
1991		
January	6.8	74
February	7.0	70
March	7.3	69
April	7.5	66
May	7.9	61
June	8.6	63
July	9.6	64
August	10.1	61
September	10.7	60
October	11.1	60
November	11.4	59
December	11.8	59
1992		
January	12.1	63
February	12.4	64
March	12.1	66
April	12.2	68
May	12.3	66
June	12.6	65
July	13.1	69
August	13.4	67
September	13.6	66
October	13.5	67
November	13.5	66
December	13.6	66

Table 1-1 (*Continued*)

	Unemployment Rate	Industrial Production (1989 = 100)
1993		
January	14.2	69
February	14.4	69
March	14.4	71
April	14.4	73
May	14.3	76
June	14.8	74
July	15.4	71
August	15.4	71
September	15.4	72
October	15.3	70
November	15.5	71
December	15.7	72
		(series discontinued)
1994		
January	16.7	
February	16.8	
March	16.7	
April	16.4	
May	16.2	
June	16.6	
July	16.9	
August	16.8	
September	16.5	

Source: Central Statistical Office of Poland, *Biuletyn Statystyczny*, various issues.
Unemployment rate = % of "civil economically active" population.

prises in Poland. Furthermore, the government has repeatedly backed away from bankrupting these industrial giants, usually by allowing them to go into arrears on tax payments.

Progress with privatization has been mixed in other countries, but both the Czech Republic and Russia have undergone more privatization than has Poland. Poland has privatized proportionately fewer of its large state enterprises than other post-communist countries, which are doing worse economically. Hence, with such limited success in privatization, it is hard to believe that this explains why Poland's economic performance has exceeded the other countries. Privatization would undoubtedly be helpful and is almost certainly necessary if Polish growth is to continue. But the fact remains that Poland's economy has improved, and privatization, to date, has not been the explanation.

Has there perhaps been a large turnaround in the 5,238 enterprises that were still in the state sector as of June 30, 1994? The Balcerowicz Plan definitely had positive effects on state firms, freeing them, to a large degree, of their dependence on various forms of subsidies. Many of these firms have responded sufficiently to avoid complete collapse, but the vast majority have struggled to fundamentally change the way they operate. The most striking (and most reliable) measure of the continuing problems in the state sector is its level of employment. In 1989–1994, 5 million jobs have been lost at a steady rate of 1–1.5 million per year. Employment in this sector fell 0.5 million from December 1992 to December 1993 (a decline of 7.6 percent).

What, then, is the difference? The source of Poland's impressive economic performance has been the new private sector, that is, firms founded from scratch and not as a result of privatization. The official numbers are subject to many biases, which is why we did not rely exclusively on them in our research. The overall picture, however, is now clear. One 1993 estimate, for example, is that the state sector's output fell over 6 percent while private sector output rose 35 percent.

The private sector had humble beginnings. In 1980 the nonagricultural private sector employed 600,000 people, less than 5 percent of urban employment. No one knows for sure, but it may have contributed around 3 percent of GDP. As a percentage of urban employment, that same sector employed 10 percent in 1988, 13.2 percent in 1989, 18.8 percent in 1990, 25.7 percent in 1991, and 34.4 percent in 1992 (data are from the end of each year). By the end of 1994, the number will be at least 40 percent. Although estimates of the private sector's contribution to GDP are less accurate, they have increased in proportion. Table 1-2 shows the rapid increase in the number of commercial law partnerships, joint ventures, and individual proprietorships.

The employment numbers in absolute terms are impressive enough to state explicitly: 1.3 million in 1988, 1.8 million in 1989, 2.3 million in 1990, 3.0 million in 1991, 3.8 million in 1992, over 4 million in 1993, and probably close to 4.5 million by the end of 1994. This is a substantial rate of new job creation in any economy.

The entire nonagricultural private sector, including cooperatives (most of which now function essentially as private organizations),

Table 1-2 Number of Private Businesses (in thousands)

End of Year	"Commercial Law Partnerships" (Limited Liability and Joint Stock Companies)	Joint Ventures	Individual Proprietorships
1989	11.7	0.4	813.5
1990	29.7	1.7	1,135.5
1991	45.1	4.8	1,420.0
1992	58.2*	10.1	1,630.6
1993	66.5**	15.2	1,783.9
1994 (forecast)	71.8	18.6	1,870.0

Source: Central Statistical Office of Poland, *Biuletyn Statystyczny*, various issues.

*New series: 3,000–5,000 higher than old series where the series overlap.

**Second new series: within 1,000 of old series.

employed 5.3 million in September 1994. By the end of 1993, again expressed as a percentage of urban employment, this sector employed 45 percent and by the third quarter of 1994, 47.8 percent. (Agriculture in Poland remained predominantly private owned under communism, and total private sector employment is now at least 50 percent of the labor force and 60 percent of total employment.)

The private sector has shown similarly impressive performance in industry, a sector in which many observers thought it would have difficulty. In 1981 the private sector accounted for about 5 percent of industry and by 1989 the private sector had risen to around 16 percent. During 1990 and the first half of 1991 this share grew slowly, from 17 percent to 19.4 percent. By the end of 1991, however, the private sector contributed 22–25 percent to industrial production. This share rose to 30 percent in 1992 and is at least 35 percent now. In the first half of 1994, labor productivity in private sector industry is estimated to have increased by 21 percent and employment by 13 percent.

In other areas the private sector has done even better. In trade, the private sector (excluding cooperatives) rose from less than 5 percent in 1989 to over 70 percent by September 1991. It is now over 90 percent. The private sector's shares of construction and services have also risen sharply, to the point where almost all operations are private.

In 1992, the private sector bought 7.5 trillion zloty ($500 million) worth of assets from the state sector. The total revenue generated for the government by selling shares through "capital privatization" in that year was less than half that amount: only 3.2 trillion zloty ($213 million).

Before the reforms began, the private sector's share of trade was small, perhaps 10 percent of exports and 20 percent of imports. The private sector accounted for 41.4 percent of exports in the first half of 1993 and 49.5 percent in the first half of 1994. Its share of imports rose from 59.3 percent in 1993 to 65.7 percent in 1994 (both figures are for the first half only). This amounted to a remarkable 84 percent increase in private sector exports and a 46 percent increase in private sector imports in one year alone.

Overall exports are up 20 percent in 1994 over 1993. Official government and banking sector foreign exchange reserves are up sharply. Last year's current account deficit has declined significantly. Poland seems poised at the beginning of a big, export-led boom fueled by new private business.

Methodology and Results

The research culminating in this book began in early 1990, stimulated by the obvious significance and interest of the economic reform unfolding in Poland—a reform effort largely unguided by received theory or empirical work at the microeconomic level. (The reform effort, however, was guided by previous experience with macroeconomic stabilization.) We were immediately convinced, first, that the establishment and growth of small private businesses would play a crucial role in the reallocation of people and capital and, second, that policymakers and analysts within and outside Poland poorly understood and underappreciated this role. In particular, with many formerly communist countries watching the Polish experience, we considered the lessons from the emerging private sector to have profound implications for reform efforts to come in other countries.

We were convinced that the best place to learn about the economic reform process was the private enterprises themselves, where entrepreneurs and managers could help us understand the broad set of issues facing managers as the reform evolved and conditions and policies changed over time. We sought the help of Polish academics in the Gdansk region who had been actively involved in small businesses as researchers, owners, and managers. With their generous assistance, we established a core group of roughly thirty small businesses whose owners or managers agreed to meet with us periodically over three years beginning in early 1990 and share with us their opinions and experiences. Our sample was by no means random: it consisted mainly of the most successful new private firms in the Gdansk-Sopot-Gdynia region at that time. Interviews with the core sample provided the framework we needed to develop a questionnaire and expand data collection to another 950 new private businesses.

In an effort to examine the other principal mechanism for microeconomic reform, state enterprise restructuring and privatization, we also undertook three intensive case studies of state enterprises: two shipyards still owned by the state (Gdansk and Szczecin) and a large garment producer (Prochnik) that was one of the first enterprises to be privatized by an initial public offering (IPO) and traded on the Warsaw Stock Exchange. These three case studies provide a detailed examination of the formidable managerial challenges associated with state enterprise restructuring, and an opportunity to evaluate alternative managerial approaches to these challenges. Unlike most large sample studies, our case studies look closely at the concrete strategic, operational, and organizational actions that leaders in each enterprise took to address a set of problems that are quite common among state enterprises in post-communist economies. The evidence suggests that successful state enterprise restructuring is remarkably difficult and, hence, likely to be rare. Although many state enterprises have survived the loss of state subsidies, the prospects for long-term viability of the vast majority are quite dim.

Moreover, our evidence suggests that while privatization is clearly a significant enabler of successful, market-oriented restructuring, it is by no means a sufficient condition for establishing a strategically aligned set of reforms to generate viable competitors in domestic and international markets. Privatized firms must still successfully overcome the wide range of difficult problems facing most state enterprises, and privatization, per se, is no substitute for a carefully designed and well-led program of pervasive organizational change. Thus, the contrast between the ability of state enterprises and privatized enterprises, on the one hand, and new private businesses, on the other hand, to adapt to the market-driven economic conditions suggests that the new private sector is the fundamental vehicle for economic transformation in post-communist countries.

The results generated from this unique collection of data go far beyond the basic conclusion about the significance of new private business in the reform process. The evidence shows that there is enormous heterogeneity in the emerging Polish small business sector. Dynamic small businesses exist in all sectors of activity, from manufacturing to trade and services, and many compete with high levels of quality and technical sophistication. After only four years, many small firms that provide basic products and services are already experiencing severe competition from hundreds of other new private businesses, and their growth is severely limited.

The data also allow us to look in detail at managerial strategies that have succeeded, in contrast with those that have failed, as the economic environment has rapidly evolved over four years of reform. The evidence shows, for example, that business strategies focused on creating excellence in a small range of products or services have come to dominate more diversified strategies, especially as competition among small firms has intensified in recent years. For example, Profilm, a company specializing in the production of public affairs and documentary television programs, has prospered while Semeco, a company that owned supermarkets, newspapers, and manufacturing firms, among others, has failed as competition has increased in each of its business segments. In an extreme fashion, successful Polish small businesses adopted a commonly discussed management principle from the West: they remain aligned with a turbulent environment by creating a flexible organization built around a focused strategy, low fixed costs, and highly adaptable human resource practices.

Many of the small firms we have studied succeeded by establishing strategic partnerships with Western firms, often organized as joint ventures. Indeed, almost all of the most successful firms have benefited through learning from various contacts with Western businesses. Collaborations with Western firms provide scarce resources such as channels for international product distribution and access to managerial skills. Styl France produces French provincial furniture, which is exported for distribution through a French furniture retailer, and Phantom Press, a joint venture involving a British investor, translates Western literature into Polish, prints the books in England, and then sells them to Polish distributors.

Implications for Economic Reform Policy

Our analysis of the small business experience provides a unique perspective on the Balcerowicz Plan, which remains extremely controversial both in Poland and throughout the post-communist world. In many countries facing the common task of transforming a planned economy with state ownership into a market-driven economy with much greater private ownership, the debate about economic reform is often cast in terms of being for or against "shock therapy."

Critics of shock therapy can be found from Eastern Europe to the United States, and among policymakers, practitioners, academics, and journalists. According to the argument most often put forward by critics of shock therapy, some of the macro measures in the Balcerowicz Plan may have been required, but these should have been accompanied by more direct microeconomic restructuring measures. The argument is that some direct intervention by the government at the level of sectors or perhaps even some firms would have helped the adjustment process. Critics maintain that a comprehensive industrial policy would have been desirable, though the best possible outcome would have been a set of policies that somehow moved more slowly or gradually to bring down inflation and force microeconomic changes. In sum, this view holds that Balcerowicz implemented strong macro measures without supportive micro policies.

In our view, the Balcerowicz Plan was successful and appropriate not only because it laid the foundation for restructuring large state enterprises, but also because its sudden stabilization and liberalization measures quickly created conditions conducive to private business development in every part of the economy. A more deliberate pace, advocated by critics of the Balcerowicz Plan and intended to gradually wean state enterprises from the old system, would have retarded economic transformation by impeding the rapid growth of new private businesses. In other words, "gradualism" is deeply flawed in part because it hinders the rapid replacement of old enterprises and ineffective work organization with new businesses better suited to a market economy. In our view, the macroeconomic changes involved in the Balcerowicz Plan were extremely well designed in terms of their effect on the micro economy. The change in macroeconomic policy was both necessary and sufficient to cause a boom in new private business and irrevocably change the organization of work in the Polish economy.

Our research also suggests that although delays in privatizing state enterprises in Poland are unfortunate, they do not signal the failure of the economic reform process. The tying up of valuable capital, labor, and managerial skills in low-productivity uses in large state firms instead of making them available for new private business acts as a brake on the pace of economic development. It would be clearly preferable to make a clean break with the previous set of property rights in the state sector—for example, through some form of voucher privatization—and thereby replace the dysfunctional incentives present in state firms with market-driven incentives for resource allocation. The emphasis for privatization programs should be on getting more productive resources into the hands of the private sector, rather than on achieving complicated balances of economic, political, and social goals. Private sector development can survive slow progress in privatization, but our evidence suggests that the failure to privatize and restructure large state enterprises increasingly slows the growth of private firms as the reform process evolves.

The key role of new private business also has important implications for financial sector reform. It is well known that efficient financial intermediation is crucial to private sector development, but failure to quickly improve and privatize the state banking systems in Poland has resulted in banks unwilling and unable to allocate funds from depositors to creditworthy borrowers. Delays in restructuring the banks are largely the result of the banks' close relationship with state enterprises that are in default on their loans, accumulated mainly during the early stages of reform. Only after 1993 did bank privatization and improvements in leading practices begin to have a significant positive impact on private sector development.

Our research, however, indicates that the most important constraint on private sector borrowing has been very high nominal interest rates. Faced with an inflation rate that has remained stubbornly high, nominal interest rates facing small business borrowers have typically exceeded 50 percent. Entrepreneurs, however, see their prices constrained by intense domestic and international competition and are rarely willing to borrow at high rates consisting mainly of an inflation premium.

In this crucial respect, the microeconomic effects of macroeconomic policy after 1990 suggest that the problem in Poland was not too much stabilization but too little. If inflation had been brought down quickly to 10 percent per year or less (Balcerowicz's original goal), small businesses would have benefited from affordable credit, and the crucial process of starting over would have proceeded more expeditiously with a significant injection of external finance.

Plan of the Book

The structure of our book is consistent with our dual objectives: (1) to provide an empirically grounded theory of economic reform focused on the role of new private businesses and (2) to derive from the Polish experience practical lessons that may help managers and policymakers navigate more effectively through the unprecedented conditions of economic transformation in Central and Eastern Europe. The book consists of three parts. In Part I we describe the economic structure inherited from communism, particularly as it existed at the end of the 1980s in Poland. We use this context to explain the Balcerowicz Plan and its consequences for microeconomic reform. Given the central role state enterprises were thought to play in the reform process, we then examine the challenges that state enterprises face in their efforts to restructure and meet the standards of international competition. We analyze these issues in depth, using the case of three large enterprises that have taken dramatically different steps toward commercial viability. Examination of these three experiences makes clear the staggering complexity, depth, and interconnectedness of the problems facing state enterprise restructuring. Because we have chosen enterprises thought to be among the most promising in Poland, the data have sobering implications for the vast majority of state enterprises.

In Part II we develop in detail our analysis of new private business in Poland. We draw on the two new sources of evidence—the core sample and the large sample surveys—to examine the origins of private business development and the regional and sectoral distribution of entrepreneurship. We examine how private business development has altered managerial and worker incentives and brought about massive changes in the organization of work. Financing plays a crucial role in the establishment and growth of new businesses, and we analyze the impact of financial sector reform on private business development. Finally, we use the case studies to look closely at the range of product market strategies and organizational practices employed by private businesses, and we attempt to distinguish among the various approaches on the basis of economic performance in the early years of reform.

We begin Part III by putting the Polish economic reform in comparative perspective. We argue that the basic issues examined in Poland are indicative of a common set of challenges extant in all post-communist economies, although the details certainly differ. We believe the evidence clearly shows that the key to economic reform is the development of new private businesses, or starting over, rather than the restructuring and privatization of existing enterprises. Interpreted in this way, the Polish experience, though clearly a function of many specific circumstances, holds powerful lessons for the reform of post-communist economies more generally.

We close Part III with a reassessment of the Polish economic reform in light of our findings. This reassessment offers a number of policy prescriptions aimed at improving what we consider to have been very effective economic reform policy in Poland, based on our view of new private businesses as the primary engine of microeconomic reform. Unlike many critics, we believe the Balcerowicz Plan was very good policy on essentially all counts and could have been improved mainly by being *more* rather than less aggressive in the achievement of its goals.

PART I

Restructuring State Enterprises

CHAPTER 2

Economic Reform and the Challenge of State Enterprise Restructuring

THE rapid growth of new private businesses in Poland has occurred in the context of dramatic changes in economic policy, beginning with reforms attempted by the Communists in the 1980s and including, in particular, the Balcerowicz Plan. The evolution of economic liberalization, which began under the Communists, had profound implications for the timing, character, and speed of private sector development in Poland. A close examination of the recent history of economic policy in Poland is therefore essential to an understanding of microeconomic reform and is also very important for policymakers wishing to adapt lessons from the Polish experience to other countries. This chapter provides a brief review of economic liberalization measures from 1980 to the implementation of the Balcerowicz Plan in January 1990.

Upon removal of the Communists, the Solidarity-led government inherited an economy poorly equipped to meet the challenges and opportunities created by the Balcerowicz Plan. In this chapter we describe the problems facing microeconomic reform at the enterprise level, and we provide a simple framework for considering the managerial tasks associated with state enterprise restructuring. Although the details of the Polish circumstances in 1990 are unique for many important reasons, we believe that the basic set of challenges associated with microeconomic reform at the enterprise level are common to most post-communist countries.

Table 2-1   Output and Inflation, 1986–1990

	Percentage Change per Year				
	1986	1987	1988	1989	1990
Real GDP Growth	4.2	2.0	4.1	0.2	−11.6
Industrial Production	4.4	3.4	5.3	−0.5	−24.2
Nominal Wages	22.3	21.3	79.4	274.3	347.9
Retail Prices	17.5	25.3	61.3	243.8	617.8

Source: Rocznik Statystyczny 1991 (Warsaw: Central Statistical Office of Poland, 1991). Particular series taken as follows: Real GDP Growth from Table 1 (195), p. 117; Industrial Production from Table 1 (385), p. 275; Nominal Wages from Table 1 (318), p. 229; Retail Prices from Table 12 (281), p. 179.

The Communist Legacy[1]

The Failure of Communist Reform

By the end of the 1970s, the Polish economic system had run into serious difficulties. The beginning of serious economic reform in Poland can be traced back to 1980–1981 when, under pressure from the newly legalized Solidarity movement, ideas about economic reform in Poland were seriously discussed, and some legislation was passed. The military coup of December 1981 interrupted implementation of these measures, but the military-backed government itself soon attempted gradual economic reform in an attempt to make state firms more efficient and to buy social peace. However, successive Polish Communist governments in the 1980s proved unwilling to follow through on their threats to bankrupt recalcitrant firms, and the effects on firm behavior were minimal. The evidence indicates that this first stage of economic reform ended with recentralization—a familiar pattern of Communist reform in which bureaucrats fought to regain their lost power and privileges. In effect, there was no significant change at the microeconomic or firm level.

Table 2-1 shows the Polish economic situation according to official statistics in the second half of the 1980s. On the surface these numbers do not look bad. Real GDP and industrial production were rising, and inflation in 1986 and 1987 was around 20 percent per year. But the reality was much less favorable: shortages of many goods, poor-quality production, and low productivity growth. A particularly pressing problem was Poland's inability to service its foreign debt.

There was a persistent current account deficit for transactions in convertible currencies at the end of the 1980s, and the slight trade surplus in transferable rubles could not be used to service debt denominated in "hard" currencies. By 1987 the Communist government considered that the situation required a further set of economic reforms.

A so-called second stage of reform was designed by the Communists during 1987 and implemented at the start of 1988. There was only weak support for this new policy, as was made quite clear when the government's economic and political proposals were defeated in the referendum of November 29, 1987. According to subsequent public statements of ministers, this defeat made the government unwilling to impose high "costs" of reform. Nevertheless, as the Communists saw matters, they had no alternative but to proceed with what they considered to be a watered-down version of the same policies.

The emphasis in the 1988 reforms was on microeconomics, which meant altering the incentive structure for firms and pushing them more toward market transactions. In particular, price controls were reduced in scope, the direct supervision of wages by ministries was abandoned, and managers were left to handle all negotiations with workers. These steps were intended to depoliticize wage bargaining, but nothing was done to strengthen the incentives for state managers to resist wage demands. Firms were now obliged to pay a tax on any "excessive" wage increase, but managers could find a number of legal ways to reduce their tax liability. In addition, this set of reforms simultaneously confused the question of who controlled managers and de facto increased the power of workers over managers. Legally and in practice the question of who owned the firms became very confused.

This second stage of reform started with a large relative price correction on February 1, 1988, in the form of a sharp increase in food prices—implying a 20 to 30 percent fall in real wages. There was quickly a "spontaneous" strike wave—not organized by the Solidarity leadership—and managers of state firms showed little inclination to resist wage claims.

There was a sharp increase in nominal wages in Poland in February and March 1988, due almost entirely to higher bonuses—discretionary payments by managers. There was also a further increase in nominal wages after mid-1988. Actual real wages, however, did not increase very much, because at this time shortages meant that an increase in nominal wages did not necessarily mean that a worker

Table 2-2   Monthly Inflation Rates, 1986–1989

	Percentage Change in Consumer Price Index			
	1986	1987	1988	1989
January	2.0	3.4	3.7	10.3
February	1.5	2.3	17.2	7.4
March	2.7	1.8	5.7	8.5
April	3.0	7.1	7.1	9.8
May	1.6	2.4	2.4	7.2
June	0.9	1.6	2.9	6.1
July	−1.8	1.8	3.2	9.5
August	0.0	0.2	0.6	39.5
September	1.6	1.2	2.8	34.4
October	2.2	1.9	2.6	54.8
November	1.0	2.3	3.8	22.4
December	1.3	1.9	4.9	11.7

Source: Central Statistical Office of Poland, as reported in part from Dabrowski, Federowicz, and Levitas (1991).

could buy more goods. In many cases the shortages worsened, and line length increased. There had been a breakdown in the financial controls that had previously limited wage increases in state enterprises.[2]

Table 2-2 reports the most important result of the second stage of reform: rapid price increases in February and March 1988, followed by further increases in the inflation rate later in the year. According to official statistics, in the first half of 1988 prices rose by close to 50 percent, and wages in every industrial branch rose by at least 50 percent. As Table 2-1 shows, officially measured inflation overall in 1988 was 61.3 percent, although this is most likely an underestimate. Higher nominal wages were financed by monetary accommodation through bank credits at low nominal interest rates. As inflation accelerated, real interest rates became increasingly negative, and subsidies to state firms that were able to borrow actually increased.

A new Communist prime minister—Mieczyslaw Rakowski—was installed in September 1988 in a last attempt to save the party's monopoly on political power. This new government did take some significant "liberalization" measures. In particular, new legislation allowed greater scope for private enterprise and relaxed the rules governing foreign investment. The government also introduced significant changes in the organization of the banking system. But these changes came too late to significantly improve the economic situation,

Table 2-3 Sectoral Distribution of GDP, 1988

		Range in OECD Countries	
	Poland	Lower	Upper
Agriculture[a]	13.1	1.3	16.3
Industry[b]	58.0	24.3	41.2
Services	28.9	46.9	68.7

[a]Includes forestry.
[b]Includes mining, manufacturing, construction, transport, and communication.
Sources: Poland—*Rocznik Statystyczny 1991*, Table 2-3 (195), p. 112; OECD statistics.

which was dominated by the breakdown of tax collections and the acceleration of inflation during 1989 (see Tables 2-1 and 2-2).

Economic problems forced the government to negotiate again with representatives of the opposition. In retrospect, the beginning of the end of Polish communism was the government's agreement to negotiate with the representatives of the opposition at "roundtable talks" from February to April 1989. As a result, Solidarity was legalized, and a partially free election was scheduled for June 1989.

The number of votes cast in protest against the Communists and their allies in the June election far exceeded expectations. Solidarity won all but one of the seats for which it was allowed to compete. Even more shocking was the realization that the Communists would not be able to form a government with a parliamentary majority if several small, previously pro-Communist parties defected to Solidarity. Intense negotiations during the summer convinced those small parties to switch their support in key parliamentary votes, and, after considerable maneuvering a Solidarity-nominated prime minister, Tadeusz Mazowiecki, was confirmed in office in early September.

The State Sector

When Mazowiecki came to power in late 1989 the state sector consisted of more than eight thousand enterprises and accounted for more than 90 percent of measured output and 80 percent of measured employment. State enterprises were heavily concentrated in the industrial sector and employed large numbers of people. Table 2-3 compares the Polish sectoral distribution of employment and GDP with the OECD average. If the transition to a market economy would involve some convergence with the OECD averages, Polish enterprise

Table 2-4   Distribution of Employment According to Firm Size, International Comparisons

	Industry (% share of total)	
Number of Employees per Firm	Poland 1989	GDR[a] 1988
1–100	1.4	1.0
101–200	18.2	2.5
201–500	18.2	8.7
501–1,000	15.0	12.2
1,001–2,500	43.1	25.9
2,501–5,000	43.1	22.6
5,000+	22.3	27.1
All firms	100.0	100.0

[a]Excluding apprentices.

	All Industrial Enterprises (% share of total)				
Number of Employees per Firm	Japan 1972	UK 1979	Hungary 1981	Yugoslavia 1981	USA 1977
5–75	90.9	81.3	7.0	22.4	76.7
76–189	6.1	10.8	18.7	32.1	12.4
190–243	0.8	1.5	9.2	12.0	3.8
243+	2.1	6.9	65.1	33.5	7.1
All firms	100.0	100.0	100.0	100.0	100.0

Sources: Poland—Polish Ministry of Industry (Promasz); GDR—Statistisches Bundesamt (1990) DDR 1990, Zahlen und Fakten, Stuttgart, Table 8 (reprinted in *OECD Economic Survey of Germany*), July 1991; Japan, UK, Hungary, Yugoslavia, USA—World Bank memo. © OECD, 1992, *OECD Economic Surveys*. Reproduced by permission of the OECD.

reform would clearly require a transformation from industrial activity to the production of services. Table 2-4 illustrates the concentration of employment in large enterprises in Poland. Comparisons with similar data from Western countries suggests that economic reform would almost certainly involve a shift in employment from large to small firms, driven both by the downsizing and fragmentation of existing firms and by the establishment and growth of new small businesses.

An additional structural legacy of communism in Poland was the large percentage of foreign trade with the Soviet Union and other countries with nonconvertible currencies. Table 2-5 shows that until

Table 2-5 Structure of Trade in the Nonconvertible Currency
Area (I) and Convertible Currency Area (II)

	Share of Trade by Trading Area (%)					
	1970	1980	1985	1988	1989	1990
Exports						
Area I	64.1	55.9	54.8	48.5	40.6	17.4[a]
Area II	35.9	44.1	45.2	51.5	59.4	82.6
Imports						
Area I	68.8	55.6	60.7	47.1	40.1	16.6[b]
Area II	31.2	44.4	39.3	52.9	59.9	83.4

Source: Jeffrey Sachs, 1993. *Poland's jump to the market economy.* Cambridge: MIT Press. © 1993
Massachusetts Institute of Technology Press.
[a]Exports to the Soviet Union were 10.3% of the total.
[b]Imports from the Soviet Union were 8.6% of the total.

the late 1980s, trade with nonconvertible currency countries (Area I)
dominated trade with the West (Area II). In most instances, trade
involved goods that were well below Western quality standards, and
the goods were exchanged at prices that did not reflect relative prices
on world markets. Consequently, large portions of Polish industry
for decades were importing and exporting under conditions that bore
little resemblance to conditions associated with competitive Western
trade markets. Accordingly, enterprise strategy, management, and
production systems were built to accommodate an environment divorced from the rigors of competitive international markets.

The concentration of employment and output in a few very large
enterprises in each industry, coupled with draconian restrictions on
foreign trade with convertible currency countries, generated a high
degree of monopoly power in many of Poland's largest state enterprises. The lack of competition from domestic enterprises or international firms, coupled with an absence of profit-based incentives from
private ownership, resulted in the widely documented problems of
dreadful enterprise productivity, chronic shortages and delays in production, and generally very poor quality output.

Table 2-6 shows that like goods made in most formerly communist countries, goods manufactured in Poland did not compare favorably with those of Western countries. The figures in Table 2-6 are
ratios of prices for various countries' products relative to the market
leader, which was typically the Federal Republic of Germany. A low
ratio reflects relatively low prices and, hence, relatively low product

Table 2-6   Indicators of Product Quality, 1977 and 1987

| | Relative Price Gaps | | | |
| | Mechanical Engineering | | Electrical Engineering | |
	1977	1987	1977	1987
Poland	0.586	0.545	0.551	0.726
FRG	1.0	1.0	1.0	1.0
Czechoslovakia	0.639	0.527	0.423	0.629
Hungary	0.667	0.670	0.488	0.776
Italy	0.982	1.020	1.083	1.083

Note: The relative price gap is a trade-weighted index of import prices in the European Community relative to the market leader, mostly Germany. In mechanical engineering, 480 products are included; for electrical engineering, 254 products.

Source: M. Landesmann and L. Székely, Industrial restructuring and the reorientation of trade in Czechoslovakia, Hungary and Poland, *CEPR Discussion Paper 546*, April 1991, London. © OECD, 1992, *OECD Economic Surveys. United States.* Reproduced by permission of the OECD.

quality. In all but a few cases, Polish exports could compete with Western products and services only on the basis of significantly lower prices. When foreign trade with the West was liberalized, Polish exports expanded simply because some new markets were open to them and prices for many Polish products were initially very low.

A major contributor to the poor quality and technological obsolescence of Polish industrial outputs was an aged and relatively backward capital stock. Table 2-7 shows that the average age of Polish capital was older than that of capital in Germany and other formerly communist countries. Hence, considerable investment was necessary

Table 2-7   Age Structure of Equipment in Industry

| | Share of Assets Under Five Years of Age (%) | | | |
	1975	1980	1985	1988
Poland	42	35	17	19
Czechoslovakia	31	32	25	23
GDR	30	30	26	29
Hungary	41	41	28	29
FRG	—	39	—	40

Sources: For FRG—1980 and 1989, Statistisches Bundesamt, Fachserie 18; Volkswirtschaftliche Gesamtrechnungen, Reihe 1. For all others—UN Economic Commission for Europe, *Economic Survey of Europe in 1989–1990* (New York, 1990), p. 13. © OECD, 1992, *OECD Economic Surveys.* Reproduced by permission of the OECD.

to catch up with the current level of technology and productivity in Western facilities.

Finally, the state tightly controlled the banking system. In Poland, as in all East European countries, there was a monobank, so called because all functions of a central and commercial bank were effectively fused into one institution. This monobank oversaw all credit in the economy. Its goal was to ensure that credit was allocated in support of the economic plan.[3] There were some supposedly independent cooperative banks—for example, for Polish agriculture—but in practice they were tightly controlled.

The Private Sector

Under communism, the private sector was generally kept under tight control, and Poland was no exception. There were episodes of relative liberalization for Polish private business, particularly in the immediate aftermath of various political crises—in 1956–1957, 1965–1968, 1977–1980, and after 1982 (Åslund 1985, ch. 2). However, until the 1980s each liberal phase was followed by some form of crackdown, and private sector activity declined.[4]

Communist regimes regularly altered their policy toward the private sector in line with their current political priorities. These regimes had almost total control over their societies, and to crush the private sector, they could use policy instruments that ranged from violent repression to altering tax rates. Nevertheless, there was a continual tension between communist ideology—which was opposed to any private sector activity—and communist governments' desire to maintain an adequate supply of goods and services, which in part could be assisted by allowing greater scope for private business.

Even when legal, Polish private business faced many constraints. One of the most significant was the difficulties associated with obtaining material inputs. Industrial supplies were hard to get, and the most desirable supplies were tightly controlled by state planning and supply agencies. Any private manufacturing operation, such as existed in the Polish handicrafts sector, relied on the state for its inputs and was therefore always vulnerable to a change in the political mood. In many cases there were also restrictions on the use of labor by the private sector—restrictions usually in the form of statutory limits on the maximum number of employees in a private firm.

There were usually onerous taxes on private business. Tax rates were both high and unstable. As a result, forecasting future private sector tax liability was hard. In some instances, important details of the tax regulations were not published, and local tax offices had considerable discretion. Private businesspeople lived in fear of an investigation by tax inspectors with draconian powers.

Thus, in addition to severe macroeconomic problems, the post-Communist government inherited a wide range of legal and institutional problems requiring massive adjustment if Poland was to move quickly to a market economy. Fortunately, the government succeeded in putting the right people in place to formulate a plan for sweeping economic reform.

Macroeconomic Reform and Privatization[5]

The Balcerowicz Plan

As a party in opposition, Solidarity had no coherent set of economic policies. But after the elections the macroeconomic situation was desperate. Inflation was beginning to spiral out of control. Within Solidarity's parliamentary group the perception was that strong measures were needed. The man selected to find and implement the appropriate strong measures was Leszek Balcerowicz, an academic economist who with a small group of associates had been working on reform ideas at least since the early 1980s. During the summer of 1989 and subsequently, the development of key concepts and the building of necessary political support within Poland and internationally was assisted by the efforts of Jeffrey Sachs and David Lipton, both American economists with proven expertise in stabilizing economies with high inflation.

The political and economic situation became clearer almost as soon as Balcerowicz began work in early September 1989. Although it took several months for the whole program to be assembled, there was immediately a sense of purpose and direction. Political events had played out in a way that pushed economic policy in a pro-market direction, but all the details remained to be resolved.

Balcerowicz quickly established the outline of an economic reform program and in late September and early October cut budget spending, limited the permissible wage increases, and tightened bank credit, all in an attempt to control inflation. These initial measures did not have immediate positive effects. Output continued to decline,

investment fell further, and the balance of trade worsened. Inflation
fell but remained high. Table 2-2 shows the monthly rates of inflation
were 54.8 percent in October, 22.4 percent in November, and 11.7
percent in December. In the view of policymakers, developments
during fall 1989 underlined the need for a radical set of policies—
which became known as the Balcerowicz Plan.

The stated goals of the full Balcerowicz Plan were ambitious: to
limit inflation within 1990 to less than 100 percent and to achieve a
monthly inflation rate of around 1 percent in the second half of the
year. Although negotiations with the International Monetary Fund
(IMF) were clearly crucial in designing the policy, the Polish government did not wait for formal approval of a standby loan. With strong
political support, the reform package implemented on January 1,
1990, had five main elements that, taken together, deserved the popular description of "shock therapy."

First, the exchange rate for payments on current account was
unified at 9,500 zloty per U.S. dollar. The new exchange rate was
based on the effective rate for exporters in the fourth quarter of 1989,
adjusted for the removal of export subsidies and tax breaks and for
estimated inflation in January, with what was perceived to be a small
margin. The IMF calculated that this rate implied a real effective
zloty depreciation of 40 percent in January on the basis of retail prices.
The stated intention was to hold the nominal exchange rate for current account transactions stable for the first three months. After that
time, the nominal rate would be adjusted to maintain a competitive
real exchange rate in terms of labor costs. The parallel (so-called
kantor) market for households was retained, and the government made
no commitment to intervene in that market. Instead, the government
promised to raise interest rates if the kantor rate rose more than 10
percent above the official rate.

Second, a very restrictive incomes policy was established for the
first four months of 1990. There were tax penalties of from 200 to
500 percent on wage bill increases that exceeded 30 percent of the
actual rate of consumer price increase in January and 20 percent of the
increase in February–April. The official expectation was that inflation
would be much reduced by the end of April, so the tax-free increase
in the wage bill was allowed to be 60 percent for May and June. This
"indexation coefficient" for the second half of the year was to be
discussed with the IMF in May 1990. The government stated that the
excess wage tax would differ from the versions used by the communist
regimes because there were to be no exemptions.

At the same time, many prices were liberalized. A price freeze was discussed but rejected because of the need for major changes in relative prices and for a brief "corrective inflation." The government hoped state sector real wages would fall by one-third, to compensate firms for the end of the massive interest rate subsidies—which some estimates had put around 25 percent of total labor costs.

Third, the goal of fiscal policy was a state budget deficit of less than 1 percent of GDP—with a small surplus on extra-budgetary funds. This represented a significant adjustment, because the budget deficit had been more than 8 percent of GDP in 1989. In the budgetary plan, subsidies were to be cut by 8 percent of GDP; the only significant subsidy would remain on coal. But higher outlays were also planned, totaling about 6 percent of GDP, primarily for new social safety nets for the future unemployed. The plan was also intended to eliminate income tax reliefs, which would give an extra 4 percent of GDP.

Fourth, on January 1, the refinance rate of the National Bank of Poland (NBP) was raised to 36 percent a month (up from 7 percent per month in December). This rate was higher than expected inflation for January and February, and the explicit goal was to adjust nominal interest rates as necessary during 1990 in order to maintain positive real interest rates. Preferential interest rates for various investments were abolished. Interest rate subsidies for housing and agriculture were retained, but their level was reduced and their cost was placed more clearly on the budget.

Fifth, trade was substantially liberalized. Almost all foreign trade monopolies were liquidated. Quotas for most goods were ended and replaced with a uniform tariff. As a result, Poland established an extremely liberal trade regime—although this soon underwent considerable modification.

Initially, Solidarity's political coalition remained strongly supportive of the program on almost all issues—with the significant exception of the government's privatization proposals. Opinion polls showed a high degree of approval for Balcerowicz and his new "professional" approach to economic policy. There was also overwhelming foreign support for the program, and part of Balcerowicz's political appeal in 1989 was his favorable standing with international creditors and with multilateral financial institutions. The program's credibility was boosted by the creation of a $1 billion stabilization fund in December 1989 from the loans and grants of 17 Western countries. Poland also received access to loans from both the IMF and World Bank.

Furthermore, at the beginning of 1990, Poland was able to suspend payments on foreign commercial bank debt without disrupting any of these external financial arrangements.

Implementation and Initial Results, 1990

The most important performance indicators at the beginning of the program were the criteria set by the International Monetary Fund. Although these criteria were initially perceived as being quite tough, on a whole range of measures the program performed "better" than required in 1990 and particularly in the first half of 1990. Real wages fell much more sharply than required, and the government budget moved rapidly into surplus. There was a much bigger fall in net domestic assets than required by the IMF, and the net foreign reserves of the banking system actually increased. For the year ending December 31, 1990, Poland's economic performance exceeded the first five IMF basic criteria.[6]

The first quarter of 1990 showed a remarkable change in economic conditions. The budget moved quickly into surplus. Real credit from the banking system fell sharply. The exchange rate remained stable, the zloty was fully convertible for current account transactions, and foreign exchange reserves actually increased. Exports rose rapidly, and the hard currency trade surplus for the first quarter was $778 million. Inflation declined quickly, even though 90 percent of all prices were liberalized. However, despite these initial successes, worries about the domestic effects of reform were growing.

From aggregate statistics, it is hard to judge whether the economic stabilization program improved or worsened the living conditions of the average Pole. *Measured* real incomes fell considerably, and there are similar results for measured real wages and consumption. But disaggregated indicators show a more ambiguous result: the average monthly salary in 1990 allowed a consumer to purchase more of some goods and less of others compared to the late 1980s. The most serious problem with these numbers is that they do not take into account the pervasive shortages of the 1980s, especially in 1988 and 1989. The fact that a good was listed at a particular price in 1988 or 1989 did not mean it could actually be bought at that price. It might have been available only after a prospective purchaser stood in line for an hour, or it might have been available only on the black market at a much higher price. Because these factors are not reflected in the statistics, real living standards in the late 1980s are artificially inflated in the official measures.

In contrast, from the beginning of 1990, there have been no shortages in Poland. The resulting rapid change from excess demand to equilibrium in the consumer goods market makes it very difficult to calculate whether average per capita consumption fell or rose.[7] However, it is true that the real purchasing power of incomes and consumption cannot have fallen by as much as official statistics suggest.

There was a sharp fall in state sector industrial output. Official statistics showed a fall in excess of 20 percent for the first quarter, much larger than had been forecast. Unemployment also rose sharply, although there was strong evidence that a large fraction of the registered unemployed had not previously been employed. At the same time there were hardly any bankruptcies—contrary to initial expectations. These developments caused a sharp debate within the government about whether the macroeconomic policy was too tight.

Two key disappointments in 1990 were that measured GDP fell by as much as 12 percent and that inflation continued to be higher than targeted. These were the first hints that the response of the Polish economy to "shock therapy" would not be as positive as had been hoped. Blame for these and subsequent disappointments was placed on the failure of state enterprises to "adjust" sufficiently to the new economic conditions. But what exactly was needed in terms of adjustment, and what prevented state enterprise managers from doing what was required?

Privatization

Most policymakers, including advisers from the West, viewed privatization as a necessary condition for enterprise restructuring. Consequently, attention focused on methods for privatizing as many enterprises as possible. Indeed, many people unfamiliar with the depth and range of management challenges associated with large-scale organizational change viewed privatization as a necessary *and* sufficient condition for enterprise restructuring. Private ownership would create the incentives, it was hoped, to liquidate unpromising companies and revitalize companies with prospects for success. With private ownership would come an injection of management skill and, perhaps, the funds necessary for working capital, training, and investment in plant and equipment.

Given substantial heterogeneity among the thousands of state-owned enterprises, the Polish government pursued a "multi-track" approach to privatization. The most promising large enterprises, whose future value was considered to be both largest and most easily discernible to investors, were slated for privatization by initial public offering (IPO). Small enterprises, with much more modest likely value to investors, were often sold or given to existing managers, workers, or both.

The most complicated privatization method addressed the need to quickly privatize a very large number of enterprises and the political desire to distribute ownership in state assets to all Polish citizens. In other words, unlike a British-style sale of enterprises to the highest bidder, the Mass Privatization Program (MPP), as it came to be called, would be a simple transference of shares at zero price to all Polish citizens above a specified minimum age. Under the terms of the MPP, citizens would receive shares in National Wealth Funds, which, in turn, would hold shares in the several hundred privatized companies. The National Wealth Funds were conceived as a mechanism for concentrating ownership (and hence avoiding the dispersed ownership otherwise associated with mass privatization), thereby facilitating the radical measures necessary to restructure, liquidate, or sell the hundreds of individual enterprises. Management of the National Wealth Funds would be contracted to mainly Western financial services firms, especially investment banks and venture capital companies. The NWF managers would be compensated largely on the basis of the financial performance of the firms in their fund, and would therefore be encouraged to take an active role in the selection of enterprise management and the development and implementation of enterprise strategies. Although the National Wealth Funds would be permitted to trade in the shares of the individual enterprises, there would be no official market for the sale of citizens' shares in the funds for a few years. Hence, although citizens would be owners of formerly state-owned enterprises, they would not have (initially) alienable property rights.

The merits of the highly complex MPP have been widely debated,[8] and the legislation required for implementation was finally passed after nearly three years of discussion in the Polish parliament. But what has been far more important than the details of the MPP is the simple fact that little privatization of large industrial enterprises occurred in the first *four* years of the reform process. As a result, only about one hundred of the thousands of large Polish state enterprises were in private hands—and therefore subject to the incentives of private ownership—as of mid-1994. The widely accepted notion that privatization was a necessary if not sufficient condition for the effective restructuring of Polish enterprises had run aground on the political rocks of the privatization process itself. And while state enterprises languished in a managerial purgatory, the best workers and managers left to seek more attractive alternatives in private enterprises, joint ventures, and foreign businesses operating in Poland and elsewhere. As the problems facing state enterprises mounted, they were left increasingly incapacitated to deal with them.

At the end of 1993, the private sector accounted for nearly half of Polish economic activity, but the privatization of large state enterprises had almost nothing to do with this otherwise promising outcome. Instead, the rapid growth of the private sector derived from the privatization of small enterprises and shops in the retail and wholesale trade sectors, and primarily from the remarkable emergence and growth of the new entrepreneurial sector. Thus, the formidable challenges facing state enterprise restructuring described at the outset of this chapter, challenges that reformers had hoped to address mainly through privatization as a mechanism for bringing about the necessary restructuring at the enterprise level, remained largely unresolved at the beginning of 1994. Indeed, in many respects the problems had worsened during the intervening four years. Indeed, Blanchard and his colleagues (1993) point out that the failure of privatization often resulted in de facto enterprise control by workers' councils vested with the power to hire and fire enterprise managing directors.[9] Actions led by workers' councils displaced roughly 20 percent of enterprise managers between mid-1989 and the end of 1990. The shift in control from ministries to workers' councils had two deleterious effects noted by the Blanchard team: (1) uncertainty about future ownership, ceteris paribus, reduced current investment; (2) uncertainty about future ownership and control inhibited the attraction of outside capital and management expertise. The result, in many cases, has been an "end-game" orientation rather than a long-term strategy for revitalization. In a recent review of the progress achieved by economic reform in Poland, Blanchard and his colleagues (1993) concluded

There were signs in early 1990 that most firms were considering partnerships with foreign firms, development of marketing activities, and various degrees of restructuring. But as the employment implications of restructuring as well as the difficulties of entering joint ventures, finding outside capital, and so on became clearer, most firms gave up such efforts. There are a few examples

Table 2-8 Characteristics of State-owned Enterprises and Market-driven Businesses

State-owned Enterprises	Market-driven Businesses
• Pervasive monopoly power	• Competition
• Output targets	• Profit
• Input allocations and hoarding	• Cost minimization
• Vertical integration	• Choice among suppliers
• Customers provided by the state	• Marketing and sales
• Broad, fixed product offerings	• Focused, flexible product offerings
• State financing	• Private financing
• Workers and ministries as clients	• Shareholders as key clients

of state firms that are adapting, sometimes with managers obtaining compensation schemes with strong incentives. But these examples remain isolated. Review of the evidence at the sectoral level does not show much heterogeneity across sectors. Sales are down in nearly all sectors.

In the remainder of this chapter we review the evidence on the adjustment of the state enterprise sector, and we present a framework for categorizing the managerial challenges associated with state enterprise restructuring.

State Enterprise Restructuring

A Basic Framework

The transition from plans to markets involves a fundamental reorientation of enterprise management on a scale that dwarfs the organizational change tasks common to large Western companies. Virtually every dimension of enterprise activity requires significant change and redirection. Table 2-8 contrasts some of the basic characteristics of enterprises under the two systems.

For over forty years, Polish state-owned enterprises (SOEs) operated as virtual monopolies and were generously subsidized by the central government. Inputs were allocated according to a central plan, full employment was a central goal of industrial policy, and managers were rewarded for achieving production targets rather than earning profits. From a free market standpoint, the results of management under communism were disastrous: output was generally of poor quality, there was relatively little innovation, and productivity—

though difficult to document because of a lack of reliable data—was typically considered to be among the lowest in the industrialized world. During the Communist era, when national industrial goals were high employment and high output, operating costs at state-owned enterprises were allowed to swell virtually unchecked. As new managers take over at SOEs and prepare their businesses for privatization and free market competition, it is clear that they will have to reduce operating costs, trim bloated labor forces, focus their product portfolios, increase productivity, and reschedule extensive debt.

To circumvent the continual supply shortages that resulted from Poland's inefficient central allocation system, SOEs manufactured many of the inputs required for the assembly of final products. State-owned enterprises thus tended to be highly vertically integrated, supporting vast manufacturing infrastructures that were often only marginally related to the firm's ultimate output. For example, it was not unusual for state-owned firms to operate manufacturing facilities that produced spare parts for the upkeep of buildings located on enterprise grounds. SOEs hoarded whatever intermediate goods could not be produced on-site as a safeguard against future shortages. In maintaining such a widespread, inefficient industrial base and financing large inventories, SOEs incurred tremendous operating costs.

State-owned enterprises hoarded not only intermediate goods to protect against supply shortages but also employees to protect against labor shortages. In a country where full employment was an industrial policy goal, labor was continually in short supply, and SOE managers, seeking to maximize production with little regard for costs, preferred to have too many workers than too few. With wages set by government planners, there was virtually no link between wages and productivity. In addition, since the early 1980s, employee unions and workers' councils in Poland often demanded higher wages, resisted decreases in employment, and insisted on extensive fringe benefits such as enterprise-subsidized vacations. This was all done with little regard for the health of the enterprise. Workers were well aware that regardless of the financial condition of the business, government subsidies assured that it would continue to function and they would continue to be employed. As a result, unions focused their efforts on extracting as many concessions as possible from enterprise management and government authorities. Managerial incentives, focused more on output than on cost, did little to offset these pressures. The result for most SOEs was an inflated wage bill and excessive social insurance costs.

Many SOEs maintained large stocks of nonproductive assets as fringe benefits for employees. These included such amenities as enterprise-subsidized housing, vacation resorts, transportation fleets, hospitals, and athletic clubs. With such extensive cost structures, it was difficult for many SOEs to become profitable. Yet government subsidies assured that these businesses would be able to function.

Many state-owned enterprises functioned as virtual monopolies and were never faced with competition. Government planners set prices as a function of cost, and hence there was little motivation for cost control. As a result, most SOEs never developed a sustainable competitive advantage. Managers were virtually assured that their firms' output would be purchased by the Polish government, Polish consumers, or COMECON (Council for Mutual Economic Assistance) trade partners, and product quality suffered accordingly. Typically, a state-owned enterprise produced a wide range of related products without ever acquiring focused expertise and without ever achieving the efficiencies associated with greater product focus.

A major setback for SOEs has been the breakdown of COMECON trade and the collapse of the Soviet Union. Many SOEs, including Polish defense contractors, were created primarily to fulfill COMECON trade obligations and to supply the Soviet Union. With the disappearance of demand in Eastern-bloc countries, reforming SOEs must develop a new clientele. This will not be an easy undertaking, for at least three reasons. First, the maintenance of a comprehensive system of protection against imports meant that enterprise managers under communism could not easily compare prices and costs with Western competitors. This inability to benchmark against international competition worsened problems with quality and inefficiency.

Second, most SOEs have had no previous marketing experience. During the communist era, all foreign trade was arranged by government trade monopolies, such as Centromor in the shipbuilding industry. These trade monopolies handled all contacts with foreign clients and negotiated all export contracts, entirely subsuming the marketing function for SOEs. When the government monopoly on foreign trade was dismantled with the introduction of Poland's free market reforms, SOEs were suddenly called on to fulfill their own marketing requirements. Thus, in addition to locating a new customer base, SOE managers had to develop a new functional capability.

Finally, after decades of building colossal, inefficient operations, and then suddenly losing access to government support and Soviet markets in 1990, state-owned enterprises have accumulated enormous debt during 1990–1993. Indebtedness has driven away banks and other lending institutions as financiers fear that loans made to insolvent SOEs will be used to pay off creditors rather than to produce goods. For the shipyards and other SOEs that manufacture products with a long production cycle, indebtedness has driven away clients who fear that the business may be shut down in the middle of a manufacturing project. Thus, many SOEs have found it virtually impossible to secure outside financing and have often been unable to exploit potential marketing opportunities.

Evidence from the Early Years of Reform

It is hard to overestimate just how much damage was done to Polish industry by more than forty years of communist rule. The widely held belief that privatization, coupled with the pressures put on state enterprises by liberalization of prices and trade and by the cessation of subsidies, would be the principal mechanism for bringing about microeconomic reform was based on a dramatic underestimate of the problems associated with large-scale organizational change. Although there was recognition that state enterprise restructuring would be difficult, there was little explicit attention to the scope, depth, or specific content of the challenges facing state enterprise managers. Blanchard and his colleagues (1991), for example, argue that "For the most part, Eastern Europe's production section is composed of large, inefficient, ex-state-owned firms. Many, if not most of them will have to close, and others will need to shed labor on a large scale." Even those firms that should expand or at least not close operations need to be reorganized (Blanchard et al., 1991, pp. 64–67). Although this analysis is accurate, it fails to address in any detail what must be done at the enterprise level to turn an inefficient producer of goods and services that few customers would purchase if they had meaningful choices into a company capable of meeting world-class competition. How, for example, will the firm develop marketing and sales expertise? How will enterprise debt be resolved and investment funds be attracted to modernize the capital stock? How will work practices be transformed to greatly enhance efficiency and quality? It is precisely such details that an enterprise manager must identify and successfully address if state enterprise reform is to contribute to the transition from plans to markets in post-communist countries.

As experience with economic reform in Poland has accumulated over the past three years, there continues to be relatively little detailed understanding of the actions taken, or not taken, by enterprise managers to improve performance and adjust to a radically different economic environment. Belka, Pinto, and Krajewski (1993) present statistical evidence from a sample of sixty-four manufacturing enterprises in five industrial sectors, stratified on the basis of enterprise profitability in the first half of 1992. After excluding the largest enterprises in each of the five sectors, they show that nearly one-half of the sample firms were profitable after taxes in the first half of 1992, and that the profitable firms are found mainly in the chemical and food-processing sectors. Using a variety of measures of real and financial activity—such as inventory movement, wage costs, employment, investment, and tax payments—they argue that "Hard budgets, import competition, and concern for managerial reputation can induce significant restructuring even when changes in governance lag behind" (p. 253). In other words, the authors argue that there is indirect evidence of significant adjustment among some Polish manufacturers *and* that the extent of adjustment is not clearly connected to privatization at the enterprise level. Although the validity of the authors' conclusions about the degree to which even the most successful firms in their (nonrepresentative) sample have restructured is open to some debate, their analysis in any case leaves the process of restructuring at the enterprise level quite opaque.

Similarly, Schaffer (1993) uses financial data reported by state enterprises and collected by the Central Statistical Office of Poland to examine relationships between enterprise profitability, macroeconomic conditions, and the government budget. Schaffer's research—along with the work of Berg and Blanchard (1994), Berg and Sachs (1992), and Estrin, Schaffer, and Singh (1992)—examines the impact of enterprise adjustment at an aggregate level on macroeconomic adjustment, and vice versa.

Although these studies are based on data aggregated from individual enterprises, much less is known about the range of actions necessary to successfully restructure a state enterprise, given recent Polish macroeconomic policies. Furthermore, large sample research based on summary measures of enterprise performance has made it difficult to examine the role of ownership changes in successfully restructuring state enterprises. The survey evidence provides little information about concrete actions taken by managers that have led to better or worse prospects for long-term viability. In Chapters 3 and 4 we address this shortcoming by presenting three detailed case studies of large state enterprise restructuring.

CHAPTER 3

State Enterprise Privatization:
The Case of Prochnik

IF state enterprise restructuring is to be a fundamental mechanism for microeconomic reform, then it is crucial to understand, in concrete empirical and managerial terms, just what is required to effectively transform a large state enterprise into a viable competitor in international markets. In an effort to fairly evaluate the prospects for successful state enterprise restructuring, we undertook detailed case studies of three large Polish enterprises. In this chapter and in Chapter 4 we focus on a detailed examination of managerial action at the enterprise level in an effort to develop an understanding of the central tasks associated with state enterprise reform *and* alternative managerial strategies for addressing these tasks. Prochnik, the subject of this chapter, was a state enterprise considered sufficiently promising to have been privatized in the first round of initial public offerings (IPOs) in 1990, and it is considered one of Poland's most successful restructuring stories.

In Chapter 4 we examine two shipyards that have been commercialized but remain state owned. The research included two enterprises in one industry to provide a comparison that controls for issues specific to an industry. We selected shipbuilding because it was a well-known industry considered by the Polish government to be among the most promising candidates for reform.[1] Shipbuilding has a long and distinguished history in Poland, and even during the years of communist rule when production was driven mainly by exports to the east, Polish shipyards maintained a level of quality and sophistication that compared more favorably with international standards than did the output of most other Polish industries. With large facilities on the Baltic Sea well positioned for trade with German, Scandinavian, and other European shippers, the Polish government had high hopes for the revitalization and ultimate competitiveness of the shipyards. Western consultants' reports, prepared in the early months of economic reform for the Ministries of Industry and Privatization, that listed the shipyards as among the enterprises most likely to be successfully restructured and privatized, bolstered these hopes.

The Polish government's belief that the shipyards were promising candidates for restructuring made them appealing research sites, because in our efforts to understand the managerial challenges facing enterprise restructuring we did not want to bias the case against large state enterprise reform by selecting enterprises with relatively dim prospects for success. Furthermore, one of Poland's three large shipyards on the Baltic Sea, the Szczecin Shipyard, had pursued a process for restructuring that was viewed by many to be a model for state enterprise reform in post-communist economies. We decided to pair the Szczecin Shipyard with another that was as similar as possible prior to the economic liberalization, in order to observe alternative managerial approaches to broadly comparable conditions. The Gdansk Shipyard, more famous perhaps for its political history than for its economic performance, shared a number of common circumstances with the Szczecin Shipyard, and a comparison of the significantly different experiences of these two enterprises reveals the central issues facing state enterprise reform and illustrates options used by state enterprise managers to address these issues.[2]

This small sample of three firms offers at least two interesting contrasts. First, it is possible to compare privatization preceding restructuring with the reverse case. Second, the study of two similar shipyards that have pursued radically different reform strategies allows an analysis of alternative managerial approaches to reform. In addition, our analysis of these three cases focuses on the need for an integrated restructuring plan that aligns changes in business strategy, marketing, operations, human resources, enterprise finances and investment, and control systems. In this respect, our study provides a concrete illustration of the theoretical insights developed by Milgrom and Roberts (1990). As they conclude from their elaborate modeling of organizational behavior, effective enterprise change follows from the adoption of a "cluster" of internally consistent reforms that are carefully aligned with business strategy. In other words, effective enterprise reforms come in packages. The effect of changing any one element of a firm's structure is greater if other elements are also being changed in a complementary fashion. Isolated changes may have no effect or may even make the overall situation worse.

Expressed in those terms, of course, the theory is plausible but not directly applicable to post-communist countries. The point of Chapters 3 and 4 and much of the remainder of this book is to provide very specific illustrations of precisely how this model of organizational change explains the post-communist reorganization of work. The experiences of the two shipyards, in particular, show how management behavior, and especially the vision of enterprise leaderships, affects the ability of the firm to benefit from complementarities of the sort identified by Milgrom and Roberts (1990). But most important, these three studies permit us to develop a richer understanding of the general scope and nature of the *managerial* issues associated with restructuring and, therefore, assess the role that large-scale enterprise restructuring may play in the reform process across many post-communist countries.

History

Prochnik was established in Lodz in 1945 as a supplier of army uniforms for Poland's postwar forces. By 1949, the company had expanded its operations to include consumer clothing, and in 1956, Prochnik began to specialize in men's overcoats. The company received its first export order from the Soviet Union three years later and soon afterward began exporting to West Germany, France, Great Britain, and the United States. During the 1960s and 1970s, Prochnik acquired five additional factories throughout Poland, and the company's output expanded phenomenally. Over time, Prochnik earned a reputation as Poland's premier producer of men's coats, and most of its output was slated for export. By the 1980s, Prochnik was exporting approximately 70 percent of its annual production to Western markets—particularly West Germany—and between 15 and 20 percent to the Soviet Union.

In 1990, soon after the communist regime was ousted, economic reformers selected Prochnik to be included among a group of five Polish companies to undergo an experimental privatization program,

on the basis of a positive assessment of Prochnik's long-term profitability. In April 1991, all five companies were registered on Poland's
newly formed Warsaw Stock Exchange and privatized through sales
of shares to the public. Privatization brought about many changes at
Prochnik, including a new market-oriented management team and a
restructured client base that was dominated by exclusive German
clothing manufacturers and high-end Polish retail boutiques.

Two years after privatization, Prochnik maintained its position
as Poland's premier producer of men's coats and had expanded its
product line to include women's wear and men's blazers. Company
headquarters were located in Lodz in a large industrial complex that
included a seven-story manufacturing and warehouse facility as well
as a new Prochnik retail shop. The company also operated large manufacturing plants in the nearby towns of Poddebice, Uniejow, and
Rawa Mazowiecka, and a growing network of boutique-style retail
shops. By April 1993, with a work force of 2,180 employees and
annual sales of 292 million zloty ($21.5 million), Prochnik was
Poland's largest private clothing manufacturer. See Table 3-1 and
Table 3-2 for Prochnik's 1991 and 1992 balance sheets and income
statements.

Customers

Prochnik had traditionally divided its markets into three geopolitical
regions: capitalist markets in the West, socialist markets in the Eastern
bloc, and the domestic market in Poland. Throughout the 1970s and
1980s, the company sold approximately 70 percent of its output to
Western clients. Approximately half of these Western sales were
made to cut-make-trim[3] clients, and all Western clients marketed
Prochnik-manufactured coats under their own brand names. Germany had always been Prochnik's predominant market in the West,
largely as a result of its geographical proximity and historical ties to
Poland. The Soviet Union and other Eastern bloc countries generally
purchased between 15 and 20 percent of Prochnik's annual output;
only 10 percent was sold in Poland.

The Polish market had never been strategically important for
Prochnik during the communist era. The central government regarded Prochnik largely as an export vehicle, either to earn hard
currency in the West or to meet COMECON trade obligations in the
East. The coats that the company sold in Poland were often originally

Table 3-1 Prochnik's Balance Sheet (in million zloty), 1991 and 1992

	1991		1992	
Assets	144,706	($13.2 million)	177,922	($11.5 million)
Fixed assets	71,557	($6.5 million)	76,146	($4.9 million)
Tangibles	63,035		64,444	
Intangibles	113		100	
Capital constructions	7,783		11,066	
Financial assets	626		536	
Current assets	72,554	($6.6 million)	101,415	($6.5 million)
Inventories	41,944		63,794	
Receivables	28,313		26,395	
Short-term savings	—		362	
Cash	2,297		10,864	
Prepaid expenses	144	($0.01 million)	—	
Other assets	451	($0.04 million)	361	($0.02 million)
Liabilities	144,706	($13.2 million)	177,922	($11.5 million)
Equity	100,399	($9.1 million)	105,760	($6.8 million)
Share capital	30,000		30,000	
Reserve capitals	70,399		75,760	
Payable	37,527	($3.4 million)	46,798	($3.0 million)
Long-term debt	—		5,131	
Short-term debt	37,527		41,667	
Accruals	731	($0.07 million)	1,932	($0.1 million)
Net profit	6,049	($0.5 million)	23,432	($1.5 million)

produced for export to the Soviet Union but for one reason or another were never purchased. "In the past, Prochnik may have manufactured a series of 10,000 coats for export to the Soviet Union," said Prochnik supervisory board member Janusz Baranowski. "Suppose that only 8,000 were sold. The remaining 2,000—the 'leftovers'—would be returned for sale in Poland. Thus, Prochnik's domestic supply was never carefully planned and was always unstable."

Prochnik's domestic distribution system was typical for an Eastern-bloc command economy. Poland was divided into forty-nine *voivodships*, or counties, and in the largest city of each voivodship, a large, state-run warehouse served as Prochnik's government-assigned distributor. Each time the warehouse received a shipment of Prochnik coats, it allocated them to state-run shops throughout the region. The forty-nine state-owned warehouses served as a buffer between

Table 3-2   Prochnik's Income Statement (in million zloty), 1991 and 1992

	1991	1992
Net sales	182,235 ($17.2 million)	292,099 ($21.5 million)
Cost of sales	163,979 ($15.5 million)	235,898 ($17.4 million)
Operating profit	18,256 ($1.7 million)	56,201 ($4.1 million)
Other income	709	100
Financial income including:	3,186	2,616
Dividends received	1,020	20
Other	2,166	2,596
Financial cost	10,247	15,433
Profit on operations	11,904 ($1.1 million)	43,484 ($3.2 million)
Extraordinary profit	1,040	3,039
Extraordinary loss	2,972	4,649
Gross profit	9,972 ($0.9 million)	41,874 ($3.1 million)
Income tax	3,902	18,442
Other taxes and claims	21	—
Net profit	6,049 ($0.6 million)	23,432 ($1.7 million)
Profit per share	4,033 ($0.38)	15,621 ($1.15)

Prochnik and the domestic market, and the company was not required to perform any marketing or promotional work.

Prochnik's export sales were channeled through a centrally administered foreign trade company called Konfexim, which allowed the government to control all business and currency transactions with capitalist countries. Konfexim managed every phase of Prochnik's export business: the trade company located foreign clients, negotiated hard currency prices for Prochnik coats, and collected all payments. Konfexim retained all hard currency earnings for the national coffers, delivering payment to Prochnik in Polish zloty after deducting a sales commission of approximately 4 percent. For exports to "soft currency" countries in the East, Konfexim did not collect payment in currency but credited its sales of Prochnik coats against Poland's COMECON export obligations. In the late 1980s, Prochnik served between 30 and 34 clients in twelve foreign countries.

The Polish government was eager to export domestically manufactured products to Western markets, even if the transactions were unprofitable. In the late 1980s, approximately 10 percent of the coats produced by Prochnik were sold to mid-quality department store chains in the United States. These department stores also purchased coats from suppliers in Korea and Hong Kong, and supply pricing was extraordinarily competitive. To maintain a market presence in the United States, Konfexim sold Prochnik coats for prices well below production costs, and the Polish government provided Prochnik with hefty subsidies to make up for losses on its export sales. Subsidizing exports was standard industrial policy in Poland until the country was swept by a wave of economic reform in 1989–1990.

Privatization at Prochnik

The prospect of privatization in 1990 generated a great deal of excitement at Prochnik, for the company would achieve several advantages by operating as a private business. To understand the role that privatization did or did not play in Prochnik's restructuring efforts, it is important to examine closely the changes associated with privatization and the managerial challenges facing senior executives after privatization. Even Longin Barski, the firm's long-time, communist-oriented director, conceded that the benefits of privatization were simply too appealing to pass up. First, and perhaps most important, government ministries would no longer direct the firm's activity. "The central government would no longer be able to tell us what, when, and where to produce," said executive committee vice president Krzysztof Trzewikowski. Thus, for example, Prochnik's exports would be freed from the control of Konfexim, its foreign trade agent.

Second, state-owned companies were required to pay an annual tax equal to 2 percent of the value of their durable assets. This tax could best be interpreted as a user's fee for state-owned equipment. Once a company's assets were privatized, however, it would no longer be required to pay the tax. In 1989, Prochnik had durable assets worth approximately 27 billion zloty ($2.8 million). Privatization would thus allow the company to decrease its annual tax bill by 540 million zloty ($57,000).

Third, private companies enjoyed greater wage flexibility than their state-owned counterparts. In late 1989, in an effort to control rampant inflation and to provide an incentive for privatization, Poland's Solidarity government introduced an excess wage tax. This tax was levied on state-owned enterprises whose total monthly wage payments (indexed for inflation) exceeded the wage bill paid in September 1989. "Excess wages" were taxed at rates of up to 500 percent. Because private companies were not subject to the excess wage tax, they could afford to pay higher salaries than state-owned firms and thus attract superior workers. Private companies could also implement pay-for-performance compensation plans that offered employees the prospect of higher earnings while boosting productivity.

Finally, Prochnik managers felt that privatization would benefit the company's marketing efforts in the West. "After all," commented executive committee vice president Boguslawa Kielan, "Western firms are not eager to do business with state-owned companies. There is something suspicious about a company controlled by a central ministry, and Western clients are much more comfortable placing orders with a private partner."

Prochnik retained two consultant firms, the British Morgan Grenfell & Company and Lodz-based Doradztwo Gospodarcze, to assist in the privatization process. The consultants organized employee meetings and rallied support for privatization. They assessed the company's financial standing, valued its assets, and performed detailed marketing studies in an effort to model Prochnik's likely private sector performance. They established contacts at the Ministry of Privatization and convinced authorities of Prochnik's financial soundness. Furthermore, the consultants produced persuasive evidence that the company would continue to be a major Polish exporter even in the absence of government assistance. When the privatization law was passed in July 1990, Prochnik management was well prepared and submitted a strong application for inclusion in the privatization program.

To establish credibility for its program, the Ministry of Privatization resolved to initially commercialize only five carefully selected state-owned companies. These companies would have to demonstrate that they would be able to compete in competitive free markets. Prochnik was a promising candidate. The company's high export volume indicated that it was able to meet Western quality standards. Furthermore, Prochnik had been profitable for many years, earning an operating profit of 9 billion zloty ($0.9 million) on sales of 36 billion zloty ($3.8 million) in 1989. Finally, encouraging marketing studies performed by the consultants projected increased demand for Prochnik products both within Poland and in nearby Western European countries, particularly Germany and Great Britain.

Having presented a compelling case for privatization, Prochnik became one of the first companies selected from a roster of twenty state-owned candidates competing for inclusion in the ministry's program. As a result, Prochnik—a company that had received little recognition in the Western world because it had so often manufactured its coats under foreign labels—was suddenly cast into the international limelight. According to executive committee vice president Boguslawa Kielan:

The promotional effect of being included in the first group of companies to be privatized in Poland was astounding. The whole world was observing our country's first attempt at privatization. Almost immediately, Prochnik's credibility increased in national banking circles, and we received offers for extensive lines of credit. The Prochnik name became known internationally. For the first time in company history, we booked orders from Italy. In fact, we managed to expand our Western client base by 10 percent over the next two years.

Eager to privatize the company, Prochnik management began to make conversion plans well before parliament passed the July 1990 privatization law. The company's consultants developed several possible scenarios for the future organizational structure of the company. One possibility was for Prochnik to form a private joint venture with a Western investor who could contribute fresh capital and possibly provide Prochnik with modern sewing machinery. This option, however, had three major disadvantages: (1) although Prochnik would be a partner in a private joint venture, the company itself would remain state-owned; (2) Prochnik would not have full managerial control of the venture; (3) the search for a suitable joint venture partner could be a time-consuming and expensive affair, significantly delaying the process of forming a private company. Another scenario that the consultants considered—converting Prochnik into a joint stock company on the basis of the plan being developed in the Ministry of Privatization—proved to be the most appealing.

Clearly, privatization offered several important advantages to Prochnik. But, as we shall see, privatization is far from a sufficient condition for the far-reaching managerial actions necessary to revitalize the enterprise.

On September 27, 1990, Prochnik was officially converted to a joint stock company. Ownership rights in the company were divided into 1.5 million shares, all of which were retained by the state treasury. The nominal value of each share was set at 20,000 zloty ($2.11). At the same time, a new management structure was introduced at the company. An executive committee and a supervisory board, both of which were elected by a shareholders' general assembly, replaced the communist-era system of government-appointed directors and managerially powerful workers' councils. Prochnik's joint stock charter prescribed the role of each constituent within the new management structure.

The three-member executive committee, which was to be responsible for day-to-day management of Prochnik's business and for representing the firm in all external affairs, would serve a term of three years. The president of the committee was to be elected by the shareholders' general assembly. The remaining members of the executive committee would be nominated by the president but required the approval of shareholders before assuming office.

The supervisory board was to be the highest-ranking management authority within the company. It would consist of between six and twelve members who would serve a term of three years. Two-thirds of the supervisory board members were to be elected by the shareholders' general assembly, and the remaining one-third was to be elected by Prochnik workers. The supervisory board would elect a director from among its own membership and was required to meet at least once per quarter. Among the board's most important management responsibilities would be ensuring the integrity of the company's balance sheet and income statement, as well as approving the executive committee's decisions for allocating profits or covering losses. The supervisory board would also have the authority to suspend the executive committee and assume managerial control of Prochnik's day-to-day operations. Supervisory board members' salaries were to be calculated as a fixed percentage of Prochnik profits, a compensation scheme that provided strong incentives for profit-oriented management. The percentage of company profits awarded to board members was to be determined by shareholders during the general assembly.

The third managerial authority in the new joint stock company was to be the general assembly. All shareholders would be entitled to participate in Prochnik's general assembly, which would be similar to an annual shareholders' meeting in the United States. Meetings of the general assembly were to be scheduled, organized, and directed by the executive committee. Business matters raised in the assembly were to be settled by simple majority vote. Each stock owner was entitled to one vote per share. All new issues of Prochnik stock, as well as the sale of corporate debt instruments, would require the approval of the general assembly. The general assembly would also be entitled to change corporate statutes and would have the authority to dissolve the company.

On September 27, 1990, the same day that Prochnik was commercialized, the company's first general assembly—made up of a panel of ministry and government officials—elected a three-member executive committee and, in conjunction with Prochnik workers, a six-member supervisory board. Unwilling to implement radical change at a company that had been successful in the past, the panel of government officials voted to retain 61-year-old Longin Barski, Prochnik's general director since 1980, as president of the executive committee. Furthermore, Barski's vice-presidential nominees, as well as several supervisory board candidates selected by the ministry, had held managerial positions at Prochnik during the company's communist era.

On November 30, 1990, only two months after the company had been commercialized, Prochnik shares were offered for public sale. To promote Prochnik's initial public stock offering, the government launched a national advertising campaign and distributed a Western-style prospectus prepared by Morgan Grenfell & Co. and Doradztwo Gospodarcze. Prochnik stock could be purchased by both domestic and foreign investors at one of four state-run banks located in Warsaw, Katowice, Poznan, and Gdansk. Prochnik had become an immensely popular company, and its stock sold quickly. Before the end of the year, 1.2 million shares were sold to over thirty thousand outside investors at a price of 50,000 zloty ($5.26) per share. The largest investor, a Lodz-based insurance company called Westa, purchased 23 percent of Prochnik's stock. Twenty percent of the stock, or 300,000 shares, was sold to Prochnik workers at half of the public offering price.

Several months later, on April 6, 1991, Prochnik's new private owners conducted the company's second general assembly. The emotionally charged meeting resulted in a far-reaching management shakeup. The assembly accepted the resignation of four members of the supervisory board. Several had been staunch communist-oriented Prochnik managers throughout the 1980s and had been pressured to resign by increasingly market-oriented colleagues within the company. At the same time, the general assembly voted to increase the number of supervisory board members from six to twelve, bringing ten successful private sector executives and free market economists

into Prochnik's management ranks. The new supervisory board selected Wieslawa Wrobel, a prominent banking and insurance executive, to serve as its chairman.

As Prochnik became increasingly influenced by market-oriented
executives, top-level management changes continued to alter the
company's operations. In December 1991, Wlodzimierza Zajdla, vice
president of the executive committee and Longin Barski's closest adviser, was abruptly dismissed by Prochnik's supervisory board. The
implications were clear for Barski, who had proved incapable of altering his old-style management practices throughout the privatization
process at Prochnik. Two months later, in February 1992, the embat-
tled Barski submitted his resignation to the supervisory board. On
the same day, the board offered the presidency of the executive committee to Wojciech Kolignan.

Developing a Business Strategy

Despite the excitement generated by the creation of the new Warsaw
Stock Exchange, Prochnik's early stock market performance was mis-
erable. Trading at approximately 56,000 zloty ($5.39) per share when
the exchange opened in April 1991, Prochnik stock fell to 25,000
zloty ($2.27) per share in September, and by October 1992, the price
per share had slipped to 17,500 zloty ($1.17). Vice President Kielan
attributed Prochnik's poor showing to external events that had made
1991 an unusually difficult year for the company. First, a deep recession in the West had resulted in severe cutbacks in Prochnik exports
to all of the company's Western client countries other than Germany.
Second, the Soviet market collapsed in late 1990. Third, Poland's
reform government canceled export subsidies for domestic manufacturing companies in 1990. In the past, the central government had
provided Prochnik with a combination of direct payments and tax
relief equal to approximately 3 percent of total export sales. For
Prochnik, with 105 billion zloty ($9.9 million) in export sales in 1991,
the loss of a 3 percent subsidy was significant. Finally, Prochnik had
begun buying much of its raw fabric in Western Europe—particularly
in Italy—in an effort to improve the quality of its products. Although
the company paid its Italian suppliers in U.S. dollars, it received
most of its export earnings in German marks. Throughout 1991, the
mark fell drastically relative to the dollar, and the result was high

relative supply prices for Prochnik. According to Kielan, Prochnik's 1991 earnings would have been 10 percent higher had it not been for the adverse mark/dollar exchange rate.

As Prochnik's stock price plummeted, managers at Westa Insurance, the company's largest shareholder, became concerned. In mid-1991, Westa hired Company Assistance Limited (CAL), an American consulting firm with a large branch office in Warsaw, to develop a new business strategy for Prochnik. For the remainder of the year and for the first several months of 1992, CAL consultants and Prochnik management hammered out a five-part business plan that would bring about significant improvements in Prochnik's performance. The plan called for Prochnik to (1) target high-income clientele, (2) focus more sales resources on the domestic market, (3) locate higher-paying clients in the West through a network of sales agents, (4) expand its product line, and (5) reduce operating costs.

Targeting High-Income Clientele

The decision to focus on the high-end segment of the clothing market resulted largely from increasingly intense competition in the middle market segments from low-cost producers in Taiwan, Hong Kong, and other countries in the Far East. When Polish import restrictions were relaxed as part of the country's economic reform program in 1990, these producers flooded the Polish market with low-cost coats, and Prochnik was unable to compete effectively on price. Far East producers also drove Prochnik from mid-quality export markets. In the late 1980s, Prochnik had sold fully 10 percent of the coats it produced to discount department stores in the United States. However, Prochnik had been able to price these exports competitively only because it received generous export subsidies from the Polish government. When economic reformers withdrew government export subsidies in 1990, Prochnik was forced to retreat from the U.S. market. Whereas the company sold 18 percent of its output to U.S. clients in 1990, by 1991, U.S. sales accounted for only 5.4 percent of total production, and by 1992, Prochnik had withdrawn from the U.S. market altogether. At the same time, economic and political reform in Poland led to the formation of a high-income class of professionals, including entrepreneurs, lawyers, and politicians. This upwardly mobile group was quick to follow Western consumer trends and began to shop increasingly for high quality despite higher prices. Poland's evolving class of fashion-conscious professionals provided Prochnik with a new target market.

Executive committee president Kolignan described Prochnik's renewed focus on wealthy, fashion-conscious consumers as a move away from the mass production market. Upscale clients demanded frequent changes in design, and they replaced coats much more frequently than customers who bought coats simply for utility. Furthermore, it was important for fashion-conscious clients to feel that their clothing was unique, that it was not available to mass market consumers. As a result, Prochnik substantially reduced the number of coats it produced in a single production run or series. Whereas in the past, a single series could range from 10,000 to 50,000 pieces, by late 1991 Prochnik began to produce a wider assortment of coats in small lots of between 300 and 1,000 pieces.

Production for a more demanding clientele called for higher-quality raw materials than Prochnik had used in the past. According to Kolignan, "Our traditional Polish suppliers were not able to fulfill the quality and time standards we set for them." As a result, Prochnik turned to suppliers in Western Europe. Imported cotton, which accounted for 25 percent of Prochnik's cotton requirements in 1991, accounted for fully 38 percent in 1992. At the same time, imports grew from 13 to 44 percent of the company's total wool purchases. Although foreign fabrics resulted in higher retail prices for Prochnik products, the company was still able to sell its coats for one-third to one-half of the price of comparable products offered by Boss, Pierre Cardin, and other fashionable Western firms that had entered the Polish market. "One of the men's coats that we make from Italian pilot-cloth sells in a local shop for 2.5 million zloty ($156)," said Kolignan. "Boss sells the same coat in its salons for 7 million zloty ($438)."

Focusing on the Domestic Market

Prochnik's new strategy called for increased focus on the domestic market. There were several reasons to concentrate marketing efforts in Poland rather than on export sales. First, the state-run chain of regional clothing wholesalers that had purchased all of Prochnik's domestic output in the communist era collapsed in 1990. To continue selling Prochnik coats to Polish consumers, the company would have to develop a new domestic distribution network. Second, Prochnik exports competed with similar products manufactured in the Czech Republic, Hungary, Portugal, North Africa, and the Far East—products that were comparable in price and often in quality. As a result, profit margins on Prochnik exports had been driven down considerably in recent years. Finally, Prochnik was interested in developing an international reputation for its own label rather than serving exclusively as a sewing subcontractor for well-established Western firms. Kolignan, however, felt that before the Prochnik label could be successfully marketed abroad, it would have to achieve stronger name recognition in Poland. The company had begun marketing its coats in earnest in Poland only in the late 1980s, and Kolignan felt that Prochnik would have to establish itself as the country's undisputed leader in coat quality and market share before it could successfully introduce its products worldwide. "Leadership in the Polish market will enable us to enter foreign markets as a trademarked producer," he said. "We will be able to sell products made from our own fabrics and cut to our own designs."

Prochnik began to develop its domestic marketing operations in 1991 largely by trial and error. Company representatives drove around the country to poll demand for high-quality coats in different regions of the country. They visited high-end retail shops and promoted the Prochnik brand name. The company participated in national trade fairs in Gdansk, Poznan, and Warsaw. Furthermore, Prochnik began an extensive advertising campaign in upscale Polish magazines, including *Biznesmen* (*Businessman*), *Playboy*, and *Twoj Styl* (*Your Style*). After extensive travel and research, Prochnik management decided that the company should market its products in Poland's largest cities; the country's wealthy young professionals and most fashionable retail shops were concentrated in metropolitan areas such as Warsaw, Wroclaw, and Gdansk.

Before privatization, Prochnik's only two "sales" employees simply took orders from the company's client base of forty-nine state-owned wholesalers. By 1992, however, Prochnik had developed an aggressive domestic marketing division staffed by fifteen young, motivated sales agents. The agents, who were paid a sales commission of 3 percent of their gross trade turnover, excelled. In fact, they were too successful. The group expanded Prochnik's domestic clientele from a base of zero in 1990 to over a thousand customers in 1992. With such a large client base, however, it became difficult to exercise control over the pricing and presentation of Prochnik products in retail outlets. "Our products must be well presented in clothing shops," said Kolignan. "We like to do business only with clients who display our products appropriately and follow our pricing recommendations. Unfortunately, we are not physically capable of inspecting retail operations at a thousand different locations." Furthermore, Prochnik had the capacity to produce only 200,000 garments per year for the domestic market, output that simply was not sufficient to effectively supply a thousand clients. As a result, orders placed by domestic clients in 1992 were often for small lots, and Prochnik's transaction costs were high.

Kolignan and his executive committee decided to limit the size of Prochnik's domestic customer base. In late 1992, they selected approximately fifty wholesale outlets and retail shops that had consistently placed large orders and had never missed payment deadlines. In the future, Prochnik would restrict its domestic trade to these fifty firms. Among this group was a high-end, Warsaw-based department store chain called Dom Towarowy Centrum (Central Department Store). Dom Towarowy was Prochnik's largest Polish client, accounting for 12 percent of Prochnik's 69 billion zloty ($6.5 million) in domestic sales in 1991.

Prochnik treated its domestic clients well. Not only did the company supply customers with free advertising and promotional materials, but twice a year Kolignan invited his twenty largest Polish clients to corporate headquarters in Lodz for two- and three-day fashion shows in the company's exhibition room. Clients were served champagne as they mingled with Prochnik management and inspected the company's new designs for the upcoming season. During the two exhibitions that Prochnik sponsored in 1992, this group of twenty clients booked orders that accounted for over 30 percent of the company's 149 billion zloty ($11.0 million) in domestic sales.

In addition to selling its products through third-party retail outlets across the country, Prochnik's executive committee decided to open its own chain of domestic retail shops. A company-owned retail chain would have several advantages. First, it would expand Prochnik's market presence in Poland and increase customer awareness of the Prochnik label. The shops would be located in Poland's largest cities and would carry only Prochnik products. Second, the new shops would allow Prochnik to further reduce the number of its domestic clients and to establish direct control over the pricing and presentation of its products on the retail market. This would eliminate much of the cost incurred in making regular visits to clients in order to inspect their operations.

Third, most shops and wholesalers that did business with Prochnik purchased only a limited number of products in a limited range of sizes. Thus, when customers visited the shops and showed interest in Prochnik wares, they were often told that a particular coat was not available in the appropriate size or color. These negative experiences reflected poorly on the Prochnik label. In its own shops, Prochnik would be able to market its entire product line, in every available size and every available color.

Finally, by operating its own retail outlets, Prochnik would be able to avoid the payment problems that had arisen with several financially troubled clients. Prochnik management generally granted customers up to one month to pay for new product deliveries, but in Poland's difficult financial environment payment delays were becoming increasingly common. In early 1993, fifteen clients were in arrears, and Prochnik had filed court suits in an effort to collect 1 billion zloty ($62,500) in overdue payments.

Prochnik opened its first retail shop in downtown Lodz in mid-1991 and added a second shop at its Lodz headquarters building in early 1992. In December 1992, in partnership with the Gdynia Wool Federation, Prochnik opened a shop in the Baltic coast town of Gdynia. Prochnik owned 40 percent of the Gdynia shop. By early 1993, the company was making plans to add retail outlets in Bydgoszcz, Wroclaw, and Poznan. After spending over 1 billion zloty ($70,000) in 1992 to remodel and stock its new stores, the company expected to invest 2 billion zloty in its retail operations in 1993.

Management's decision to focus its sales efforts on the domestic market proved unexpectedly rewarding. From 1990 to 1991, Prochnik experienced a 27 percent increase in the quantity of goods sold domestically and a 204 percent increase in revenue. In the following year, the number of items sold domestically increased by 20 percent, and domestic revenue increased by 104 percent. Domestic sales exceeded export sales for the first time in over thirty years. In 1991, domestic sales accounted for 40 percent of total sales value; by 1992, sales within Poland had risen to 51 percent of the total.

Furthermore, domestic sales proved to be much more profitable than export sales: in 1992, Prochnik's gross profit margin on domestic sales was approximately 37 percent, but the export margin was closer to 12 percent.[4] Sales on the Polish market in 1992 were concentrated

Table 3-3   Prochnik Sales by Value and Volume, 1991 and 1992

a. Sales by Value

Market	1991		1992	
	Value (million zloty)	%	Value (million zloty)	%
Domestic	72,894 ($6.9 million)	40	148,970 ($11.0 million)	51
Prochnik-Designed Export	60,138 ($5.7 million)	33	40,894 ($3.0 million)	14
Cut-Make-Trim Export	51,026 ($4.8 million)	28	102,235 ($7.5 million)	35
Total	182,235	100	292,099	100

b. Sales by Volume

Market	1991		1992	
	Volume	%	Volume	%
Domestic	172,790	30	208,471	34
Prochnik-Designed Export	153,292	26	64,684	11
Cut-Make-Trim Export	258,290	44	333,697	55
Total	584,372	100	606,852	100

in five cities: Gdansk, Kielce, Lodz, Poznan, and Warsaw—these areas accounted for 120,000 of the 208,000 items sold domestically and 60 percent of total domestic sales value. As a result of intensified Polish marketing efforts, Prochnik management estimated that the company had captured at least 30 percent of the domestic market in men's coats by the end of 1992. For a description of Prochnik's domestic and export sales in 1991 and 1992, see Table 3-3.

Locating High-Paying Clients in the West

Prochnik's new business strategy called for the acquisition of a higher-paying client base in the West. Initially, the need to look westward for new clients occurred as a result of the collapse of Eastern markets—particularly the Soviet Union—in the early 1990s. However, even in the West, many countries were suffering a deep recession, and many Western clients had begun to insist on prices that resulted in dangerously low profit margins for Prochnik.

No longer required to channel its exports through Konfexim, Prochnik saved the 4 percent sales commission but had to develop its own network of foreign sales agents. Much as it had done in Poland,

Table 3-4 Prochnik Exports by
Volume (%), 1991 and 1992

Market	1991	1992
Germany	57.5	73
Great Britain	14.3	8
United States	5.4	—
France	4.9	—
Finland	4.6	3
Netherlands	3	4
Italy	—	3.5
Other	10.3	7.5

the company hired aggressive sales representatives to travel the countries of Western Europe with large stocks of Prochnik promotional materials, locating new clients largely through intuition. By late 1992, Prochnik had two agents operating in Germany, two in Great Britain, and one each in France and Finland.

However, just as Prochnik was transferring resources from Eastern to Western markets in the early 1990s the recession, particularly severe in Great Britain and France, resulted in pressure on prices that scarcely allowed Prochnik to recoup its production costs. Thus, CAL recommended that the company shift its Western marketing focus to regions that had not been as critically affected by the recession and were able to pay higher prices for Prochnik products. The primary target of these marketing efforts would be Germany.

The decline of Eastern markets, the development of a Western sales force, and the disparate effects of the recession in the West altered the composition of Prochnik's West European export markets. Sales to French clients, which accounted for 5 percent of total export volume in 1991, disappeared altogether in 1992. At the same time, sales to Great Britain decreased from over 14 percent to approximately 8 percent of Prochnik's export volume. These export losses, however, were offset by increased sales to high-paying German clients. Between 1990 and 1992, sales to Germany increased from 41 to 73 percent of total export volume. In 1992, Prochnik's German sales amounted to 93 billion zloty ($6.9 million), fully 32 percent of the value of the company's total sales. For a description of Prochnik's exports to Western markets in 1991 and 1992, see Table 3-4.

Cut-make-trim clients booked most of the new orders emanating from Germany. Among Prochnik's most significant German clients were Brinkmann, Philips, and Boss. By 1992, when total production at Prochnik was slightly over 600,000 pieces per year, Brinkmann alone was ordering up to 50,000 cut-make-trim pieces annually. In fact, in April 1993, the six main production teams in Prochnik's Lodz factory had all been dedicated to cut-make-trim production for German clients: two teams were manufacturing exclusively for Brinkmann, two for Philips, and two for Boss. Cut-make-trim sales increased from 44 percent of total sales volume in 1991 to 55 percent in 1992. "Cut-make-trim sales may not be a glamorous business," said Kolignan, "but it allows us to see the latest in Western fashion trends." Most attractive, however, was the approximately 50 percent gross profit margin on cut-make-trim sales.

Expanding the Product Line

Another key element of the strategy that CAL consultants and Prochnik management developed was an extension of Prochnik's traditional product line. In the past, the company had manufactured men's coats almost exclusively, routinely producing light cotton jackets and trench coats in the spring and thick wool jackets in the fall. However, increasing domestic demand in other high-quality clothing segments provided additional opportunities for growth. In 1991, the company began producing coats for the women's market and, soon afterward, women's suits for the rapidly increasing number of female professionals.

The move to women's wear was a logical one for Prochnik. For two years Kolignan had served as director of production at Dom Mody, Poland's leading manufacturer of fashionable women's apparel. By the time Wojciech Kolignan came to Prochnik in 1992, he had acquired extensive technical experience and market knowledge in the women's segment of the industry, and Prochnik's sales of women's accessories exploded. In 1992, women's coats and suits accounted for 33 percent of the company's total sales of 292 billion zloty ($21.5 million), and Kolignan predicted that this figure would rise to 40 percent within a year. In addition to women's wear, Prochnik began producing men's blazers for the domestic market in mid-1992. "We want to be known as more than a high-quality coat manufacturer," said Kolignan. "We want to be known as a high-quality *garment* manufacturer. For a description of Prochnik's product sales by market segment in 1992, see Table 3-5.

Table 3-5   Structure of Prochnik Sales in 1992

Product	Value (million zloty)	%	Volume	%
Men's Winter Overcoats	127,960 ($9.4 million)	44	229,943	38
Men's Summer Overcoats	31,723 ($2.3 million)	11	32,625	5
Men's Short Coats	31,088 ($2.3 million)	11	31,990	5
Men's Blazers	4,955 ($0.4 million)	2	9,610	2
Women's Overcoats	53,732 ($4.0 million)	18	117,321	19
Women's Short Coats	17,158 ($1.3 million)	6	47,742	8
Women's Suits	11,285 ($0.8 million)	4	25,608	4
Women's Blazers	11,130 ($0.8 million)	4	42,522	7
Total	292,099 ($21.5 million)	100	606,852	100
Domestic Sales	148,970 ($11.0 million)	51	208,471	34
Export Sales	143,129 ($10.5 million)	49	398,381	66

Reducing Operating Costs

Prochnik's new business plan called for efforts to reduce operating costs. The firm was not only overstaffed but had accumulated a large number of expensive, nonproductive assets. Kolignan and his executive committee were committed to eliminating nonproductive expenditures.

On CAL's recommendation, Prochnik management reduced the number of workers not directly employed in manufacturing. Between 1990 and 1992, the company released over 300 administrative employees, and total employment fell from 2,485 to 2,180. This cut resulted in savings of approximately 1.05 billion zloty per month ($77,400 per month at 1992 exchange rates).

In addition, after privatization, Prochnik divested many of the assets that Longin Barski and his socialist-oriented management team had acquired and operated at a loss for over ten years. Among these was a "workers' hotel"—a housing complex in Lodz that provided free apartments for employees who lived outside the city. The building, which provided living space for one hundred Prochnik seamstresses, proved too expensive to maintain and was sold in 1992. The company also closed an employee cafeteria at the Lodz factory that served subsidized meals and had never been able to cover its own operating expenses. Furthermore, when Barski had served as director, he had always maintained large inventories of raw materials, often hoarding enough fabric to fill Prochnik's production lines for over six months. To store his supplies, Barski had acquired a cavernous three-story warehouse in Lodz. By 1992, the warehouse was empty, and Prochnik sold the building soon after Barski was replaced by Kolignan. Finally, since 1946, Prochnik had operated in Lodz a small coat factory that employed approximately 150 workers. Overhead costs at the aging factory were high, and the operation was simply too small to be profitable. In 1991, management sold the building and transferred its 150 workers to the nearby plant at Prochnik headquarters.

Kolignan felt that employment cuts and asset sales were only the beginning of a true cost reduction program. "What we really need is a change in workers' mentality," he said. He felt that the most effective way to lower operating costs was to increase productivity. "In communist times," he said, "workers were guaranteed a job and a salary, and they had little incentive to put effort into their work. Now that must change." Ownership of 20 percent of the company's stock, which provided workers with a vested interest in Prochnik's profitability, was a step in the right direction. Employees worked faster, became conscientious about conserving energy at the factories, and made efforts to reduce the amount of fabric wasted in the manufacturing process. Improved productivity was reflected in the fact that net sales at Prochnik increased by 60 percent from 1991 to 1992 and the cost of sales grew by only 40 percent. In addition, net sales per employee increased from 100 million zloty ($9,455) in 1991 to 140 million zloty ($10,320) in 1992.

Prochnik in 1993: Continued Change and New Challenges

By early 1993, Prochnik was Poland's preeminent producer of high-quality coats and business wear. The company had been successfully privatized and was one of seventeen firms traded on the Warsaw Stock Exchange. Although the majority of the company's output continued to be exported to Western countries, Prochnik had become a major player on the Polish market. Other Polish coat producers were unable to match Prochnik's quality. Boss, Pierre Cardin, and other Western producers were unable to compete with Prochnik on price. As a result, Prochnik had been able to capture 30 percent of the Polish market for men's coats. The company was also quickly making inroads into the women's fashion segment, capturing over 1 percent of this highly competitive market only one year after introducing its line of women's wear.

Market-oriented changes that Prochnik management had implemented over the past year had resulted in a 300 percent increase in profitability. Prochnik's share price had also improved dramatically, rising from a low of 17,500 zloty ($1.17) in October 1992 to 135,000 zloty ($8.44) in May 1993. Encouraged by these results, Kolignan planned to continue refining Prochnik's operations. A priority in 1993 would be investment in new machinery. The average machine age in Prochnik's factories was approximately fifteen years, and most of the company's equipment was at least 70 percent amortized. Prochnik plant managers were eager to acquire automated fabric-cutting tables and modern steam presses. Whereas the company had spent 500,000 DM ($330,000) for new stitching equipment in 1992, management would invest four times as much in new machinery in 1993. Furthermore, Kolignan planned to computerize Prochnik's design department. Computerization would allow designers much more flexibility in sketching patterns for new clothing models, and it would allow them to correct imperfections almost instantaneously. Computers would also be useful in determining the most cost-efficient layout for individual component patterns on a sheet of fabric. Computerization of the design office, which the company began in late 1992 with the purchase of an IBM workstation, would cost Prochnik a total of 3 billion zloty ($221,000 at 1992 exchange rates). Prochnik's third investment initiative in 1993, of course, would be the 2 billion zloty ($147,000 at 1992 exchange rates) expansion of its growing chain of domestic retail shops.

At the same time that Kolignan was making plans to expand Prochnik's in-house manufacturing capabilities, he had begun to subcontract sewing jobs to idle state-owned plants with excess capacity. Many state-owned clothing manufacturers were unable to compete in Poland's new free market environment, and by 1992, their order books were empty. Desperate to bring work into their factories, these firms were willing to sew Prochnik's designs for little more than the cost of their seamstresses' labor. Prochnik began subcontracting work to state firms in the summer of 1992, and by the end of the year, six outside companies had sewn five thousand Prochnik garments, or 1 percent of the company's total output. In 1993, Kolignan planned to subcontract 8 percent of Prochnik's output to the same six Polish firms and an additional 2 percent to a state-owned firm in Belarus. Boguslawa Kielan, executive committee vice president, estimated that the subcontractors were manufacturing Prochnik's designs for 70 percent of what it would cost Prochnik to perform the work in its own factories.

Although Prochnik's new investment and subcontracting initiatives appeared promising, two major challenges threatened to slow the firm's growth. First, bank financing had become extraordinarily expensive in Poland. Second, Prochnik was having difficulty attracting qualified manufacturing workers.

For Prochnik, bank financing was essential. The tight macroeconomic policies introduced at the beginning of 1990 resulted in very high nominal interest rates, including rates on commercial loans of over 70 percent in the second half of 1990 and in 1991. High rates resulted in unprecedented financing charges for Prochnik. In 1992, the company had an average of from 15 to 17 billion zloty ($1.1 to $1.3 million) in bank debt on its books on any given day, resulting in financing charges of 8.8 billion zloty ($0.6 million) over the course of the entire year.

Fortunately for Kolignan, however, the financing problem began to solve itself as a result of the large increases in cut-make-trim orders from Western clients. Because these orders did not require Prochnik to make investments in raw materials, cut-make-trim expenses were minimal, and bank loans were unnecessary. Furthermore, income from cut-make-trim sales could be used to subsidize inventory purchases for manufacturing that Prochnik performed under its own label. Cut-make-trim sales increased from 27 percent of total sales in 1991 to 33 percent in 1992, and Kolignan expected this trend to continue in 1993.

Another fundamental challenge for Kolignan in 1993 would be increasing employment in Prochnik's direct production areas. Prochnik's factories were operating at capacity, and the firm had received more export orders than it could fill. Kolignan thus wanted to introduce second shifts in several of the plants, hiring an additional three hundred stitching workers in Lodz alone. However, despite an unemployment rate of 26 percent in Lodz, this would not be an easy undertaking. The average monthly salary at Prochnik's factories in 1992 was 2.6 million zloty ($192), well below the national average of 2.9 million zloty ($214). Prochnik seamstresses had expected to receive much higher pay once the company was privatized and compensation was no longer constrained by the excess wage tax. When wages remained suppressed, many of Prochnik's manufacturing workers became disillusioned. "How is it possible that for the wage I earn in a private company I can hardly make ends meet?" lamented a sewing machine operator in the Lodz plant. Kolignan, however, feared that salary increases would reduce Prochnik's competitiveness on international markets. "If we were to raise workers' wages, which account for half of a garment's manufacturing cost, Western clients would choose to have their products sewn in Bulgaria or even the Far East," he said.

Furthermore, many of Prochnik's competitors on the labor market were small, privately run sewing shops with low overhead costs. These small manufacturers were often unregistered and operated illegally, avoiding hefty income and wage taxes. Prochnik, in contrast, not only had to meet overhead expenses for four large factories but had to pay an annual income tax equal to 40 percent of its gross profit and wage taxes equal to 48 percent of its annual gross wage bill. As a result, small sewing shops were able to pay higher salaries than Prochnik and to attract the most talented seamstresses in the Lodz area, particularly those who had completed three-year training programs at local textile schools. Kolignan was committed to reducing operating costs, but in 1993, he would have to consider increasing salaries if Prochnik were to continue its growth.

Assessment

Prochnik, one of the most successful privatization and enterprise restructuring experiences in Poland, demonstrates the range and depth of issues managers must address successfully to create an enterprise that has long-term viability in domestic and international markets. Prochnik would never have survived without the selection of a highly competent leader (Kolignan) *and* his subsequent retention of skilled strategy consultants. The installation of new, profit-driven management was a result of Prochnik's privatization early in the reform process. Although privatization itself neither provides nor guarantees solutions to management problems, it has the clear benefit of putting in place managers and governance processes that are driven by profits and accountable to private shareholders.

After being installed as president, Kolignan pursued an impressive, multifaceted approach to restructuring that began with an overhaul of Prochnik's business strategy and included (1) targeting high-income customers, (2) focusing on the domestic market, serviced in part by a number of retail stores, and (3) the introduction of new

product lines. With a new strategy in place, based on careful analysis
of the relevant market, Kolignan thoughtfully reformed production
operations, shed assets and cut unnecessary labor, improved inventory management, changed suppliers, and introduced new technologies in many parts of the business. The results of these initiatives
were impressive in virtually every respect, as sales and profits soared
while efficiency improved significantly.

The tightly aligned set of actions that Kolignan took are illustrative of the "complementary" changes necessary to successfully restructure a large, formerly state-owned enterprise. A clear, market-
driven leadership vision was carefully combined with a sound
business strategy based on Prochnik's relative advantages in international and domestic markets. Marketing plans and distribution
channels were created to support the various dimensions of the strategy, and production operations were rationalized to deliver higher
value at lower cost. Assets and labor that were unnecessary, in light
of the strategy, were eliminated, and others were redeployed. New
technologies were introduced to enhance performance and cut costs.
Each of those changes reinforced all of the others. In fact, it is unlikely
that Prochnik would have enjoyed the same success had any element
been sacrificed or altered dramatically.

The challenge of conceiving and implementing such complementary organizational reforms is common to managers of state enterprises, as well as to newly privatized enterprises, in all post-
communist countries. The evidence suggests that Prochnik is a rare
example of rapid and long-lasting success. But, despite remarkable
progress since privatization, the wage pressures facing Kolignan in
1993 suggest that Prochnik's future viability is by no means assured.
Given the vigorous worldwide competition in the garment industry,
Prochnik must continue to significantly improve its performance if it
is to remain competitive with *lower-cost* producers in other countries.
In this respect, the Prochnik experience clearly shows that, first, successful restructuring is enormously difficult and hence unlikely in all
but exceptional cases and, second, enduring viability in the mature
industries that characterized Poland's industrial structure is a constant
long-term struggle for even the most capable managers.

CHAPTER 4

State Enterprise Restructuring:
A Tale of Two Shipyards

Prochnik is a leading example of privatization (through initial public offering) preceding restructuring, and it illustrates the range and depth of managerial actions necessary to make one of Poland's most promising state enterprises competitive in international and domestic markets. Despite remarkable progress, Prochnik's long-term viability is by no means secure. Szczecin and Gdansk shipyards, in contrast, were not part of the early privatization process and as of late 1994 remained fully owned by the state. Hence, unlike Prochnik, the shipyard managers are attempting to restructure *before* privatization. The Szczecin and Gdansk stories show the diversity of approaches undertaken in response to a similar set of problems facing managers in post-communist countries.

The newly installed managing directors of the Szczecin Shipyard pursued a radical, market-driven restructuring plan involving debt forgiveness, the establishment of an export-oriented marketing function, focus on a single product line, dramatic changes in production operations and in human resource practices, the shedding of unproductive assets and unnecessary labor, and new mechanisms for ship financing. Consensus among key stakeholders, especially workers and creditors, was gained by making a persuasive case that a smaller, viable shipyard was preferable to a bankrupt shipyard.

The newly installed managing director of the Gdansk Shipyard had no market-driven vision for his enterprise. He sought to maintain a large yard operated mainly for the benefit of the workers, despite the yard's inability to be economically self-sufficient.

The results from a comparison of these two enterprises are quite disparate and are typical of the range of outcomes associated with very different managerial strategies for state enterprise restructuring. Regrettably, the Gdansk experience is quite common, if not typical. The Szczecin experience, though impressive and clearly preferable to most observers, is nonetheless more troubling because it suggests that heroic management actions may not be enough to save the vast majority of state enterprises from failure in competitive international markets. To better understand the circumstances facing managers at the time of economic and political liberalization, we begin with a brief historical review of the shipbuilding industry.

Background

The Polish shipyards' major customers were Eastern-bloc countries, particularly the Soviet Union, which accounted for over 60 percent of the Polish shipbuilding industry's total output. Poland's central government played a fundamental role in locating clients for the national shipbuilding industry; the shipyards never interacted directly with fleet owners. Rather, a large, state-operated trade company called Centromor received all customer inquiries and negotiated contracts on behalf of the shipyards for a commission of 2 percent of a ship's selling price. Centromor paid the yards in domestic currency on completion of each shipbuilding project.

The government's influence in shipbuilding operations was pervasive. The government not only screened clients through Centromor but provided virtually all financing for new ship construction. Most financing was channeled through the National Bank of Poland (NBP), a state-owned banking monopoly, which provided the yards with inexpensive loans that often covered as much as 90 percent of total ship construction costs. In the late 1980s, when the interest rate charged by the NBP was well below the rate of inflation, Polish shipyards actually profited by borrowing from the National Bank. Furthermore, although most orders filled for foreign clients were unprofitable, direct government subsidies ensured that the shipyards would have sufficient funding to complete each project. These subsidies often reached 50 percent of total construction costs.

During Poland's communist era, the national shipbuilding industry was administered by the Industrial Shipbuilding Union (Zjednoczenie Przemyslu Okretowego), which was directly accountable to the Ministry of Industry. Strategists at the Shipbuilding Union felt that it was important for each shipyard to manufacture a wide range of vessels in order to ensure that all yards would be able to maintain full employment even during off-peak demand periods for particular types of ships.[1] The three largest yards—located in Gdynia, Gdansk, and Szczecin—boasted product portfolios that contained over thirty types of ships. Competing shipyards in Korea and Japan, for example, were much more highly specialized. By producing a series of ships of the same type, those shipyards gained tremendous cost and productivity advantages through learning, refinement of the design, and economies of scale in materials acquisition and capital utilization. Conversely, by maintaining such a diverse product portfolio, the Polish shipyards were unable to develop world-class expertise or world-class manufacturing efficiency in any one particular model.

With unfocused product portfolios and cost structures inflated by an array of social services for employees, the Polish shipyards were unable to build ships efficiently and were forced to rely on government support to meet operating expenses. The Polish government was willing to pump money into the loss-making industry because it supported thousands of workers and because Polish shipbuilding had become a point of national industrial pride. As a result, managerial strategy in the shipbuilding industry was based on extracting government concessions rather than earning profits. The shipyards' easy access to the government till, however, was abruptly severed when Poland was swept by political reform in 1989.

Mounting Crisis and New Management

National political and economic reforms resulted in important changes at Polish state-owned enterprises. Sweeping management changes were introduced as government officials and employee groups sought to remove all vestiges of the former communist leadership structure. At the Gdansk Shipyard, union leader Hans Szyc replaced staunch communist Czeslaw Tolwinski as general director. At the Szczecin Shipyard, the top job was awarded to former labor activist Krzysztof Piotrowski. The similarities between the shipyards' new market-era managers were striking: they were close in age, had received similar academic training, had extensive experience in the ship-building industry, and were long-time leaders of shipyard employee unions. On paper, at least, Szyc and Piotrowski seemed to be cast from an identical mold.

Hans Szyc had been a dedicated employee at the Gdansk Ship-yard for thirty-two years. After completing his studies in ship design and heavy industry at the Gdansk Polytechnic Institute in 1970, he joined the yard as a production worker and became well acquainted with the grueling manufacturing work on the slipway. From his front-line job in the production bay, he was promoted to manufacturing brigade foreman, then to engineer, and eventually to chief ship de-signer before being named general director in 1990. Szyc's appoint-ment to the top job in the shipyard resulted largely from his stellar work record and from his broad-based support among the shipyard's employee unions.

Krzysztof Piotrowski's personal history closely resembled that of Hans Szyc. The 45-year-old Piotrowski had been an outstanding student at the Polytechnic Institute in Szczecin, where he specialized in underwater engineering and designed pressure-resistant steel saws and other tools for shipyard divers. When he completed his studies at the Polytechnic, Piotrowski took a laborer's job in the production bay at the Szczecin Shipyard and rose quickly through the manufac-turing hierarchy. Much like Szyc, he was an outspoken union leader and served as the chairman of the workers' council. He was dismissed from the yard in 1985 for his aggressive pro-labor activities. From 1985 to 1991 Piotrowski lectured and studied at the Polytechnic Insti-tute in Szczecin, where he was awarded the doctorate degree in un-derwater engineering in 1991. With the introduction of economic reforms, Piotrowski was called back to the shipyard by a management search committee whose members included government officials from the Ministry of Industry and a panel of shipyard union representa-tives. The panel considered four people who entered the competition for the managing director position. Piotrowski presented the commit-tee with an impressive plan for market-oriented reform and was of-fered the position of general director in April 1991.

The disappearance of the Soviet market resulted in staggering financial setbacks at both the Gdansk and the Szczecin shipyards. In Gdansk, the Soviet Union placed its last order in 1988, but by early 1993 the yard still housed three unfinished fishing vessels that the Soviet Union had ordered but was unable to pay for. Because these ships had been built to nonstandard Soviet technical specifications, the yard was unable to sell them to Western clients even at prices well below production costs. The unmarketable ships generated millions of dollars in losses at the shipyard. A similar scenario was played out in Szczecin, where in 1990, eight of the eleven ships in the yard's production bay were being built for Soviet clients. On short notice, all eight orders were canceled. Furthermore, the yard had recently completed three ships that the Soviets could not afford to purchase. Just as in Gdansk, the Szczecin yard was unable to locate Western fleet owners willing to buy the Soviet-ordered vessels. The Soviet Union's inability to meet its contractual obligations in Szczecin cost the shipyard 700 billion zloty ($74 million) in losses.

In 1991, Poland's second year of economic reform, the Gdansk Shipyard suffered losses of 57 billion zloty ($6 million) on sales of 732 billion zloty ($77 million). Meanwhile, in the construction bay at the Szczecin Shipyard, three ships destined for clients in India and the United Kingdom were in various stages of production. When contracts for the ships were signed in the late 1980s, Poland's communist government had agreed to subsidize 50 percent of all ongoing construction costs. However, when the new Solidarity government canceled shipbuilding subsidies in 1990, the yard, unwilling to abandon its Western clients and sacrifice its reputation on the world market, was forced to finance the projects with bank credit. At the time, the annual interest rate on commercial loans in Poland was nearly 120 percent, and the cost to the Szczecin yard for completing the ships was enormous, resulting in losses of approximately 1.1 trillion zloty ($116 million).

Thus, in Poland's shipbuilding industry, two new managers, both of whom enjoyed broad union support, took over the leadership of two similarly troubled shipyards. Despite nearly identical circumstances, management at the Gdansk and Szczecin shipyards pursued radically different reform strategies. Szyc lobbied strongly for a policy of government-industry cooperation and maintained the high employment, high wage line of his union days. Piotrowski introduced a demanding restructuring plan calling for reduced employment, highly focused product selection, and a complex rescheduling of his shipyard's massive debt. The disparate results achieved by the Gdansk and Szczecin yards by early 1993 provide compelling evidence about the effectiveness of alternative strategies for the restructuring of state-owned enterprises.

The Gdansk Shipyard

Recent History

Post–World War II reconstruction of Gdansk's shipbuilding operation was completed in 1947, and the 146-hectare industrial giant was christened the Lenin Shipyard. Supported by government subsidies and Soviet clients, the Lenin Shipyard experienced phenomenal growth, becoming a self-contained industrial city by the time it reached its productive peak in the 1970s. With a work force of 17,000, the yard was producing over 30 ships per year, 60 percent of which were exported to the Soviet Union. The shipyard's six slipways were capable of launching vessels of up to 265 meters in length and weighing up to 18,000 tons. The Lenin Shipyard was also endowed with dozens of towering industrial cranes, manufacturing facilities for producing shipbuilding inputs, maintenance facilities, office buildings, employee shops, cafeterias, and a hospital. The yard not only assembled ships but also manufactured almost all internal components, and it even served as a supplier of diesel engines and boilers to other Polish shipyards. The Lenin Shipyard's product portfolio was extraordinarily diverse: the yard produced roll-on/roll-off cargo ships, floating fish-processing factories, tankers, research vessels, refrigerated transport ships, and many other specialty ships demanded by the yard's Soviet overlords. Although the business was never profitable, government subsidies ensured the shipyard a comfortable existence.

The Lenin Shipyard was a source of industrial pride for Poland, but in early 1980–1981, shipyard workers transformed it into a hotbed of opposition. Striking workers overran the yard, demanding better working conditions and the right to unionize. Led by Lech Walesa, they formed the Solidarity trade union. By the end of 1981, the Communist party had proved unable to reach agreement with the newly organized labor movement, and the government responded by imposing martial law and banning solidarity. The Lenin Shipyard was taken over by military forces, and a policy of political retaliation was instituted against the shipyard.

Throughout the 1980s, the government systematically lowered shipyard wages relative to the wages of other professions in the area, and shipyard workers abandoned the yard in droves for better opportunities elsewhere. Employment fell from 16,000 in 1980 to 12,000 in 1985. At the same time, Centromor directed fewer orders to the defiant shipyard, and the value of annual production fell from $196 million in 1980 to $111 million in 1985. In a final act of political vengeance, the government liquidated the Lenin Shipyard in 1988, allowing it to complete current building projects but forbidding it from booking new orders. With the shipyard under a death sentence, an additional 3,500 demoralized workers abandoned their jobs to seek a more promising future.

The business environment at the Lenin Shipyard was dismal. After the liquidation order, customers, mainly Polish and Russian state enterprises, canceled 29 of the 44 orders on the yard's books, resulting in an estimated loss of 100 billion zloty ($21 million), and Bank Gdanski demanded immediate repayment of loans that it had made to finance shipyard inventories. However, in late 1989, just as the shipyard appeared to be on the brink of ruin, Barbara Johnson—a Chicago resident, native Pole, and heiress to the Johnson & Johnson Co. fortune—made an unexpected bid to buy the shipyard. It was an unprecedented event in postwar Polish history.

The market-oriented Johnson proved to be a demanding investor. She proposed an ambitious strategy to reduce shipyard employment, limit the scope of production to the core shipbuilding business, and decrease the number of projects undertaken by the shipyard at any one time. She would establish stringent compensation policies, capping shipyard wages at their 1989 level of 50 cents per hour. Johnson's regimen of free market reforms was demanding, but it offered the doomed enterprise a realistic opportunity to finally become a profitable business. Johnson's advisers, however, estimated the value of the shipyard to be only $6.5 million, far below the $100 million reported by shipyard management and optimistically propagated in the Polish press. To ease disappointment, Johnson offered to create a joint venture with shipyard management—rather than purchase the entire yard—for an investment of $6.5 million. In a shocking display of the managerial conservatism that would plague the shipyard well into Poland's reform process, a negotiation committee consisting of shipyard management and union representatives rejected Johnson's offer. As Prime Minister Jan Krzysztof Bielecki would comment several years later, "The Gdansk Shipyard squandered a golden opportunity to become a free market competitor when it rejected Barbara Johnson's offer."

Nevertheless, the shipyard was soon granted a second opportunity to privatize. In January 1990, Poland's newly installed Solidarity government rescinded the 1988 liquidation order, and the Ministry

of Industry recommended the yard for government-directed commercialization—the process whereby a state-owned enterprise is transformed into a joint stock company whose shares are all owned by the
state treasury before some or all of them are sold to private investors.
The shipyard therefore continued to be a state-owned enterprise, but
commercialization was the first step toward privatization. This time,
however, absent were the two most important components of Johnson's offer: an immediate injection of capital and a free market vision.
The commercialized shipyard would receive fresh capital only if it
could be transformed into a profitable enterprise, providing investors
with an incentive to purchase shares. The shipyard, in turn, could
become profitable only if it were led by highly disciplined, market-
oriented management. On January 24, 1990, Szyc replaced Tolwinski
as general director of the shipyard. When Szyc began to stubbornly
pursue the high-wage, high-employment managerial policies of the
1970s, the shipyard's chances for successful free market reform appeared as remote as ever.

Hans Szyc's Approach to Reform

Despite the excitement surrounding Poland's economic transformation and the far-reaching privatization program, Szyc was concerned
that changes at his shipyard were occurring too quickly. When he
was ushered in as shipyard manager in 1990, 50 percent of shipyard
management was replaced. Szyc felt that the purge of previous management was largely an emotional reaction against the displaced communist regime. He complained that the shakeup was too radical a
change; it did not allow for continuity at the yard. "I am not against
reform," he said, "but I do not want to do it simply for the sake of
making changes. If we are to make effective changes, they need to be
implemented slowly and with a great deal of foresight."

Szyc was also reluctant to make rapid reductions in the size of
his shipbuilding operation. For example, for financial reasons, Szyc
realized that the yard would eventually have to shut down one of its
four hull construction departments, but he planned to wait several
years before doing it. The delay would give workers who were to be
displaced ample time to make adjustments and to prepare for the
change. A devoted union member for thirty-two years, Szyc realized
that it would be difficult to dismiss his long-time colleagues in the
hull department. "How can I convince these people that firing them

is for the good of the yard?" he wondered. "For all the excitement they have generated in our country, capitalism and democracy are not good systems."

In advocating slow change, Szyc focused his managerial efforts on accomplishing three objectives: (1) he would maintain the historical scope of the shipyard's operations; (2) he would hire more labor and increase wages; and (3) he would make a strong case for government intervention. At a time when the Polish economy demanded market reforms, Szyc's management style clearly bore the stamp of Poland's socialist era.

Large Institutions. Hans Szyc's vision for the future was shaped largely by his memory of the shipyard during its golden era in the 1970s. Szyc was pleased that he had been able to manage the 146-hectare shipyard through its first three years in a market economy without reducing its physical dimensions or its extensive base of industrial assets. "We produce as many ship components as possible on our own grounds," said Szyc. "We do not want to become overly reliant on outside suppliers." This was clearly a management principle that had been learned during the communist era. "The transformers and the boilers that we produce at the shipyard could be purchased at lower cost in Western countries," commented shipyard board member Stefan Szpalerski, "but we have strong unions, and we cannot simply lay off the workers."

Closely related to Szyc's autarchic production strategy was his insistence on maintaining a highly diversified product portfolio. Although product focus had become a popular and important manufacturing concept in many free market economies, Szyc said, "I do not want to become dependent on a single type of client and close doors for the shipyard." Of the nine vessels under construction at the shipyard in early 1993, two were roll-on/roll-off cargo ships, three were container ships, and four were refrigerated transport ships. Furthermore, the prospectuses that the shipyard's marketing department sent to foreign fleet owners touted the yard's expertise in fishing factory vessels, reefer carriers, and large-scale sailing ships.

The large-institution mentality prevalent among Gdansk shipyard management was clearly manifested in Szyc's strategy for setting financial goals. Growth targets were always expressed in terms of revenues rather than profits. Szyc was convinced that high gross income was the most important indicator of industrial success. Indeed, under Szyc's leadership, revenue at the yard steadily rose from 523 billion zloty ($55 million) in 1990, to 847 billion zloty ($77 million in 1991), to 2.4 trillion zloty ($171 million) in 1992, yet the shipyard was still unable to turn a profit. "If I can double my production every year and still not earn a profit, there must be something wrong with the economy," claimed Szyc. "My goal is to achieve annual sales of $300 million," he said. "At this level, the shipyard will certainly break even." Szyc focused on revenue rather than profit largely because he felt that within his sprawling "industrial city," fixed costs played a more significant role than variable costs.

Labor Policy. Crucial to increasing production at the shipyard and spreading fixed costs over a large number of projects was increasing the size of the work force. "We are currently operating at only 50 percent of capacity," said Szyc, "but we have a full order book. If I could hire more workers, we would be able to build more ships." The shipyard's declining fortunes in the 1980s had a significant impact on Szyc's management philosophy. As a direct result of a 50 percent reduction in employment during an eight-year span after the shipyard uprisings in 1981, production plummeted from over thirty ships per year to less than ten. By hiring more workers, Szyc intended to increase capacity utilization at the shipyard to at least 80 percent. Unfortunately, during his first three years as general director, Szyc was unable to expand his work force because of Poland's excess wage tax, which severely restricted a state-owned enterprise's total wage bill.[2] In early 1993, however, repeal of the wage tax was under discussion in parliament, and Szyc hoped that he would soon be able to bolster shipyard employment from its current level of nine thousand to its 1970s level of seventeen thousand.

Szyc was a firm believer in the principle of full employment. He felt that this was especially important for a country like Poland, where low wages often made high employment more cost-effective than other capital investments. Thus, for example, Szyc maintained a staff of a hundred accountants rather than computerizing the shipyard's bookkeeping operations. In addition, rather than investing in modern automated welding equipment for soldering hull sections, Szyc hired workers who could perform the same task manually. The danger of this strategy was that by neglecting investments in modern equipment, the Gdansk Shipyard risked ceding significant productivity advantages to more progressive producers.

Szyc had strong sympathies for the social plight of his workers, often becoming involved in employees' difficulties on a personal level:

"Last March, I increased a production worker's pay by about 50 percent. He approached me again in April to request another pay raise because his wife had lost her job, and it was difficult for them to live on his 4 million zloty ($250) monthly salary. In this situation, I would ideally hire his wife to work in the shipyard. This would solve both his problems and mine. This is an issue that can be worked out between the shipyard and the local employment administration once the excess wage tax is removed."

In a costly display of solidarity with employee interests, Szyc continued to operate a vast infrastructure of workers' amenities that had been put in place by previous shipyard managers. These included shipyard-owned hotels, health spas, and vacation resorts; subsidized housing; free hospital and day-care services; and a shipyard-sponsored sports club. The shipyard also maintained an expansive fleet of buses and automobiles that managers and employees used for personal transportation. "These services are important for the workers," said Szyc. "And they constitute only a small percentage of the total cost of operating the shipyard."

Government Intervention. Shipbuilding was big business in Poland; however, it was also highly unprofitable. For both of these reasons, Szyc felt that the Gdansk Shipyard belonged within the protective realm of government rather than in the uncompromising world of a free market. "If you look at the shipbuilding process," he said, "the real business is not in the shipyard, it's in my eight hundred suppliers. I give them the business, and then we simply assemble the parts." Because his shipyard incurred huge losses in supporting such an expansive economic infrastructure, Szyc insisted that the yard merited government support. Thus, much as the Ministry of Education funded public schools because they fulfilled a social function, Szyc felt that the government should subsidize the country's business-generating shipyards.

In arguing for government financial support, Szyc stressed the difficulties that Polish shipyards faced in obtaining financing. Financing requirements for shipbuilding projects were enormous, and the ability of the Gdansk Shipyard to repay loans was anything but certain. Although shipyard management had been able to partially finance manufacturing operations after 1990 by demanding that clients provide prepayments both before and during the shipbuilding process, this solution was hardly comprehensive. Since prepayments rarely exceeded 50 percent of total shipbuilding costs, additional sources of financing were still necessary. Furthermore, Western fleet owners insisted that their prepayments be guaranteed by Polish commercial banks. Once again, however, Polish banks were usually unwilling to tie their financial fortunes to the Gdansk Shipyard; the risk that the shipyard would use prepayments to pay off creditors or to cover operating costs rather than to build ships was simply too high. The lack of financing became a major problem for Szyc. In January 1993, he lamented, "We do not have access to credit." No longer able to pay for shipbuilding inputs with subsidized government loans, the shipyard had accumulated debts of over $20 million to outside suppliers. Without government financial assistance, Szyc feared that the shipyard would not be able to escape its fiscal crisis.

The longer the shipyard struggled with its finances, the more convinced Szyc became that privatization was a poor industrial strategy for Poland's shipbuilding sector. He claimed that nowhere in the world was shipbuilding a profitable industry and that private investors would never buy into the business.[3] "Why should we expend energy trying to find investors?" wondered Szyc. "Who would possibly want to be a shareholder in a loss-generating shipyard?" That the shipyard's most important government contact had become the Ministry of Privatization rather than the Ministry of Industry was baffling to Szyc. He felt that the shipyard's interaction with government should be focused on the development of a cooperative industrial plan rather than on efforts to sell shares to an unwilling public. He pointed out that in Germany, where shipyards were operating at only 20 percent of capacity, the federal government was providing the industry with massive subsidies in an effort to fill production capacity.[4] As a result, German shipyards were able to achieve significant cost advantages on world markets. Furthermore, the governments of other ship-producing countries provided fleet owners with inexpensive long-term loans—generally ten- or fifteen-year loans at annual interest rates of from 3 to 5 percent—in order to attract new shipbuilding orders.

Szyc felt the government should bear other costs for the shipyard. Paramount among these were the losses that the yard had sustained in building Soviet ships that were never purchased. The contracts for these ships had been negotiated and signed by the central government's foreign trade monopoly, Centromor, yet the shipyard was forced to suffer the financial consequences when the deals went sour. "How can the government justify its decision to simply abandon the shipyard?" asked Szyc.[5]

Even more appealing to Szyc than industrial shipbuilding policy at the national level was government cooperation at the *voivodship*—or county—level. In February 1993, unemployment in the Gdansk Voivodship had reached seventy thousand. At the same time, Szyc claimed that he needed over a thousand new workers. He was convinced that by working together, the Gdansk Shipyard and the Gdansk Voivodship could establish a suitable employment policy. "How could an issue like this possibly be resolved in Warsaw?" he asked. Szyc envisioned a number of other cooperative arrangements that would benefit both the shipyard and the voivodship. He suggested, for example, that the shipyard could construct local roads in exchange for tax reductions.

Finally, Szyc's argument for government intervention appealed to a sense of political justice. The ruling government, after all, had its roots in the Gdansk Shipyard. Now, with Solidarity representatives occupying the most important political offices in Warsaw, Szyc felt that the Gdansk Shipyard was entitled to special benefits as recompense for the hardships that it had suffered on the current government's behalf.

The Szczecin Shipyard

Events at the Szczecin Shipyard closely mirrored those at the Gdansk Shipyard prior to the introduction of economic reforms in Poland. However, the restructuring strategy pursued by Krzysztof Piotrowski's management team resulted in fundamental differences in the yards' operations and performance.

The Past Forty Years

Just as in Gdansk, the Szczecin shipyards—which had been retooled for German submarine production—were largely destroyed during World War II. After Poland annexed Szczecin and its shipyards in accordance with the Yalta peace settlement in 1945, the government combined operations of the town's three German yards and invested heavily in new capital equipment. The new Polish-owned Szczecin Shipyard launched its first vessel in 1948, the first ship to be built in Poland after the war. After delivering a single ship in 1948, the yard delivered 11 ships in 1957, and by the 1970s, the shipyard was producing up to 18 ships per year with a maximum deadweight of 15,000 tons. Meanwhile, shipyard employment had reached 13,000 by the mid-1970s, and the yard's production employees were among the most highly paid workers in Poland.

The shipyard's fortunes, however, declined throughout the 1980s, and after the first year of free market reforms, financial crisis engulfed the business. From a debt level of nearly zero in 1990, expensive bank loans and Soviet insolvency had pushed the yard's total debt to approximately 1.8 trillion zloty ($190 million) by 1991. The cash-strapped shipyard had been forced to delay payments to over fifteen hundred suppliers and to a number of commercial banks, and uneasy creditors had begun to threaten legal action when it appeared that the yard would be unable to repay its debts. Distressed shipyard workers appropriated megaphones to provide colleagues with daily updates on what appeared to be the yard's impending bankruptcy. Rather than attempting to implement reforms, Zenon Grabowski, the yard's last communist manager, appealed to old-line tactics and demanded that the Polish government bail out the shipyard with unconditional cash transfers. Word of the Szczecin Shipyard's financial difficulties quickly spread throughout the world shipbuilding industry, and international fleet owners began to express serious reservations about placing orders for fear that the business would be shut down in the middle of a shipbuilding project.

As crisis at the shipyard mounted, a management search committee installed Krzysztof Piotrowski as general director in 1991. When he assumed office, Piotrowski unveiled an ambitious, market-oriented vision for the shipyard that was based on two broad objectives. First, he would reduce the shipyard's massive debt; then he would streamline the yard's wasteful production operation.

Financial Restructuring: Debt Reduction

At a time when the cash-strapped shipyard owed 1.8 trillion zloty ($190 million) to over fifteen hundred suppliers, banks, and government revenue departments, debt restructuring was crucial for successful reform. Piotrowski thus enlisted the cooperation of the Polish Development Bank, a newly created government bank designed to assist in large-scale enterprise restructuring. The Development Bank became deeply involved in restructuring efforts at the Szczecin Shipyard because bank directors believed that Piotrowski had assembled the Polish shipbuilding industry's most competent and market-oriented management team.

After a month of strategizing, shipyard negotiators and Development Bank experts initiated a series of debt-rescheduling negotiations with the shipyard's largest creditors in the fall of 1991. The results were disastrous. Stubborn creditors demanded immediate repayment of all outstanding debts, an impossible request for the shipyard to fulfill, and for eight months the talks dragged on with little hope for a resolution to the shipyard's financial crisis. Finally, in the summer of 1992, with creditors threatening to initiate bankruptcy proceedings, Piotrowski abandoned all hope for an out-of-court settlement.

In the meantime, enterprising shipyard lawyers had uncovered an obscure 1934 law, the Arrangement Proceedings Act, designed to offer relief to indebted companies that had become insolvent as a result of developments beyond management's immediate control. The act permitted the indebted firm to renegotiate debt payments with creditors in a court of law, and, if a majority of creditors could be persuaded to accept a repayment plan, the terms of the plan would be binding for all debt holders. Piotrowski argued that the Szczecin Shipyard qualified for arrangement proceedings because its indebtedness resulted primarily from the collapse of COMECON trade and the withdrawal of government funding, developments that were certainly beyond managerial control. In June, in what was perhaps the largest court proceeding in Polish history, Piotrowski and his Development Bank colleagues subpoenaed over fifteen hundred ship industry suppliers and creditor banks to renegotiate the shipyard's debt under the Arrangement Proceedings Act. For two months, shipyard counsel vehemently argued that if suppliers initiated bankrupty proceedings, the yard would be forced to shut down its operations and would be unable to repay outstanding debts, and most creditors would leave the process empty-handed. Furthermore, shipyard representatives pointed out that many suppliers were dependent on orders from the Szczecin Shipyard for their own survival, and successful debt restructuring would assure future orders.

As creditors eased their demands for immediate reimbursement, Piotrowski unveiled a payment plan that he had formulated with his advisory team from the Polish Development Bank. According to the plan, creditors would agree to a universal reduction of 33 percent in the shipyard's total debt of 1.8 trillion zloty ($190 million). The remaining 66 percent, or 1.2 trillion zloty ($126 million), would be repaid in equal quarterly installments over a five-year period beginning in December 1993. Finally convinced that debt restructuring offered the only realistic prospects for repayment, a majority of creditors signed into the plan, and the Szczecin Shipyard's monumental debt rescheduling deal became official in August.

The shipyard's complex debt-restructuring plan was the first of its kind to appear in Poland. By holding creditors at bay and diminishing the threat of bankruptcy, it allowed the yard to focus its efforts on finding customers and building ships. The deal was touted in the national press as a resounding success, and Poland's Ministry of Finance hoped that it would become a restructuring model for the other financially troubled state-sector enterprises.

Industrial Restructuring

While struggling with creditors in debt-restructuring negotiations, Piotrowski began to implement sweeping changes in the Szczecin Shipyard's production operation. In an effort to transform the yard into an internationally competitive shipbuilder, he planned to focus the yard's product portfolio, minimize production cycle times, boost productivity through changes in compensation policies, shift the yard's target market from the Soviet Union to the West, trim bloated operating costs, and locate viable sources of financing for new ship construction. It was an ambitious restructuring program, but Piotrowski made rapid progress on many fronts.

Product Focus. Piotrowski felt that it was essential for the shipyard to narrow its product focus and develop a niche market. He assembled a market research team, instructing its members to analyze trends in the world shipbuilding industry and to recommend a niche market for the Szczecin yard. Piotrowski's analysts discovered that world prices for container ships were relatively high and demand was substantial, particularly in a medium-size class that the Szczecin Shipyard was well outfitted to supply. With the support of his research team's analysis, Piotrowski dedicated virtually all of the shipyard's manufacturing capacity to the production of container ships. His decision proved to be wise: by early 1993, of the forty-eight orders on the Szczecin yard's books, forty-four were for container ships. From an insignificant market presence in 1990, the Szczecin Shipyard gained 40 percent of the international market for 12,500-ton container ships and became the world's dominant producer of vessels in this category.

Reducing Product Cycle Times. Once he had established product focus at the shipyard, Piotrowski turned his attention to reducing the time required to build a single vessel, commonly referred to as the product cycle time. Reducing the product cycle time would serve two purposes. First, it would accelerate the business's cash flow and thus would allow the yard to decrease its borrowing and to become more financially independent. Second, shorter production cycles would attract customers who needed ships to be delivered quickly. Decreasing cycle times required major operating changes at the yard. Piotrowski limited the number of shipbuilding projects that the yard undertook at any one time, and production operations were performed in serial rather than in parallel. Of the yard's six slipways, two were removed from operation. Furthermore, fifteen hundred redundant workers in other departments at the yard were transferred to direct manufacturing jobs in the production bay. Piotrowski was thus able to concentrate the efforts of a larger number of workers on a smaller number of projects.

The results of Piotrowski's reorganization efforts in the production bay were phenomenal. Turnaround time for a single ship was cut from between two and four years to eleven months. "We believe that we now have the shortest production cycle in the world," remarked Technical Director Ryszard Kwidzinski. These efforts were a clear example of dramatic improvements from the reorganization of work—improvements that are necessary for successful restructuring. The reduction in cycle time was also a crucial complementarity for Szczecin's overall reform program.

A New Compensation Scheme. A key component of Piotrowski's strategy to reduce production cycle times was an overhaul of the shipyard's compensation system, which resulted in profound productivity gains. In the past, all workers at the shipyard had been paid a piece rate wage—that is, they had been paid for each task accomplished rather than for the total number of hours worked. Although this system was designed to provide workers with an incentive to work quickly and at high productivity levels, the results were often just the opposite of what was intended. Production workers often did work quickly under this system, but they also worked carelessly, and poor-quality workmanship resulted in substantial corrective work. As a result, productivity at the shipyard was unacceptably low. For example, under the piece rate system, welders who were required to make three welding passes to close a seam on a ship's hull often used thick electrodes and made only two passes to save time. The thick electrodes, however, generated more heat than standard electrodes and warped the steel in the vicinity of the welded seam. Consequently, metal shop workers often spent hours smoothing the steel seams after welders had completed their work. The additional time spent correcting the low-quality welding work resulted in substantial productivity losses.

It was clear to Piotrowski that if productivity was to be improved at the shipyard, employee compensation would have to be radically restructured. Piotrowski and Jan Kiryluk, the shipyard's director of human resources and compensation, developed an entirely new wage scale. In a series of detailed discussions in mid-1991, Piotrowski and Kiryluk assigned each shipyard worker to a professional qualification category that reflected occupational training and total years of work experience. An hourly wage was then assigned to employees in each qualification category. The highest wages were allocated to the most highly qualified workers. Employees could advance to higher qualification classes by passing a series of occupational exams. Each advance in professional qualification resulted in an automatic 50 percent increase in a worker's hourly wage, and each additional year of work experience resulted in a 10 percent increase through the eighth year of employment and every other year thereafter.

In previous years, under communist management, physical labor had been valued much more highly than intellectual labor, and production workers had earned more than managers, engineers, and even members of the shipyard's supervisory board. Under Piotrowski's new system, managers and engineers attained higher professional qualification ratings, and the compensation hierarchy at the shipyard was reversed. Piotrowski was able to persuade the shipyard's four employee unions to agree to this change in relative wages and thus avoided the strikes that had paralyzed Poland's shipyards during wage negotiations in the past.[6] All workers were required to work eight hours per day, and no overtime was permitted. Under the new system, the average salary was 4.5 million zloty ($280 in February 1993) per month, well above the national average of 2.5 million zloty ($155).

The shipyard's production employees were divided into workers' brigades, each of which was directed by a foreman and was assigned specific tasks by shipyard management. The shipyard's engineering department carefully analyzed every job to be performed and allocated to each a fixed number of labor hours. Workers' brigades were expected to complete their assignments within the time frame that the engineering department established, and the foreman was required to organize the work that his brigade performed and to ensure that all time targets were met. If a worker was unable to complete a job within the prescribed time period, he was not paid for overtime he spent finishing the assignment. According to shipyard engineer Jan Bielecki: "Under the new compensation system, a welder will seal a seam three times rather than two, because he will be paid for eight hours of work no matter what he does. It does not make sense to avoid work simply to save time. Furthermore, if he has to go back and rework a seam, he will exceed his allocated number of hours and will not be paid for the additional work." The new compensation system eliminated incentives to cut corners by performing substandard work. It also facilitated production scheduling, because all employees were required to work at the same pace and production deadlines for each step in the shipbuilding process were firmly established.

In October 1991, the new hourly wage scale was introduced as a pilot project in one of the shipyard's steel shops. Over the next several months, productivity at the steel shop soared, and in April 1992, Piotrowski's management team implemented the new compensation system throughout the yard. The Szczecin Shipyard was soon operating at unprecedented productivity levels. The yard planned to sell fourteen ships in 1993, nearly the same number that it sold during its best years in the 1970s. Only now, the fourteen ships were being built with a work force of five thousand rather than the bloated 1970s work force of thirteen thousand.

Developing a Marketing Capability. Since Centromor had lost its monopoly on foreign trade, the Szczecin Shipyard was left to pursue clients on its own. The Szczecin yard created a marketing office in 1989—earlier than any other Polish shipyard—when it became clear that there would be no further orders from the Soviet Union. The marketing department quickly began to pursue Western clients. In developing a new client base in the West, the shipyard's geographic location proved to be an advantage. Located on the German border, only two hours from Berlin, Szczecin was easily accessible to German fleet owners. In fact, German shipowners had already become frequent customers at the shipyard. Since the early 1970s, the Szczecin yard had built a total of nineteen freight ships for German-owned shipping companies. An early foothold in the German market proved crucial at a time when the shipyard was attempting to redirect its marketing efforts westward.

In 1988, the Szczecin Shipyard signed contracts for four container ships to be built for Hamburg Sud and Rederei B. Rickners, German fleet owners renowned for placing stringent technical and quality demands on ship producers. Because they were able to maintain fleets of extraordinary quality, Hamburg Sud and Rederei B. Rickners had become opinion leaders among German shippers, and word that they had contracted the Szczecin yard to build four container ships spread quickly through the German market.[7] When the first of these vessels was delivered to Hamburg Sud in December 1991, it received widespread acclaim for its highly developed technology and timely delivery, solidifying the Szczecin Shipyard's reputation in Germany. Container ship expertise and brisk production cycles became major selling points for the yard's new marketing division, and new orders followed in rapid succession. In the first ten months of 1992, the shipyard signed contracts with German fleet owners for an additional thirteen container ships worth $300 million. As the yard's German business continued to expand, Piotrowski made plans to open a trade office in Hamburg.

Another advantage for the Szczecin Shipyard as it launched its new marketing campaign was its long-standing relationship with the Polish Steamship Company (PZM). Over the previous forty years, the Szczecin yard had built seventy ships for PZM, two-thirds of the Polish shipping company's fleet. Even after Poland's economic transformation and the collapse of many state-owned enterprises, PZM continued to be an important shipyard client. In 1992, the Szczecin yard delivered four ships to PZM and signed contracts for five more, to be completed in 1994 and 1995. The only real change in the restructured shipyard's relationship with PZM was that PZM was to be billed for all future ship construction in U.S. dollars rather than in Polish zloty.

As a result of the shipyard's penetration in Germany and its long-term relationship with PZM, the new marketing department was able to fill its order book with remarkable speed despite the breakdown on COMECON trade. In 1992, the shipyard produced thirteen ships worth a total of 2.6 trillion zloty ($185 million), three times the value of the five ships that it produced in 1991. By July 1992, the Szczecin yard had been contracted to build forty-eight ships valued at a total of $1.2 billion through 1995, and A. T. Kearney/Hestia Consultants of Gdynia ranked the yard twenty-second in the world in total number of contracts for new ships.

Cost Control. In addition to streamlining production and developing a marketing operation, Piotrowski slashed inflated operating costs at the shipyard. He eliminated many of the employee amenities provided in the past: fully paid vacations at shipyard-owned vacation resorts, free employee housing in local apartment complexes, and highly subsidized meal plans, among others. In addition, Piotrowski sold an entire transportation fleet, replete with buses and luxurious automobiles, that previous shipyard management had used for personal travel.

Piotrowski also attacked labor costs. Employment at the shipyard had fallen substantially throughout the 1980s, from a peak of approximately 13,000 in the late 1970s to slightly less than 6,000 by the time Piotrowski became the shipyard's general director in 1991. Piotrowski eliminated an additional 700 jobs, primarily administration jobs and positions not directly related to ship production, and was able to significantly reduce the shipyard's total wage bill.[8] Piotrowski was able to successfully curb employee privileges and reduce employment because he had established a high level of credibility with the shipyard's four employee unions. By virtue of his past, he was in a unique position to convince workers that changes that benefited the shipyard also benefited its employees.

In addition to downsizing the shipyard's labor force, Piotrowski sought to reduce materials costs in the production process, primarily by eliminating the vast inventories of shipbuilding inputs that had characterized production under communist management. Piotrowski was careful to order inputs only as they were needed, rather than acquiring them months in advance and storing them in shipyard warehouses where they would tie up precious capital. No longer constrained by a system of centrally allocated inputs, Piotrowski was free to make purchasing decisions solely on the basis of cost and time considerations.

Finally, as Piotrowski eliminated unnecessary shipyard services and removed costly production facilities from operation, pockets of unused space became available on the shipyard's expansive grounds. Piotrowski decided that rather than allow the space to remain idle, he would lease it to other companies. Thus, for example, he was able to strike an attractive deal with Denmark's Burmeister and Wain

Skibsvaert A/S shipyard in late 1991. Burmeister and Wain was interested in decreasing its labor costs—which accounted for approximately 65 percent of the total cost of building a ship in Denmark—in order to compete effectively with Korean and Japanese producers; average Polish wages were only 30 percent of Danish wages. Burmeister and Wain approached Piotrowski in the hopes of leasing two idle Szczecin Shipyard production halls where it planned to produce heavy metal inputs, including masts, ladders, and steel doors. Piotrowski offered the Danish concern a lease, thus converting costly idle space into a profit center for his own yard. On the Szczecin Shipyard grounds, Burmeister and Wain established a private company called PolFab Ltd. with an initial capital investment of $100,000. The Danish shipyard planned to invest an additional $500,000 in modern capital and equipment for PolFab, as well as $500,000 in training Szczecin Shipyard employees who would eventually operate the new equipment.

Ship Construction Financing. With a restructured debt portfolio, a vastly improved production system, and a tightly controlled cost structure, Piotrowski turned his attention to locating sources of financing for new ship construction. Soviet clients and Western clients had paid for their ships on different terms. The Soviets often bartered raw materials or credited Poland's trade account in "transferable rubles." The Polish government then credited the shipyard's account with the zloty equivalent of the Soviet payment. Soviet clients were never required to provide working capital and, instead, paid a single lump-sum fee on completion.

Western clients, in contrast, paid the shipyard 10 percent of the total on signing the contract. The client then paid approximately 15 percent of the ship's selling price once the yard's design office had completed a detailed engineering plan, and an additional 20 percent once hull construction was completed on the slipway. The Western fleet owner paid the remaining 55 percent when the completed ship was delivered. Because the shipbuilding cycle was long and unpredictable, Western clients demanded that their prepayments be guaranteed by the government-owned National Bank of Poland. The National Bank of Poland always provided guarantees, regardless of the shipyards' financial condition or the profitability of a particular shipbuilding project.

However, with the introduction of banking reform in 1989, ship construction financing changed dramatically. No longer required to carry out a centralized industrial plan, the Polish banks had no incentive to provide guarantees for customer payments to the Szczecin Shipyard, which had accumulated an alarming debt load of 1.8 trillion zloty ($190 million). The risk that the shipyard would use prepayments to pay off creditors rather than to finance ship construction was simply too high.

Furthermore, interest rates for commercial loans ranged from 50 to 80 percent per year as the liberalized banks responded to very high inflation rates and increases in the National Bank of Poland's benchmark lending rate. As a result, bank lending became an unrealistically expensive option for financing future ship construction. Unable to obtain guarantees for customer prepayments and unable to afford commercial credit, Piotrowski was desperate for a financing mechanism that would allow him to continue laying keels on the slipways of his newly restructured yard.

Once again, the Polish Development Bank intervened. Confident that the Szczecin Shipyard was destined to become a profitable producer, the Development Bank agreed to provide guarantees for fleet owners' prepayments, but under a special set of conditions. In late 1991, the Development Bank and the Szczecin Shipyard created a joint stock company called Kontenerowiec (Container Ship) in which each was a 50 percent owner. The company was formed to build a single ship—a 12.4 thousand ton, $18 million container ship for a Hamburg-based freight company called Hansa Treuhand. Shipyard managers and Polish Development Bank officials required that Hansa Treuhand provide an unusually high 65 percent of total construction costs in prepayments. The Development Bank would provide guarantees for the prepayments from Hansa Treuhand, which would serve as working capital for construction of the vessel. The remaining 35 percent, or $6 million, would be provided in the form of loans from the Polish Development Bank. Because the ship would formally be built by Kontenerowiec and not by the Szczecin Shipyard, the Szczecin yard's creditors would have no claims on the working capital channeled through the Development Bank.

Construction of Hansa Treuhand's ship began in December 1991 under a regimen of stringent cost control. The Polish Development Bank released working capital to Kontenerowiec only as it was needed. Workers maintained a tight production schedule, and the finished vessel was delivered in November 1992, eleven months after initiation of the project and several months ahead of the promised completion date. Harald Block, a Hansa Treuhand representative, was ecstatic about performance at the Szczecin Shipyard: "I'm paying 20%–30% less and getting delivery six months earlier than I could have got in Germany last year," he said (Bobinski 1992).

The Kontenerowiec financing experiment.was a tremendous success for the shipyard. Not only did it enable the yard to obtain badly needed working capital, but it allowed Piotrowski to display the capabilities of his revamped production process to great effect. Confidence in the yard's future prospects soared, fleet owners placed new orders, and, most significant, Polish banks proved willing to issue guarantees for working capital provided by Western clients.[9] Of the fourteen ships that the yard was scheduled to deliver in 1993, all were financed by customer prepayments guaranteed by major Polish banks.

Privatization

Szczecin Shipyard made phenomenal progress in its restructuring program. Production cycle times and operating costs were substantially reduced, financing was available, and the yard's order book was filled through mid-1995. Although the yard was still unprofitable in 1992 as a result of debt repayments, Piotrowski predicted that it would turn its first postwar profit in 1993 and believed that it was ready for privatization.

In January 1993, Poland's Ministry of Privatization, Krzysztof Piotrowski, and the shipyard's four workers' unions signed a letter of intent to privatize the yard. According to the privatization plan, the yard would be turned over to a consortium of banks, industrial firms, workers, and management. Of the shipyard's 10 million shares (which were assigned a nominal value of 70,000 zloty but were to be sold for a symbolic price of 1 zloty), 30 percent would be allocated to four Polish banks, 30 percent to shipyard employees, 9 percent to shipyard management, and 15 percent to the yard's ten largest suppliers; 10 percent would be retained by the state treasury, and 6 percent would be offered for sale. The shipyard's new owners would not be permitted to sell their shares for a period of six years—the delay would allow the yard sufficient time to complete its restructuring program.

Transferring ownership of the shipyard to a consortium of private investors had several distinct advantages for Piotrowski and his management team. Ever since the shipyard had been commercialized, Piotrowski had been uneasy about the prospect of the state treasury owning 100 percent of the enterprise's stock. He knew that it was in the government's best interest to sell the shares of commercialized companies as rapidly as possible to raise revenue and to accelerate the national privatization program. Shipyard management had little influence over stock sale decisions undertaken by the treasury, and Piotrowski feared that the yard would be sold to a foreign investor and reduced to the role of a low-cost provider of prefabricated keels for a large Western shipyard. By transferring a majority ownership stake to private hands for a minimum of six years, however, the shipyard eliminated the near-term threat of a takeover by Western competitors. In the intervening six years, Piotrowski believed that he would be able to develop a powerful integrated shipbuilding operation of his own.

Comparative Results from Szczecin and Gdansk

Hans Szyc and Krzysztof Piotrowski embarked on the difficult road to enterprise restructuring in Poland with very different management philosophies. By February 1993, though still early in the reform process, their varied approaches to free market reform had produced equally disparate performance results. In evaluating the effectiveness of the restructuring programs implemented at the Gdansk and Szczecin shipyards, it is useful to examine changes in productivity and competitiveness, as well as to compare the yards' prospects for future development.

Productivity

Although both shipyards had taken several slipways out of operation to concentrate workers' efforts and decrease production cycle times, productivity at the Gdansk yard remained far below that of the Szczecin yard. Table 4-1 shows that in 1992 the total production value at the Gdansk Shipyard was $171 million and the value of the Szczecin Shipyard's output was a slightly higher $185 million. The Gdansk yard required 9,000 workers to achieve this level of output; the Szczecin yard, however, required only 5,000. In addition, at the Gdansk Shipyard, productivity was 20 cgt (corrected gross tons) per

Table 4-1 Performance Results at Gdansk and Szczecin Shipyards, 1990–1993

a. Gdansk Shipyard

Year	Ships Built	Sales	Profit
1990	6	$55 million	Negative
1991	NA	$77 million	Negative
1992[a]	7	$171 million	Negative

b. Szczecin Shipyard

Year	Ships Built	Sales	Profit
1991	5	$46 million	Negative
1992	13	$185 million	Negative
1993[a]	14	$260 million	Positive

[a]Projected.

employee in the 1970s but only 10 cgt in 1992. At the Szczecin Shipyard, where production cycle time was reduced to eleven months, productivity in 1992 was 28.5 cgt per employee.[10]

Competitiveness

The degree to which a restructured state-owned enterprise is able to compete effectively on fiercely competitive international markets is perhaps the most important indicator of the success of its privatization program. Given the large number of producers and the high degree of specialization in international shipbuilding, development of a sustainable competitive advantage is essential for effective performance.

Piotrowski attributed the Szczecin Shipyard's success to three significant competitive advantages: (1) container ship expertise, (2) an extraordinarily short production cycle, and (3) the relatively low cost of Polish labor. By focusing on container ship production, the yard was able to garner 40 percent of worldwide orders for mid-size container vessels, and the yard's eleven-month production cycle was a major attraction for clients at a time when the industry average was closer to two years. Also, shipyard workers in Western Europe earned approximately $20 per hour, but the average hourly wage in the Szczecin yard was $1.75. Low labor costs were particularly important for the shipyard at a time when almost every Western industrialized country provided substantial subsidies to its shipbuilding enterprises.

While management at the Szczecin Shipyard was focusing production efforts on mid-size container ships and the yard was becoming a world leader in this niche market, Hans Szyc was unable to build a lasting competitive advantage at Gdansk Shipyard. He made no efforts to develop a specialty, preferring to manufacture a wide range of ship types. With its highly diversified product portfolio, however, the Gdansk Shipyard had difficulties competing with Western producers. Instead of developing a sustainable competitive advantage, Szyc relied heavily on low Polish labor costs, and in fact, the majority of the ships under construction in the yard's production bay in early 1993—such as refrigerated transport ships and roll-on/roll-off carriers—had complex designs that required a high degree of manual labor. The Gdansk yard, however, was unable to compete with highly automated Japanese and Korean producers in markets for vessels of more standard design, such as tankers. As Szyc passively relied on low Polish labor costs, it appeared that his shipyard's competitive position would deteriorate even further if Polish shipbuilding wages were to rise to world levels, or if Japanese and Korean shipyards developed methods to automate the production of more sophisticated vessels.

Szyc complained bitterly that the Polish Development Bank had provided a great deal of assistance to help the Szczecin yard restructure its debt but the government had provided no restructuring assistance to the shipyard in Gdansk. Yet, according to former prime minister Jan Krzysztof Bielecki, the government was willing to help those enterprises that helped themselves:

The Szczecin Shipyard had undertaken a program of massive internal restructuring. They eliminated all activities not directly related to ship construction, laid off redundant employees, improved production cycle times, and proved that they could build ships profitably without government subsidies. We felt that the Polish Development Bank could help them in a constructive way by assisting in negotiations with creditors. The Gdansk Shipyard, however, has been much less self-sufficient in adapting to the new free market.

Future Prospects

Although neither shipyard had completed the privatization process by early 1993, events had progressed far enough to make conjectures about their future performance. At the Gdansk Shipyard, Hans Szyc seemed to be playing a waiting game. He was anticipating the repeal of the excess wage tax, at which time he would be able to hire more workers and increase production. In the meantime, however, he had made no plans to decrease operating costs or limit the scope of his behemoth operation. Although the shipyard had managed to secure orders from Western clients that would enable it to operate at 50 percent of capacity through 1994, it had been able to do so largely because it was producing the ships at attractive prices, often below production cost. As a result, the shipyard had sustained substantial losses during each of its first three years in its new free market environment. With Szyc unwilling to decrease costs and unlikely to receive government assistance, it appeared that the losses would continue. After three years of reorganization at the Gdansk Shipyard, the future remained bleak.

In stark contrast to management at the Gdansk Shipyard, Piotrowski continued to develop his detailed vision for the future of the Szczecin yard. He took into account the state of the industry in Poland, as well as international shipbuilding dynamics, and he sought to establish a profitable role for the Szczecin Shipyard. Despite the uncertainty that Szyc claimed rendered business planning impossible, Piotrowski continued to plan. He was willing to accept the retreat of government from big business, and he realized that progress at the Szczecin yard could be achieved only through the market-oriented efforts of its own management.

Piotrowski's plans for the future were ambitious. He envisioned the formation of a national shipbuilding consortium, structured much like the Mitsubishi and Hyundai conglomerates in Japan and Korea, that would combine disparate enterprises in Poland's shipbuilding industry in a joint effort to produce high-quality, low-cost ships for the international market. In February 1993, management at the Szczecin Shipyard had already begun preliminary negotiations with a group of approximately ten suppliers and other enterprises closely affiliated with Poland's shipbuilding industry. The cast of potential consortium partners included Cegielski, the country's largest producer of ship engines; Towimor, an industrial crane manufacturer; Ustka, Poland's only producer of life boats; Huta Czestochowa, a large steel mill in southern Poland; the Odra Shipyard; and the Polish Steamship Company. Piotrowski planned to guarantee orders to consortium partners in exchange for low prices for shipbuilding inputs. Eventually, he hoped to invite Polish banks into the industrial group in order to facilitate ship construction financing. This consortium not only would provide a boost to the Polish shipbuilding industry but would enable the Szczecin Shipyard to achieve substantial cost reductions and would facilitate access to credit.

Piotrowski was also focusing planning efforts on the shipyard's future production requirements. The improved financial condition of the Szczecin Shipyard enabled management to consider new capital investments. Recent developments in world container ship markets called for substantial upgrades in the shipyard's capital equipment base. Although the Szczecin yard had become the world's leading player in the market for mid-size container ships, Piotrowski predicted that after 1995, demand for these ships would be largely filled. Market analysis revealed that fleet owners would need to upgrade their stock of larger container ships. As a result, Piotrowski embarked on a capital investment program that would enable the Szczecin yard to produce larger vessels. In order to increase the maximum attainable ship width at the yard from 25.3 meters to 40 meters, Szczecin engineers fused two of the idle slipways in the production bay. The single enlarged slipway would allow the shipyard to produce container ships in the 20,000-ton class but would require new investments of approximately $15 million in heavy-duty cranes and related dock equipment. By early 1993, with the capital investment program well under way, the shipyard had already secured new orders for six 20,000-ton vessels.

Lessons for State Enterprise Reform

The Prochnik case presented in Chapter 3 and the shipyard cases presented in Chapter 4 clearly illustrate the range and depth of the challenges facing managers in their efforts to change state enterprises, designed to suit the conditions of a centrally planned economy, into competitive businesses capable of meeting the demands of an international market for goods and services. Most research on state enterprises analyzes summary income and balance sheet data. Our three case studies, in contrast, are detailed examinations of what managers must accomplish if they are to succeed in enterprise restructuring.

Prochnik is an encouraging example of a business that so far has succeeded in fundamentally altering its business strategy, operations, human resource practices, financial management, and distribution systems in a manner that yields a sensibly aligned organization for a market economy and delivers value to customers commensurate with what is available from competitors in other countries. It merits emphasizing that the dramatic changes that have occurred at Prochnik were not the immediate result of privatization per se. Instead, the creation of private ownership generated the demand for performance that, in turn, led to the hiring of a new chief executive and the engagement of expert counsel for strategy formulation and implementation. In this respect, privatization appears to have been a necessary condition for Prochnik's success but certainly not a sufficient condition. It is easy to imagine any number of examples of large, privately owned enterprises in the West that have failed to execute profound reform, despite resources far greater than the resources available to Prochnik. The secret to Prochnik's success has been the combination of privatization and exceedingly effective leadership by managers determined to establish Prochnik as a self-standing competitor in carefully chosen domestic and foreign markets.

The more far-reaching issue, however, is the degree to which Prochnik's experience will likely be replicated on a large scale across the thousands of Polish state-owned enterprises. Put differently, the question is whether many other enterprises will be able to attract talented and inspiring leadership; identify promising markets and attract (new) customers; develop and execute a well-aligned business strategy; significantly reorganize work and enhance efficiency; cut costs; recruit, motivate, and retain motivated employees; manage cash flow; and acquire any necessary outside funding. Simply assembling such a list, which does not do justice to the real magnitude of the task, suggests that Prochnik's experience will likely be much more the exception than the rule.

Such a conclusion is supported by the three years of restructuring at the Gdansk and Szczecin shipyards—years that have revealed important lessons about the nature of large state enterprise restructuring in post-communist economies. Both shipyards faced the same bleak circumstances in 1990. They had suffered the disappearance of the Soviet market and the withdrawal of government subsidies and had been forced to enter the free market era with millions of dollars in losses on their books. Both yards were awash in operating costs, nonproductive assets, and unfocused manufacturing operations, and both were forced to abruptly reorient their marketing focus to Western clients. Finally, both received new management teams with strong union-based support. So similar only three years ago, why have the two shipyards achieved such disparate results? The answer lies in radically different approaches to managing the reform process.

At the Gdansk Shipyard, management has based its reform strategy largely on the perceived successes of the enterprise in the past. In the 1970s, the shipyard was able to produce an impressive thirty ships per year. This output, however, required seventeen thousand workers, an inefficient vertically integrated infrastructure, and financial and marketing intervention from the central government. Gdansk management has attempted to replicate the organizational structure of the 1970s in an international market that demands efficiency, cost control, specialization, and, above all, profitability. As a result, performance at the shipyard has been dismal. Hans Szyc has demonstrated that socialist management methods are not readily transferred to a free market. Investors have been unwilling to participate in the ailing enterprise, and the privatization process at the Gdansk Shipyard has stalled.

At the Szczecin Shipyard, Krzysztof Piotrowski introduced a detailed and compelling vision for a competitive shipbuilding operation, and his intentions were well understood by shipyard managers and employees. Piotrowski was able to establish financial credibility by rescheduling the shipyard's overwhelming debt. He developed a competitive advantage by focusing production on mid-size container ships. He reduced production cycle times by concentrating a larger number of workers on a smaller number of slipways and by implementing a performance-enhancing compensation scheme. He decreased operating costs by shedding nonproductive assets and reducing the number of employees not directly involved in ship assembly. Finally, he eliminated most intermediary manufacturing at the yard and focused workers' efforts on building ships. Piotrowski was able to implement these changes because he had the support of shipyard workers, who were well aware of the sacrifices he had made for the labor movement in the 1980s. However, rather than allowing his labor ties to impede his market strategy, Piotrowski used his influence to persuade union members that difficult restructuring decisions that included large layoffs would provide long-term benefits for the remaining work force by enhancing the shipyard's competitiveness. Piotrowski succeeded in convincing labor that creating a viable shipyard with a few thousand jobs was a more attractive option than precipitating the shipyard's demise in an effort to avoid job losses.

The Szczecin and Gdansk shipyards have taken radically different approaches to restructuring, and a review of the basic differences is given in Table 4-2. There can be little doubt about which approach has the greater likelihood for success. The Szczecin Shipyard has

Table 4-2 Alternative Approaches to State Enterprise
Restructuring

Management Challenge	Approach of Szczecin Shipyard	Approach of Gdansk Shipyard
Debt Overhang	Radical Restructuring	Inaction
Financing	Innovative Buyer	Inaction
Product Mix	Focused	Diffuse
Production Methods	Restructured	Unchanged
Labor Relations	Consensus for Rationalization	Resistance to Rationalization
Compensation	Redesigned System	Unchanged System
Modernization	Likely	Unlikely
Strategy	Competitiveness	State Intervention
Leadership	Visionary and Consensual	Protective and Backward-looking

made substantial progress toward self-sufficiency and international
competitiveness, but the Gdansk Shipyard's future hinges on the
Polish government's willingness *and* capacity to subsidize its loss-
producing operations. Piotrowski and his colleagues at the Szczecin
yard have clearly done a remarkable job of managing a change process
of enormous scope and magnitude, and they deserve a great deal of
credit and emulation.

The Prochnik case and the contrasting experiences of the
Szczecin and Gdansk shipyards have a number of implications for
research on the process of economic reform. First, when presented
with data showing considerable variance in state enterprise performance within industries, some observers have questioned whether
the superior outcomes are the result of good management or good
luck. The evidence in this chapter indicates in concrete, empirical
terms that superior outcomes almost always result from superior management actions along a number of interrelated dimensions.

Second, enterprise managers must successfully address a range
of issues if enterprise restructuring is to lead to long-term competition. As shown in Tables 2-8 and 4-2, the transformation from plans
to markets requires enterprise managers to completely reorient management systems and practices, articulate sensible market-based strategies, create new functions and disband others, and, most important,
develop and communicate a compelling vision of the enterprise as a
competitive, self-supporting organization. Furthermore, the nature of

the managerial challenges is not fundamentally a function of whether or not the enterprise has been privatized. Although privatization, or the expectation of privatization in the near future, plays a crucial role in installing managers—and managerial incentives—conducive to effective action, privatization itself does not generate solutions to the range of problems facing state enterprises. This argument is consistent with the work of McDonald (1993), and Belka, Krajewski, and Pinto (1993), who report that ownership form is not an effective predictor of enterprise performance in cross-sectional data. In most instances restructuring may be so overwhelmingly difficult that managerial skill dominates ownership as a short-term determinant of success. In the longer term, managerial skill and private ownership will likely go hand in hand, regardless of the causality.

Third, the shipyard experience is consistent with the "complementarities" theory recently developed by Milgrom and Roberts (1990), which suggests that enterprise effectiveness depends on a coherent and comprehensive alignment of strategy, system, and structure. Both Piotrowski at Szczecin and Kolignan at Prochnik articulated and implemented strategically aligned plans based on their respective organizations' operation as self-sustaining competitors in international markets. The creation of focused marketing and product strategies was driven by careful assessments of the fit between market conditions and the company's relative advantages vis-à-vis worldwide competition. Changes in production and labor practices and in financing enabled the successful implementation of the strategies. In the absence of the "complementarity" among all these dimensions, neither Piotrowski nor Kolignan would have succeeded in vastly improving his firm's performance.

Nevertheless, for the purposes of evaluating the prospects for state enterprise restructuring more generally, the experiences of Prochnik and the Szczecin Shipyard are more troubling than inspiring. The dramatic improvements that these two enterprises achieved have come only as a result of positive outcomes on a series of highly interconnected issues, each of which was complex and fraught with potential for failure. Reflection on the incidence of successful large-scale reform within the far better resourced large corporations in the United States suggests a low rate of success. The experience with state enterprise reform in Poland so far indicates that very few firms will be able to replicate the progress achieved by Prochnik and the Szczecin Shipyard because very few will be able to harness the skills, leadership, ingenuity, and cooperation that characterized their experiences. This rather grim conclusion is supported by the evidence from Poland, which so far shows very few cases of competitive viability among the country's roughly eight thousand state enterprises, and from Eastern Europe and the former Soviet Union more generally (Carlin, Van Reenen, and Wolfe 1994).

Moreover, intense international competition in both textiles and shipbuilding requires Prochnik and Szczecin Shipyard to meet very high standards for quality, efficiency, and cost. Despite relatively low labor costs for a European country, Prochnik's labor costs are higher than, for example, labor costs in some Asian countries, whose garment industries are expanding rapidly. And Prochnik's employees are already agitating for substantial wage increases that management fears would seriously damage the company's ability to compete internationally and domestically. Likewise, despite the Szczecin yard's progress to date, the odds of its long-term survival as a private company are mixed at best. Despite dramatic improvements in productivity, Szczecin's productivity rate of roughly 28.5 cgt per employee does not compare favorably with rates of roughly 40 and 80 cgt per employee in Korea and Japan, respectively. Poland's low wages are also vulnerable to competition from rapidly growing shipbuilding industries in Brazil and China. In fact, in 1992, China's production of cargo ships exceeded Poland's. Given the magnitude and scope of the challenges facing large state enterprise reform, even the remarkable experience of Prochnik and the Szczecin Shipyard suggests that entrepreneurship and the growth of small businesses may continue to fuel the reform process.

PART II

Private Business Development

CHAPTER 5

The Nature of the Polish Private Sector

The Importance of Starting Over

The task of economic reform requires a massive reorganization of work at the enterprise level. There are two alternative ways to achieve the necessary reorganization: restructuring state enterprises and starting over through the creation of new private firms. In Part I we demonstrated the grave difficulties associated with restructuring even the most promising state enterprises. Four years into the economic reform process in Poland, there has been relatively little success in the restructuring of large state enterprises. Yet while the post-communist state enterprise sector has struggled to meet the requirements of a market economy, the new private sector has grown dramatically. In Part II we examine the emerging private small business sector in Poland. We use a unique combination of official statistics, large sample interview data, and detailed case studies of businesses in the Gdansk region—all of which we developed through repeated visits and in-depth interviews. These data, the results of four years of intensive fieldwork by us and our Polish associates, tell a rich and evolving story of the emergence, growth, and subsequent consolidation of small businesses driven by entrepreneurs who responded quickly and flexibly to the liberalized economic environment.

According to the evidence that we have been able to uncover, the formation of these new private businesses has proved to be the most effective way to reallocate labor and capital into productive uses in a market economy, for three reasons. First, the collapse of communism implies and creates a need for an essential economic and managerial change: almost every aspect of the organization of work needs to be changed, often completely. The previous organization of work made sense within the old central planning system, but that system disintegrated during the 1980s and has disappeared. The restructuring of Polish shipyards, discussed at length in Chapter 4, is a good example of what needs to be done after communism. An organization that can arrange the reorganization of work will see increased profits and will grow. An organization that inherits the old work process and cannot make the necessary adjustments will contract and eventually die. The same is true for any kind of service or manufactured output. Very occasionally one finds state enterprises that start with the right product and the right organization, but they are only the exceptions that prove the rules.

The second reason for the importance of the private sector is the difficulty of restructuring large state enterprises. In theory, essential changes in the organization of work could be made within state enterprises, but in practice this has proved far from easy. As we argued in Part I, every state enterprise inherits a great deal of baggage, be it incompetent managers, difficult management-labor relations, or all other aspects of its internal structure and strategy. State enterprises can change, but change takes time and produces job losses in almost every case.

Very few state enterprise managers have matched Krzysztof Piotrowski's success at the Szczecin Shipyard. It has proved incredibly difficult to change state enterprises effectively. The reason lies with the secret of Piotrowski's success: he recognized the important "complementarities" involved in reorganizing work. Changing just one aspect of a firm's operation is not likely to do much. Changing a few elements may have some effect but probably will not make a great deal of difference. Only if and when the strategy, structure, and compensation systems are changed simultaneously is there a major impact on a firm's performance. Coordinating the implementation of these complementary measures, however, is difficult, and essential changes can be opposed from any number of directions—such as by workers, other managers, or creditors. The end result is usually delay and only partial, ineffectual change.

The third reason for the relative importance of the private sector is precisely that these new firms naturally and automatically make complementary changes in the organization of work. Private sector firms, after all, are set up from scratch, and the founding entrepreneurs choose all aspects of the firms' operation anew, without directly inheriting the constraints of old organizations.

Entrepreneurship offers powerful incentives for the flexible allocation of labor and capital to profitable activities in the rapidly changing context of an economy in reform. Unlike state enterprises, entrepreneurial companies have little inherited organizational baggage, simple governance structures, very low fixed costs, and the motivation to exit unpromising markets quickly and pursue attractive ones. Starting over gives any new private sector firm a chance to create from scratch a business strategy, together with a consistent internal organizational structure and an appropriate compensation system. In other words, private sector firms can solve the complementarities problem much more easily than can state-owned enterprises.

Nevertheless, to many outside observers it has seemed that there are disadvantages to starting over in the private sector. Concern has been expressed about whether the private sector will have enough capital, whether it can move beyond merely trade activities, and whether it will generate high-paying jobs. Our research indicates that these disadvantages are quite small and far outweighed by the advantages of starting over. Our work indicates that, on the whole, the state sector will struggle to reorganize work but the private sector will do it quickly and pervasively.

Even though our evidence is drawn from a detailed examination of the Polish experience, the arguments should apply more generally. In every post-communist country, reform requires a massive reorganization of work. State enterprises everywhere have the same problems making effective change.

In Part II we analyze the development and organization of the private sector in Poland. Chapter 5 examines the origins of entrepreneurs and how the private sector developed before 1990. Chapter 6 explains the precise nature of the surge in private sector activity from 1990. Chapter 7 looks at financial constraints on private sector growth.

Methodology

The dynamics of private sector development in Poland are complicated and rich in confusing details. Early in the reform process it became evident to observers that official statistics were inaccurate measures of what happened in the private sector. The official statistical apparatus was designed to monitor the performance of state enterprises in a stable planned economy and, as a result, had difficulty collecting accurate information on private sector development. We present some of this data below but recommend that it always be used with great caution.

To provide a different perspective, we wanted to survey private sector firms directly ourselves. Doing so turned out to be a difficult task. Many registered businesses were not in operation, some businesses that were in operation were not registered, and many other businesses were registered to conduct one type of activity but were actually involved in different activities. Putting together a representative sample was far from easy. We were fortunate, however, to have an astute Polish entrepreneur on our side. When we first met Piotr Strzalkowski, he taught at the University of Warsaw and had his own market research firm—one of the first to pioneer a "yellow pages" type of business directory in Poland. Piotr and his colleagues compiled data on all aspects of the private sector. These data were usually up-to-date and had an accurate classification of firms according to their principal activity.

Our survey work began in 1991 with a preliminary sample of 294 firms in Warsaw, selected from a database of firms that had advertised. The second survey, completed in spring 1992, interviewed private firms in Monki, a small Polish town. We included this town, situated in the Suwalki region, which has not done well recently, so that we would have a point of comparison with the large cities that we deal with in the rest of our work. We attempted to speak with every entrepreneur in Monki, and we put together a sample of 102 firms.

At the end of 1992, we conducted two more detailed surveys, based on an improved questionnaire, in the cities of Krakow and Lodz. In these cases the "yellow pages" database was available for use in selecting the sample, and we were also able to use the database to choose the proportions of sectors. These surveys are the mainstay of our empirical results, both because we feel confident about the way the samples were constructed and because we were able to improve our questions based on our previous experience. Altogether we have 418 firms in these samples: 226 are from Lodz and 192 are from Krakow. For this work we sampled by sector, with the proportions of sectors as listed in the comprehensive "yellow pages" database.

In spring 1993, in a subsequent survey of 133 private firms in Krakow, we used a questionnaire with more detail about the entrepreneurs and their workers, in addition to the questions that had been asked in the previous Krakow and Lodz surveys. This survey also used the "yellow pages" database for both sample construction and selection of enterprises.

The 947 observations in our five samples provide insight into the structure of Poland's private sector. The samples are probably not fully representative, particularly when the data from Warsaw and Monki are included, but the samples from Lodz and Krakow measure private sector performance in large cities quite well.[1]

A survey, like a photograph, captures certain aspects of reality at a moment in time. The cross-sectional data do not capture the dynamics of firm births and deaths; instead, they reveal the character-istics of the existing population at a particular time. Accordingly, a survey cannot tell the story of a firm's development, and attempts to infer facts about time series developments from cross-sectional evi-dence are extremely dangerous. Thus, an essential source for our research is information from the entrepreneurs themselves, gathered in detailed interviews over several years. Working with these Polish private business people and following their developments has allowed us to obtain unique information about the managerial challenges fac-ing new private businesses and about the range of responses under-taken to create and develop businesses in a post-communist economy.

We draw heavily on cases that were approved for publication by the entrepreneurs.[2] These cases were developed for Harvard Business School and followed the usual stringent procedures, which require that information gathered and written cases may be released only after review and written authorization from the entrepreneur. The advantage of these procedures is that the entrepreneur's review of what we have written often reveals errors of fact or interpretation. The disadvantage is that the case becomes official history and a form of advertisement for the firm. We never knowingly misrepresent what happens, but some biases probably emerge in these histories.

In summary, our empirical methodology is one of careful obser-vation of the private sector, using published secondary information and various small and large samples that we ourselves assembled. We do not claim to have captured and reported the entirety of the Polish private sector experience, but our version is more complete and, we believe, more accurate than previous work.

The New Entrepreneurs

Our large-sample evidence confirms that the private sector was well established before the implementation of the Balcerowicz Plan in 1990 and that it is based primarily on people who worked in the state sector for a while and quit during the 1980s. Most of the entrepreneurs currently operating in the Polish private sector left the state sector and were employed in private business before the Balcerowicz Plan began. During the 1980s, the private sector was easy to enter. Barriers to entry, at least in terms of initial capital requirement, were very low. But sufficient human and financial capital, above a minimum level, has helped entrepreneurs to do better in absolute terms and relative to each other—at least when we measure performance by the number of employees in a firm, referred to below as the "employment equation." It has also been easy for these people to stay employed—less than 10 percent of them has ever been unemployed.

Although almost anyone could enter the private sector, success was not assured. We find that people who started out with sufficiently large amounts of financial capital, or who had private sector employment experience before starting their own firm, created significantly larger firms than others. Success during the Balcerowicz Plan period seems very much related to how people spent the 1980s and the amount of human and financial capital they were able to accumulate.

Personal Background

The average (mean) age of interviewed entrepreneurs was 40½, and median age was 40.[3] There was a considerable range of ages in our samples, from 19 to 80 years old, but 80 percent of the entrepreneurs were between 28 and 52, and 50 percent were between 33 and 47.[4] These results suggest that the private sector consists predominantly of people who were between 20 and 35 years old in 1980–1981, during the first Solidarity period. Our small sample evidence strongly suggests that many of these people were caught up in the Solidarity movement from the beginning and had become extremely disillusioned by socialism in general and state sector employment in particular by the early 1980s.

Our evidence also suggests that during the 1980s, as the state sector attempted to reform and steadily declined, this generation progressively moved into the private sector. For example, in our samples people who entered the private sector during the 1980s and 1990s have very similar demographic characteristics. Regardless of how the overall sample is broken down by groups according to the specific years in which entrepreneurs founded their firms, the average age remains between 38 and 42, and the distribution of ages is very similar. This finding suggests that most of those who entered the private sector during the 1980s belonged to roughly the same generation, although they differed in when they left the state sector. There is a clear contrast between entrepreneurs who started their firms before and after 1980. In 1992, the before-1980 group had an average age of 51.

Not surprisingly, given their ages, these entrepreneurs have substantial work experience—an average of twenty years per person.[5] Almost all (83.5 percent) have more than ten years of post-education work experience.[6]

Table 5-1 cross-tabulates information on entrepreneurs' previous jobs with the period in which they founded a firm (in the upper part of the table) and with the period when they left the state sector (in the lower part). The first and second columns in the upper part of this table show that most people worked in at least one job before starting their own firm, and for firms founded after 1980, the majority of people had held two or more jobs. The average number of previous jobs per person was 2.14, although only 56.6 percent had held more than one job. The same pattern is seen in the lower part of the table.

As far as we can ascertain, most of these entrepreneurs have worked continually since they finished education. Relevant evidence on this point is that less than 13 percent reported they were ever unemployed and only 8.8 percent were registered as unemployed. Anecdotal evidence suggests that when these entrepreneurs were unemployed, they were out of work for only a brief period.

Only 47.6 percent of entrepreneurs (253 of the 415 for whom we have this information) had worked in the sector in which they set up their enterprise. This proportion was 44.6 percent for people starting firms before 1980, 53.0 percent for those starting firms from 1980 to 1987, 53.7 percent for those starting firms from 1988 to 1989, and 45.7 percent for those starting firms in and after 1990.

Family Traditions

Some observers have suggested that the relatively recent experience of a private market economy helped private sector development in Poland. Our interviews provided three measures of family links to

Table 5-1 Entrepreneurs' Previous Work Experience

	Previous Jobs			Previous Private Sector Jobs		
	Average Number of Places Worked (Mean)	Percentage with One or More Job	Percentage with Two or More Jobs	Number of Places Worked (Mean)	Percentage with One or More Job	Percentage with Two or More Jobs
Period in Which Firm Was Founded						
Before 1980	1.64	73.9%	43.9%	0.35	24.6%	8.6%
1980–1987	2.06	89.3	60.4	0.36	28.9	7.2
1988–1989	2.44	95.8	64.6	0.4	28.0	8.5
1990–	2.28	90.4	58.1	0.5	31.3	11.8
All periods	2.14	87.6	56.6	0.45	29.7	10.3
Period When Person Left the State Sector						
Never worked in state sector	0.92	56.4	23.1	0.74	48.1	15.6
Before 1980	2.9	98.7	74.9	0.79	45.3	20.0
1980–1987	2.77	99.3	80.3	0.49	32.1	12.5
1988–1989	2.43	100	66.7	0.33	25.3	5.7
1990–	2.34	100	67.4	0.16	11.4	2.1
All periods	2.14	87.6	56.6	0.45	29.7	10.3

the private sector. In terms of directly continuing a family tradition, there is only a limited effect. Just 13.8 percent of entrepreneurs said their business was established as a family tradition.

Answers differ according to when people founded their businesses. Of those who started their companies before 1980, 37 percent said their business was a family tradition. The percentage of people giving the same answer fell to 21 percent of those who started their company between 1980 and 1987, to 6 percent of the 1988-to-1989 group, and to 5 percent of the 1990-and-after group.[7]

A slightly different pattern is shown by answers to the question of whether the entrepreneur's family was active in business before 1948—when the communists took complete power in Poland and began to crack down on the private sector. Overall, only 23.6 percent said their families were active in business before 1948. The proportion of respondents with this kind of family history was 45 percent among firms founded before 1980, 19 percent among firms founded between 1980 and 1987, and 15 percent among firms founded from 1988 to 1989. However, among firms founded in and after 1990, the percentage of such responses was up to 22 percent.

Using a third measure, we find that 33.3 percent of respondents said they had family members who were active in business during the last ten years. The pattern across founding-year groups is similar to the pattern of family activity before 1948. Fifty-four percent of the group of entrepreneurs founding their enterprise before 1980 said they have family members active in the private sector in the last decade. This percentage declines to 40 percent among those founding between 1980 and 1987, to 22 percent among those founding from 1988 to 1989, and to 26 percent among those founding in and after 1990.[8]

Overall, 41.5 percent of the 947 entrepreneurs who answered this question reported at least one of the three forms of family links to private business, although if we exclude people whose only connection was family members active in private business during the past ten years, the percentage of people with a family link (either before 1948 or who started the firm as a family tradition) falls to 23.2 percent. There is evidence of family links to private business, but their importance should not be overestimated. This last point is confirmed by regression analysis. There is no specification of the employment equation in which we find a significant effect of dummies representing the three measures of family ties to the private sector. Each is insignificant when included by itself, and they are jointly insignificant when included together.

Entry into the Private Sector

Overall, our samples indicate that 85 percent of the entrepreneurs worked at some point in the state sector. The exceptions were older people who founded firms before 1980, usually continuing a family tradition, and younger people who founded firms after 1990.

We also found that the entrepreneurs had a considerable amount of work experience in the private sector, although this is not evident from the numbers on when their current firms were founded. A relatively high proportion of our sample—49.7 percent—started their current business in 1990 or more recently. However, 73 percent of respondents had left the state sector before the beginning of the Balcerowicz Plan—that is, by the end of 1989—and 56 percent had left before the second stage of communist reform began in early 1988.

Of those 314 firms founded in and after 1990 for which we have relevant data, 41 percent were started by people who left the state sector before 1990. People who had never worked in the private sector accounted for 15.6 percent of the firms founded after 1990, and people who left the state sector in 1990 and later constituted 43.3 percent of the total. Given that it was rare to leave the state sector and (1) work anywhere other than in the private sector or (2) return to the state sector, we assume that the time these people have spent in the private sector is equal to how long ago they left the state sector. So, according to our calculations, by the end of 1992, these entrepreneurs had worked a mean of 7 years in the private sector.

Almost 30 percent of the entrepreneurs in our samples worked for at least one private firm before starting their own operation. Among the 545 entrepreneurs to whom we asked this question, there was an average of 0.45 previous private sector jobs per person. The average number of previous private sector jobs was highest for people who founded their firms most recently (see the last three columns in the upper part of Table 5-1).

In contrast, the lower part of Table 5-1 also shows that entrepreneurs who left the state sector most recently on average worked in the fewest private sector firms. Just over 45 percent of the people who left the state sector before 1980 had at least one private sector job, but the same was true of only a third of the people who left between 1980 and 1987, a quarter of those who left from 1988 to 1989, and just over 10 percent of those who left during and after 1990.

The difference between the two parts of Table 5-1 is due to the fact that until 1988 it was less common for entrepreneurs to leave the state sector and directly start a company. Thus nearly a third of the people who left the state sector before 1988 worked in at least one private sector job before they founded their own firm—often in 1989 or 1990. The important and not surprising finding from Table 5-1 is that people who founded firms more recently have, on average, more private sector experience and those who quit the state sector more recently have, on average, less private sector experience.

Once these entrepreneurs started their private sector businesses, they did not continue to work in the state sector. Our samples found almost no cases in which entrepreneurs had their own private business part-time while working in the state sector. Furthermore, of the 141 people who quit the state sector for the last time after 1990, only 5 founded their current business before 1990.

Overall, we find that nearly 33 percent of entrepreneurs formerly held a high-level management position in the state sector. We purposely used a fairly restrictive definition of such positions to ensure that we received responses only from members of former top management teams.[9]

Given that the condition of the state sector declined steadily in the 1980s and more rapidly from 1990, it is not surprising that the proportion of entrepreneurs who were previously high-level managers rises for businesses founded more recently. Of entrepreneurs who started their firms before 1980, only 25 percent were previously state sector managers. This proportion rises to 32 percent for those who founded firms between 1980 and 1987, to 43 percent for those who founded from 1988 to 1989, and to 42 percent for those who founded after 1990. However, regression analysis shows no evidence of former state managers having different performance from other entrepreneurs.

Initial Capital

Anecdotal evidence suggesting that many Polish entrepreneurs began their operations with only small amounts of capital is confirmed by our larger samples. We asked 796 entrepreneurs in our sample how much initial capital they had. Their responses were as follows: 31.4 percent started their firms with less than $100, 57.2 percent had less than $500, and 65 percent had less than $1,000.[10] The pattern according to when entrepreneurs started their firms is striking. Table 5-2 shows that almost 80 percent of firms founded before 1988 began with capital worth less than $500.[11] This proportion declines to 60 percent for firms founded from 1988 to 1989 and to 35 percent for firms founded in and after 1990.

More generally, Table 5-2 indicates that most firms started with very little capital. For example, less than 25 percent began with more than $5,000, and less than 10 percent began with more than $20,000. Initial capital requirement was a very low barrier to entry into the private sector. It is true that average wages in the state sector during the 1980s were low—typically ranging from $10 to $20 per month. However, in this period there were always small transactions, usually various forms of trade or services, through which a determined person with a little skill could earn a couple hundred dollars. After stabilization in 1990, the purchasing power of the dollar fell, so the average monthly wage rose from $10 or $20 to more than $100 within a year, and the opportunities for accumulating money through small-scale trading (especially importing goods) actually increased. Only in 1992 and increasingly in 1993 did it become hard for a person to gather enough capital to start a private business.

We also asked about sources of initial capital, allowing two answers per person. Almost all respondents said they used their own capital which they had earned exclusively inside Poland. Only 18.2 percent of entrepreneurs said they had earned some of their initial capital abroad. Although the role of foreign contacts and business dealings was important for the Polish private sector, this result indicates that its importance should not be exaggerated.

Measures of Performance

One way to test the importance of various personal characteristics of entrepreneurs is to run regressions that have measure of firms' performance on the left-hand side. Ideally, we would want to have precise measures of the size, profitability, and efficiency of private sector firms. Unfortunately, such precise information is not available. Instead, we have to make use of what facts can be obtained from respondents.

Table 5-2 Crosstabulation of Initial Capital and Period When Firm Was Founded

Initial Capital	Before 1980		1980–1987		1988–1989		1990 and After		Total	
	N	PCT	N	PCT	N	PCT	N	PCT	N	PCT
Less than $100	68	60.7%	51	46.8%	54	47.8%	77	20.6%	250	35.4%
$101–$500	21	18.8	28	25.7	13	11.5	54	14.5	116	16.4
$501–$1,000	7	6.2	10	9.2	4	3.5	40	10.7	61	8.6
$1,001–$5,000	8	7.1	4	3.7	19	16.8	74	19.8	105	14.9
$5,001–$10,000	4	3.6	8	7.3	10	8.8	50	13.4	72	10.2
$10,001–$20,000	1	0.9	4	3.7	7	6.2	33	8.8	45	6.4
$20,001–$50,000	1	0.9	2	1.8	3	2.7	32	8.6	38	5.4
More than $50,000	2	1.8	2	1.8	3	2.7	13	3.5	20	2.8
All firms	180	19.1	149	15.8	144	15.3	468	49.7	941	100.0
Total	112	100.0	109	100.0	113	100.0	373	100.0	707	100.0

Note: N is the number of firms. *PCT* is the percentage of firms in a founding-year group that had the indicated amount of initial capital. Columns were rounded to 100.

The best measure available is total employment because it indicates the size of enterprises in a way that is easy to compare across firms. Given that all private sector firms started from zero employment quite recently, this measure gives a rough but useful indication of overall firm performance. Firms that employ more people have probably, on average, done better than firms that employ fewer people. Successful firms typically grow in size—that is, employment—while unsuccessful firms struggle along with just a couple employees. The employment measure is also attractive because we have employment information for almost all firms we interviewed (945 out of the 947). The mean level of employment was 8.5 workers, and the median was 3—both figures do not include the entrepreneur as an employee. Fifty percent of the distribution had employment between 1 and 7. Only 5 percent of the distribution had employment equal to or greater than 30 people.

We do not find any specification in which age or total years of experience is significant in the current-employment-level regression. The *lack* of a result is interesting. If entrepreneurs' ages cannot contribute to the explanation of the pattern in employment levels, this suggests that there is no advantage to being older or younger in the Polish private sector. Age is also not significant in either regression when we use on the left-hand side the firm's value or whether the firm received credit.

In the employment regression, the value-of-firm regression, and the credit regression, we were also not able to find a significant effect of the number of places where people worked earlier.[12] The effect of never having worked anywhere else is also not significant in the employment regression. Our econometric analysis, however, indicated that private sector experience does influence firm performance. In our employment regressions, dummy variables for having held either at least one or at least two private sector jobs are consistently significant with positive coefficients.[13] This important result suggests that previous private sector experience, rather than experience per se, has helped entrepreneurs build larger firms.

Interestingly, three of the dummies for the level of initial capital are not significant in the employment regression. These are dummies for initial capital less than $100, less than $500, and less than $1000. However, the dummy for initial capital greater than $5,000 is positive and significant. This suggests that the amount of initial capital, if we control for all other plausible variables, does not affect employment for low levels of capital. But it seems there is a critical level of initial capital that, if possessed, makes it easier to develop a larger business.

Summary of Survey Results

The 1980s were an important training period for private sector entrepreneurs. This view is supported by the fact that people who worked in the private sector before setting up their own firm have significantly higher employment now. The overall amount of work experience does not have a significant effect, but having worked in the private sector appears to have been excellent training for opening one's own firm. Our sample evidence is consistent with the hypothesis that the experience gained by entrepreneurs during the 1980s was extremely important in enabling them to take advantage of the opportunities presented by the Balcerowicz Plan.

In general terms, we can claim that the mid-1980s saw the rapid accumulation of managerial skills and human capital necessary for private sector growth. But what exactly did Polish entrepreneurs learn? How were these skills acquired? For a more detailed understanding of how people built business and acquired management skills, we need to understand the role of new Polish cooperatives during the 1980s.

Early Cooperative Structures

The new Polish "cooperatives" were a hybrid legal structure that included features of both state-owned enterprises and worker-managed firms. Cooperatives were important vehicles for new private initiatives during the 1980s, and they had a great deal of influence over private sector development both before and after the Balcerowicz Plan.

Under the partially reformed communist system of the mid-1980s it was risky and difficult to start up a purely private firm. Existing Polish law, however, allowed the existence of cooperatives. Most of them were state enterprises by another name. These cooperatives were particularly important in trading activities and controlled most of the wholesale and retail food trade in the communist period.

Strictly speaking, anyone could form a cooperative, but prior to the 1980s the communist government used extralegal measures to prevent the creation of cooperatives that were anything other than state initiated and state controlled. Permission to operate was withheld on various pretexts, and it was obvious that official harassment would either prevent registration or drive an unapproved cooperative out of business very quickly. Then, at the beginning of the partial economic reforms in the 1980s, the government made it known that it would accept cooperatives founded by individuals (in contrast to the cooperatives founded by the state), provided the law was followed precisely. The law called for each new cooperative to be established by a group of no fewer than ten founding members, who were required to submit an official statement of purpose that was to be approved by local government authorities. Although cooperatives were often established on private initiative, they were not treated as private enterprises. All of a cooperative's assets and business operations were owned by society at large.[14]

Cooperatives were entitled to select a field of business activity and to create a company, but founding members were not permitted to alter the cooperative management structure, which was precisely spelled out in Poland's commercial code. Stringent rules also governed membership and wage policies. Workers hired by the cooperative were entitled to become members only after a full year of service. Each month, cooperative members were required to submit 5 percent of their earnings to a cooperative wage fund, which was used for investment and business development purposes. Although long-time members had larger capital stakes in a cooperative than new members had—because they had contributed wages to the fund over a longer period of time—all members had equal voting rights in management issues raised at the annual general assembly.

A cooperative's capital was derived from worker's wages and company profits, but all capital investments made by a cooperative were considered state property. Thus, a cooperative had no ownership claims on any of its assets, and, if a cooperative was dissolved, all of its property was appropriated by the state treasury. The lack of ownership rights became a major obstacle for cooperative management boards that wanted to privatize their businesses after the introduction of economic reforms in Poland in 1990.

Cooperatives constituted a remarkably complicated and cumbersome legal structure, given that most new entrepreneurs were trying to start small businesses. While deterring the formation of new firms, this structure did not present an insurmountable obstacle. In fact, as our cases show, there may even have been a side benefit, because it forced people to form informal coalitions of at least ten people, and this mobilization of talent could prove essential to a firm's success.

The Gdansk Cooperative

At the beginning of our interview work we met with managers of the Gdansk Cooperative, a firm that was unusually influential because of the impact of its practices on the local labor market and because it provided a demonstration of how private business can operate success-fully. Several of the entrepreneurs we studied got their first taste of private business in this firm. Among other things, the Gdansk Cooperative provided excellent training ground for future busi-nesspeople.

The cooperative had precisely the right kind of product focus for the mid-to-late 1980s. It had several profitable niches in the prod-uct market, an informal internal structure based on teams, and an appropriate compensation scheme. The cooperative also provided an idealist view of how a private economy might operate if only commu-nism could be done away with. Workers shared common noneco-nomic goals, and the company was more a community than a profit-seeking firm. This philosophy was fine while communism lasted, but it became much harder to sustain when political and economic condi-tions began to change in 1989.

The development of this cooperative also illustrates the way in which the inefficiencies of the state sector created new opportunities for private business, at least at the very beginning. The origins of the Gdansk Cooperative, and of many other Polish firms in the mid-1980s, were more social and political than strictly economic. The story of one of the key figures in this cooperative, Jaroslaw Czarniecki, provides an indication of how people first became involved in the private sector.

Gdansk was the center of Solidarity's political activity in 1980–1981 and its strongest base of popular support. As a politically active student at that time, Jaroslaw developed a widespread network of Solidarity contacts, whose diverse ranks included historians, dock workers, rail workers, and physicists. However, as the Polish govern-ment intensified its efforts to break the opposition movement, Jaros-law's Solidarity acquaintances were summarily ousted from their state-sponsored jobs and blacklisted for anticommunist political activity. By the time he completed his studies in 1983, the politically zealous Jaroslaw had become unemployable in Poland's state sector.

Jaroslaw resolved that he would find a way for himself and his colleagues to earn a living outside the state sector while continuing to pursue Solidarity's political agenda. At the time, Poland's private sector was largely restricted to agriculture, so Jaroslaw thought his best option for employment outside the state sector would be through the establishment of a cooperative. Though subject to various burdensome state controls and regulatory requirements, a cooperative in the early 1980s provided a legal vehicle for independent, nonstate economic initiative. At Gdansk University, Jaroslaw had worked in a student-run maintenance cooperative, washing windows and sweeping hallways at state-owned enterprises in and around Gdansk. With no other work experience and no manual skills to his credit, Jaroslaw decided that if he were to start a cooperative, it would have to be similar to the low-skill, low-profile operation that he had joined as a student.

In the fall of 1983, Jaroslaw Czarniecki assembled a group of ten politically active colleagues to serve as cooperative cofounders. He secured statements from several local state-owned enterprises asserting that they would use the new cooperative's maintenance services (a precondition for cooperative registration), and he was granted permission by the local authorities to establish the Gdansk Cooperative. Lacking capital and management experience, the founders of the Gdansk Cooperative began the business by gathering whatever simple tools they could bring from home. Jaroslaw and his colleagues realized that rudimentary cleaning and maintenance services would produce a meager income, but their primary concern was providing employment for blacklisted Solidarity activists and a supportive environment for underground political activity. Thus, when the founding members of the Gdansk Cooperative arrived at Jaroslaw's apartment with buckets, rags, soap, and the odd hammer or rusty saw, they sat down to plan not only the company's business development strategy but also its political agenda. From the beginning, one of the cooperative's main objectives was to provide members with a subsistence-level income so that they would not have to worry about living expenses while pursuing political activities outside the workplace.

The basis of the cooperative's competitive advantage was that it could provide good service at reasonable prices. The members were willing to do jobs that employees in state enterprises were not willing to do. They were sensitive to the needs of customers—primarily managers in state firms—and tried to address them (this was all quite new in Poland). Business expanded rapidly, and the cooperative quickly established a reputation as a reliable provider of routine maintenance services.

At the large state-owned buildings that contracted the cooperative to perform industrial cleaning services, towering smokestacks and rooftop spires were often in need of repair. Few companies in Poland had the equipment or the training necessary to perform high-altitude cleaning and maintenance services, and, for the most part, smokestacks, towers, and other high-altitude structures were simply allowed to deteriorate. Sensing opportunity in an underdeveloped market, Jaroslaw became convinced that the Gdansk Cooperative should specialize in high-altitude maintenance. Although this work was dangerous and required a highly specialized set of climbing skills, it would enable the cooperative to move away from amateur cleaning jobs and to differentiate itself from low-skill competitors.

As the cooperative accumulated capital from its basic cleaning and maintenance activities, Jaroslaw began to invest in rope, mountain-climbing gear, and scaffolding, which would allow cooperative members to scale the smokestacks and towers that other maintenance companies had routinely avoided. Cooperative managers soon organized monthly mountain-climbing and rapelling seminars in the mountains of southern Poland, where cooperative members developed skills that would enable them to maneuver dexterously and safely in their new assignments atop industrial chimneys. "Chimneys," said Jaroslaw. "Industrial chimneys. Smokestacks. Tall cranes. Radio-transmission towers. Church spires. All over the country, there were tall structures in regular need of painting and maintenance. So we just taught ourselves to perform those tasks—you know, scaffolding, rope and pinion, that sort of thing—and we began hiring ourselves out."

Poland's state-owned industrial sector was full of massive factories and towering buildings, and the demand for high-altitude services quickly became overwhelming. Customers flocked to the cooperative for high-rise maintenance. Petrochemical companies with coal-stained smokestacks, local shipyards with rusty 120-meter-high industrial cranes, refineries with punctured oil towers, and churches with crumbling steeples flooded the Gdansk Cooperative with orders. Growth at the cooperative was explosive, entirely financed out of retained earnings. Annual sales at the Gdansk Cooperative rose dramatically.[15]

As demand for the cooperative's services expanded and cooperative members honed their high-altitude construction skills, the company began to offer increasingly sophisticated services. By the late 1980s, the cooperative was performing helicopter-assisted construction, as well as overhauling complex cooling systems in industrial chimneys. The Gdansk Cooperative was one of three companies in Poland to offer such a sophisticated repertoire of high-altitude industrial services.

Growth enabled the company to expand geographically as well. Within a year, the cooperative had moved its operations out of Jaroslaw's private apartment and into a rented warehouse in a Gdansk suburb. By the mid-1980s the company had opened four branch offices throughout Poland, and in 1990 cooperative management purchased an elaborate three-story, 700 million zloty ($74,000) headquarters building in a fashionable Gdansk business district. The Gdansk Cooperative's corporate logo was rapidly earning recognition around the country.

This newly prosperous private sector firm owed its success to its willingness to fill the gaps ignored by state enterprises. State enterprises were not profit motivated and did not have an incentive to compete with the private sector. The members of the Gdansk Cooperative were motivated by more than profit and were driven to find new customers and to expand. The Gdansk Cooperative, like the private sector in general, was willing and able to organize work differently from the state sector.

The flexible work environment at the cooperative was based on a brigade system. Each time a new order for a maintenance or construction job was received, cooperative managers organized a team of members—a brigade—to perform the work. The size of the brigade depended on the job. Cooperative management appointed members with strong entrepreneurial talents to serve as brigade foremen. The foremen supervised workers on the job, arranged for the delivery of supplies, and established deadlines for project completion. Several of the cooperative's most effective brigade leaders had gained valuable managerial experience as organizers of Solidarity activity at the Lenin Shipyard in Gdansk during 1980–1981.

Management paid brigades as a group for each job performed, and it was the foreman's responsibility to divide the payment among team members on completion of an assignment. Each brigade functioned as an independent unit, on its own time schedule. Its only directive from management was that it "must maintain the good name of the Gdansk Cooperative." Under this system, cooperative members often earned up to five times the average Polish salary. Jaroslaw Czarniecki himself worked on the brigades for the first two years of the cooperative's existence, and he earned more as a worker than he earned later when he served only as the company's director.

The brigade system and piece rate compensation had great appeal for the cooperative's politically active work force. Under this flexible arrangement, members could earn a large amount of money in a short time, and they could take extended leaves of absence, during which they could devote all their energies to political activities.

As the Gdansk Cooperative expanded, it continued to hire new employees through informal Solidarity networks. Membership expanded from 10 in 1983 to over 250 in 1990. Much like the cooperative's founders, the new hires were political activists who had been blacklisted from state sector jobs for antigovernment activity. The odd mix of business and politics created a distinctive corporate culture at the cooperative. Asked to describe the firm in 1990, Jaroslaw replied, "We do anticorrosion work, high construction, helicopter montage of electrical-transmission towers. Generally speaking, any sites difficult to get at. And then, of course, all manner of social activity underground."

The success and prominence of the Gdansk Cooperative during the 1980s meant that many of its best people moved on to other careers once the political environment changed. From the summer of 1989 on, many members were recruited by the new Solidarity government. Cooperative members moved into an impressive array of government positions, and the company lost its most ardent Solidarity supporters.[16] Furthermore, in light of the clearly pro–private sector orientation of the new government, its further liberalization of entry into private business, and the overall change in the macroeconomic environment as a result of the Balcerowicz Plan, many of the Gdansk Cooperative's best managers left the firm to establish their own companies.

Managerial experience earned at the Gdansk Cooperative proved invaluable, and companies created by cooperative-spawned entrepreneurs were often highly successful. In 1990, for example, Jarek Poloczanski left the cooperative to establish Citrus Wholesale, the first private sector banana-importing operation in northern Poland. Within six months his weekly turnover reached 60 tons of bananas, and his weekly take-home pay exceeded $10,000 (we discuss Citrus Wholesale in more detail in Chapter 6). Another brigade foreman, Slawomir

Wejner, left the cooperative to open a pharmaceutical warehouse in Gdansk.

Rather than discouraging employees from creating their own companies, Jaroslaw often provided departing members with start-up capital from the cooperative's investment fund. Thus, for example, the Gdansk Cooperative became a 55 percent owner in Polmar, a local construction company, and a 60 percent owner in Mix, a domestic trade company. Of the fifteen private firms that were established by former members, the Gdansk Cooperative had large ownership stakes in six, which accounted for a total investment of 1.3 billion zloty ($137,000).[17]

Because of the political and economic changes in Poland, the Gdansk Cooperative became a launching pad for both administrators and private businesses. Firms like the Gdansk Cooperative played a critical role by providing training to future private sector entrepreneurs. It was in these firms during the 1980s that Poland's human capital—its managerial ability—really developed.

Educated Entrepreneurs

The story of private sector development in Poland is about scarce managerial talent and the way it is used. The change in economic system requires people who can develop market-oriented management skills, and educational attainment is an important indicator of that ability.

Of the 549 people who answered our question about education, 37 percent had completed university and another 6 percent had some university education but had not earned a degree. Only 1 percent said they had no education beyond elementary school. The remainder had completed either special or general secondary school courses.

We find that university education has a positive effect in the employment regression—our benchmark regression for private sector performance. A dummy variable for whether an entrepreneur completed university has a positive sign and is significant in all the specifications we tried.

In our second Krakow survey, we found that university-educated entrepreneurs are most likely to pay especially high wages to their best-paid group of employees and to make a higher proportion of all employees' salaries dependent on performance.[18] Educated entrepreneurs also appear to be a relatively high proportion of entrepreneurs starting firms during the 1980s (and surviving to 1992 for our interviews). Of the 71 firms in our sample founded before 1980, only 18 percent were started by entrepreneurs with a university degree. This proportion rose sharply to 31.9 percent for the period 1980–1987 and to 50 percent for 1988–1989. In and after 1990, university-educated entrepreneurs—that is, those who completed university—declined to just under 39 percent.

Educated entrepreneurs are more common in some sectors than in others. In the second Krakow sample, the proportion of university graduates is highest in three sectors: modern services (72 percent of all entrepreneurs in our sample are university graduates), transport (67 percent), and production (47 percent). The proportion of university graduates is lowest in traditional services (17 percent), restaurants (13 percent), and wholesale trade (25 percent).

When education level and prior work experience are cross-tabulated, university graduates stand out. Of university graduates in the second Krakow sample, 69 percent of those who worked previously did so in a sector different from the one in which they work now. Of other people who worked previously, only 47 percent worked in a different sector. This finding suggests that higher levels of education enhance individuals' ability to enter new lines of activity. Supportive evidence for this claim is the fact that, compared to non-university-educated entrepreneurs, a higher proportion of university-educated entrepreneurs previously worked in a different sector: the proportions were 58 percent of those who completed university and 49 percent of others. These survey results support the hypothesis that entrepreneurs who have a higher level of general human capital, as measured by a university education, have some advantages when it comes to solving the complex and ever-changing problems of business administration in an environment as unstable as that of Poland.

What advantages are conferred by education in this context, and what possibilities does it create? The case study in which we examine these issues in detail is that of Doradca, a consulting firm that is interesting not only for its own sake but because it influenced the development of many other firms in our study. Some of the founders and original members of the Doradca cooperative went on to become leading politicians and spokespeople in the emergent private sector.

We are also interested in the relationship between general human capital and the ability to start up and survive in the private sector.

Doradca, a consulting cooperative, provides an excellent example of a services firm based on a high level of human capital and offering products never before seen in Poland.

Doradca

In the late 1970s, Jan Krzysztof Bielecki was an economist working for the Center for Heavy Industry, an applied research institute in Gdansk. Like many other academics in Gdansk, Bielecki became active in Solidarity's opposition to the communist government in 1980–1981 and spent much of his time providing logistical support for Solidarity activities. When martial law was declared, Bielecki was arrested, detained briefly, and dismissed from his position at the Center for Heavy Industry. Blacklisted from state jobs, he was unemployed for eight months before finding work as a truck driver for an agricultural cooperative. Meanwhile, as a member of the Gdansk underground Solidarity, he published dissident pamphlets and monitored the secret police.

After martial law was lifted in 1983, there were a number of well-educated young graduates and professors from Gdansk University who, like Bielecki, wanted to work outside the state sector and continued to support underground Solidarity. In 1985, a group formed around the idea of starting a consulting business that would provide financial advice to state enterprises and to newly established cooperatives and private firms. The communist government had recently instituted reforms whereby direct administrative control of state enterprises by ministry bureaucrats was replaced by written rules limiting the actions of enterprise managers. Bielecki and some former colleagues from Gdansk University recognized these complicated and convoluted rules as a consultant's paradise: complex financial and tax regulations full of loopholes applied to managers who had strong incentives to circumvent the regulations.

For advice and guidance, the group approached a friend and former teacher, Professor Jan Majewski, who had considerable experience with the implicit and explicit regulations governing the establishment of cooperatives. Majewski also had close connections with Polish Ocean Lines (POL), part of Poland's merchant marine and one of Poland's most successful state enterprises. He suggested that the most visible positions (president of the cooperative and head of the executive committee) be given to people without strong ties to underground

Solidarity. Bielecki, the de facto managing director of Doradca, was given the low-sounding post "chief of operations."

Doradca was established with virtually no capital or sources of financing. Accordingly, overhead had to be minimal and all costs made variable. Doradca began with only two employees: Bielecki and a secretary. The business strategy was to solicit state enterprises for consulting services and then form teams of consultants on a project-specific basis to perform the work. The cooperative relied on its founders' connections with state enterprise managers to generate business. Majewski was especially important in this regard because several of his former students held senior management positions at POL.

Because there were no experienced consultants in Poland at that time, and Bielecki wanted to build the cooperative's reputation for high-quality service, the involvement of his Gdansk University colleagues was critical. The seemingly cumbersome organizational structure of a cooperative actually facilitated this network approach to client development. The cooperative form meant that Doradca had a democratic decision-making apparatus, which facilitated the recruiting of other intellectuals, many of whom were active in underground Solidarity and were suspicious of any form of hierarchical authority.

Doradca's first engagements involved "attestation" work, a product of President Jaruzelski's economic reforms in the early 1980s. To receive their wage allocations, state enterprises were required to, in Majewski's words, "check each post in the enterprise and document whether the person works." Majewski said, "Enterprises did not know how to do 'attestation' well and get it approved. 'Attestation' really did nothing—it was just a matter of fulfilling the government order. We learned this from Russia."

Tax consulting was the mainstay of Doradca's first years. Piotr Konwicki, a Doradca consultant, described how the Polish tax system generated so much work for the cooperative: "When a tax law passed parliament, the Finance Ministry was responsible for the details. One could read these ordinances, providing you had some acquaintances in the local fiscal office. Very often the interpretation was left absolutely up to them."

The decentralized and opaque nature of the Polish tax system created many opportunities for experts with good connections to assist clients. Doradca was particularly successful with advising state enterprises on how to minimize their wage tax liabilities. It was in the state enterprise manager's interest to both overstaff and pay high wages to attract the best workers and ensure industrial peace, because he or she was accountable only for the production target, not for production cost or profit. In an attempt to slow the growth in wage costs, a tax was introduced that penalized firms when they exceeded some preset level of growth in total wage costs from year to year. The regulations were complicated and left managers with a variety of ways to get around the restrictions—such as paying employees for "foregone" vacation time. In addition, the regulations were revised frequently. Doradca became expert at helping firms to increase individual wages without tax consequences. In 1987, Bielecki organized a group of Doradca employees to write software that enabled state managers to simulate the effects of different strategies on their wage tax liabilities. The software was very successful and was purchased by many of Poland's largest enterprises.

Doradca's practice of maintaining minimal overhead and using subcontractors on a project-by-project basis proved exceptionally effective in the cooperative's early years. The tax-consulting projects earned revenues of from 100,000 to 300,000 zloty per engagement (roughly $150 to $450 at the shadow exchange rate). Approximately half of the fees went to compensate the consulting team; Doradca retained the other half. The teams were free to distribute their share of the fees among themselves as they saw fit, and the compensation typically exceeded the average monthly wage of $20 to $30 for white-collar workers in state firms.

This system of collaboration with a network of trusted consultants was not only efficient but also extremely flexible in responding to new opportunities in the marketplace. When a member found a new market or a new product for the cooperative, there was no impediment to Bielecki assembling a group to pursue it. For example, prior to 1988, Polish law made joint ventures between Polish enterprises and Western firms nearly impossible. Legal reform in 1988 permitted such ventures, and Doradca quickly became active in working with Western consulting, accounting, and investment banking firms to locate and evaluate joint venture targets in Poland. After more than forty years of communist rule, there were very few English-speaking Poles conversant with Western accounting methods and financial analysis. Doradca's proficiencies in this regard soon made joint venture consulting the largest part of the cooperative's business.

The arrival of foreign businesses in Poland presented new opportunities. Work with Western consulting firms was attractive to Doradca, Bielecki said, "because it generated fees of three to five times what Polish state firms could pay per hour. In communist countries you do not pay for knowledge, only for workers and goods." By late 1990, Doradca had completed work on foreign equity participation in more than twenty companies and had fifteen more in process. The joint venture work was connected with a large engagement with the International Finance Corporation (the World Bank group member responsible for lending to private organizations) to prepare feasibility studies for loans to Polish cooperatives.

The growth in Doradca's volume and scope of activities led to a sharp increase in employment. While continuing to perform most of its engagements with teams composed of individuals on contract, Doradca's staff grew from two to eight in its first year, and by 1987 the cooperative had twelve employees. Retained earnings had financed several microcomputers, which were provided for a fee to the engagement teams. The organizational structure remained unchanged. Pay continued to be based on project performance, and very small dividends were paid to the cooperative's members.

The lack of a formal career system was not a major problem for two reasons. First, the individuals who worked for and with Doradca were involved, in one way or another, with underground Solidarity, and Doradca provided a vehicle for them to support and coordinate their Solidarity activities. Members and contracted consultants often worked for a few weeks and then took a few weeks off to work for Solidarity, taking on jobs ranging from writing pamphlets to organizing strikes. Second, as Konwicki put it, "the main attractions of Doradca were not monetary; they were independence and freedom on the job, flexibility in activities and in working time, and the general atmosphere here." The atmosphere, in turn, was largely the product of loyalty to Bielecki and to the Solidarity resistance.

Why was Doradca so successful? From the beginning, the management demonstrated brilliant strategic vision. They saw opportunities to apply a high level of human capital profitably. They found an ideal alignment of product strategy, organizational structure, and human resources—including the people they hired, their shared values, and the way they were paid. One of the first companies to offer high-quality consulting services in the Polish market, Doradca made effective use of its knowledge of regulations and of the operating environment. As market conditions changed, Doradca was able to change the consulting products it offered. Furthermore, the management of Doradca made effective use of its internal structure, even though the regulations pertaining to cooperatives made that structure more complicated and controlled than would usually be the case for a start-up company. The cooperative ethos actually supported the team-based and contingent compensation system inside Doradca.

The development of management skills among key people in Doradca can be traced back at least to their political activities connected with Solidarity. Without a doubt, however, these skills developed further during the early days of Doradca's operation. This company is an excellent example of highly educated people who, over a period of time, converted their knowledge into management skills and, more generally, into human capital having commercial value.

Assessment

Throughout Part II, we try to qualify conclusions that can be drawn from our case work by looking at the extent to which they are supported by general survey evidence. In this context, it is important not to exaggerate the extent to which people worked initially for one private firm, such as the Gdansk Cooperative or Doradca, learned how to operate in the private sector, and then moved on to start their own company.

As we already discussed, just under a third of all entrepreneurs in our samples actually had a private sector job before starting their own firm. However, our large-sample evidence suggests that those people have been among the most successful, in the sense that they now employ more workers.[19]

Although it is hard to be sure, the balance of our evidence suggests that there is probably an important difference between generations. People who in 1980–1981 were young and active in Solidarity were more likely to become involved in a new form of cooperative, as described above. At least in the mid-1980s this involvement offered a way to be independent and display initiative without breaking completely with the collectivist ideas that were central to socialism and that Solidarity also represented. In contrast, people who entered the labor force in the late 1980s were less likely to be politically active and more likely to start a purely private business, such as a limited liability company. Of course, the legal situation had changed by the late 1980s, and we often find there was a core group of founders who worked together closely, just as did those who started cooperatives, although the ethos is different. These later entrants were more interested in profit and less interested in politics. If they were concerned with politics, they were more likely to see a clear division between political activity and business.

Gdansk Cooperative, Doradca, and the other cooperatives we studied provide important examples of how firms operated successfully at this time. An assessment of these examples is valuable not only for understanding the 1980s but also for understanding what came next.

Both the Gdansk Cooperative and Doradca had the right combination of strategy, structure, and people to succeed in the difficult operating environment of the mid-1980s. Both found ways to turn difficult elements of the environment to their advantage. Shortages made it difficult to get supplies but also gave rise to niches in the product market in which state enterprises were not interested in operating. Bureaucratic barriers to entry slowed expansion but also limited the number of potential competitors. As these barriers were gradually reduced during the 1980s, new opportunities were created, and competition often increased. Nevertheless, important advantages were usually associated with being the first to enter a particular market or market niche.

Good people were hard to come by and often had priorities other than making money. Both cooperatives recognized this difficulty explicitly and worked through networks of political contacts to find the right people and to provide ways to generate income while supporting rather than hindering their political activities. Note, however, that the managers in both cases say the firms themselves were never directly engaged in political activities. Such activities were employees' choices, although management respected and perhaps even encouraged them.

The right people often resisted working in hierarchical structures. But again the cooperative form, seemingly cumbersome for small start-up firms, also served a purpose. The positions that were available, often on flexible work teams—with remarkable similarities despite the different nature of work in the Gdansk Cooperative and Doradca—fit the people well.

The contingent compensation pay systems were tightly aligned with the strategies and other organizational characteristics of the Gdansk Cooperative and Doradca. Contingent compensation provided incentives to find business, maintain high-quality standards, and work efficiently. It also supported sufficiently high pay rates to attract talented and motivated people into the cooperatives' activities.

Furthermore, contingent compensation kept fixed costs very low and thus made it easier for the cooperatives to respond quickly to new business opportunities.

The pattern of development shown in the Gdansk Cooperative and Doradca was far from unique. Two other cooperatives that we studied closely started as cooperatives providing basic services, but with the intention of raising capital so they could move into manufacturing. Initially, both found the cooperative structure conducive to this pattern of development, but both subsequently complained of the constraints it imposed.

By 1990, in the aftermath of the Balcerowicz Plan, almost all relevant interviewees complained that the disadvantages of their cooperative structures greatly outweighed the benefits for at least four reasons. First, all cooperative assets belonged to the state, despite the fact they had been acquired with company profits and the workers' wage fund. Second, the decision-making process was too diffuse to be efficient. Under the cooperative structure, most important managerial decisions had to be accomplished by consensus at the general assembly meeting. Successful cooperatives had too many members for this structure to function smoothly. Third, in 1990, wages at the cooperative were restricted by a stringent excess wage tax, so, for example, Gdansk Cooperative members complained bitterly as their monthly salaries fell from four times the national average in 1989 to approximately the $200 average in 1992. Finally, managers frequently claimed that cooperative members, with no real ownership stake in the business, were losing motivation. In a private company, workers would be able to buy shares and, as owners, would be motivated to improve company performance.

CHAPTER 6

The Private Sector Breakthrough

T HE growth of the new private business sector is closely connected to macroeconomic reform in post-communist countries. In Poland, "shock therapy" succeeded precisely because it created the necessary conditions for the emergence and growth of new private businesses. Widely criticized for being too aggressive and for inflicting great pain on large state enterprises, shock therapy was the right medicine. State enterprises had to be forced to restructure, and entrepreneurship, the real engine of reform, needed the liberalization and stabilization measures of shock therapy in order to flourish. Precisely how this worked in and after 1990 is the subject of this chapter.

Official Statistics

To some extent we can use official statistics to track what happened to the Polish private sector. A company with at least 51 percent of its shares privately owned is officially defined as private. To fully understand these statistics, however, it is necessary to appreciate the difference between "trade law companies" and "individuals" who operate as firms. So-called trade law companies have their legal basis in the amended 1934 Commercial Code.[1] Both limited liability and joint stock companies are trade law companies. We will refer to these companies by their common collective Polish name: *spolka* (singular) and

133

spolki (plural). Polish official statistics define a *spolka* as private when at least 51 percent is owned by private individuals.

For most of the communist period it was not possible to create new spolki, but this situation changed after 1987, when the communists tried to encourage some private business.[2] Up to 1989, the minimum capital required to start a limited liability company was 1,000 zloty—a significant amount in the 1930s but worth only a few dollars by the late 1980s. It is not unusual to meet people who registered several spolki at that time. Some of those spolki may still be "sleeping"—if they are not active, then no taxes need to be paid.[3]

The number of incorporated spolki rose from 1,275 in 1988 to 11,693 at the end of 1989, 33,239 at the end of 1990, and 38,516 by mid-1991. A small part of this total is joint ventures between Polish and foreign partners, which at this time required a minimum investment of $50,000 in hard currency. The total number of joint ventures rose from 32 in 1988 to 429 in 1989 and to 1,645 by the end of 1990.

The growth of spolki tells only part of the story of the Polish private sector. Many private entrepreneurs, even those with substantial businesses, have preferred to operate as individuals.[4] There are several reasons for this preference. First, it takes only a few days to start an individual business, because it is necessary to complete only a simple registration procedure. In contrast, forming a spolka is relatively complex and usually takes more time.[5] Second, there is no minimum starting capital for an individual, whereas for spolki by mid-1991 the minimum starting capital had risen to 10 million zloty (about $1,000) for a limited liability company and 250 million zloty (about $20,000) for a joint stock company. Third, if the accounting is handled properly, there are fewer taxes on an individual entrepreneur than on a spolka. In addition, a one-year tax holiday was available to individuals in 1990, as long as they were "newly" involved in wholesale trade.[6]

Official statistics give the total number of unincorporated firms, rounding to the nearest thousand, as 357,000 at the end of 1980, 418,000 at the end of 1985, 660,000 at the end of 1988, 814,000 at the end of 1989, and 1,136,000 at the end of 1990. Of the 813,485 "unincorporated firms" registered on December 31, 1989, 482,020 were in handicraft, 71,802 were in trade, and 259,663 were classified as "others." After that date, statistical information was published in a more detailed form, and by September 30, 1991, official statistics show totals of 44,226 private spolki, 3,512 joint ventures, and 1,365,644 individual entrepreneurs.

By the end of 1991, official estimates were that the private spolki and joint ventures together employed 0.5 million people, in addition to the 2.5 million employed by individual entrepreneurs. The Polish urban labor force is about 12 million people, so these numbers implied that the private sector accounted for 25 percent of jobs outside of agriculture.

Early Problems

The Polish private sector has performed phenomenally well, but this fact was initially obscured by the problems that some private firms encountered when the Balcerowicz Plan was introduced. For example, in the late 1980s Semeco was a successful exporter of Polish produce to Sweden. By the fall of 1989, Waldemar Staszak and his partners decided that the export operation would be more profitable if they were to grow their own produce rather than rely on a widespread network of independent farmers. In October, the company leased 25 hectares of greenhouse space in Szczecin and created a subsidiary called Semeco-Okmess Co. Ltd. to run the operation. In its Szczecin greenhouses, Semeco-Okmess gew apples, tomatoes, peppers, cucumbers, and flowers, which it exported to Svenska Corab AB in Sweden, just as Staszak had done after collecting produce from his network of private farmers. The company's first season was highly successful, and the company earned a net profit of two billion zloty ($211,000) through its produce sales in Sweden. But when the Polish government tripled energy prices in 1990, operating costs at the greenhouses skyrocketed, and Semeco-Okmess was forced to withdraw from the business.

That is an excellent example of how a change in relative prices could have negative effects on private enterprise. At least in the case of Semeco, however, the human and even financial capital accumulated by the failed venture was not lost. Semeco was sufficiently flexible and diversified that it was able to employ those resources productively in other activities. The same company that operated the greenhouses also ran supermarkets. While the greenhouses were profitable, they generated a surplus that could be invested in the relatively capital-intensive process of developing commercial real estate for the stores. When the greenhouse operation had to close, the shutdown did not drag down the rest of Semeco's business.

Ironically, Semeco profited from subsidies provided by the state in the form of cheap energy and was able to use this money to fund its overall development. This form of subsidy was not the basis for sustainable development of either the state or the private sector and should be criticized for inducing private investment in businesses—such as greenhouses—that were not viable when energy prices rose closer to world levels. Semeco faced problems in 1990 because its product strategy no longer made sense at the new relative prices in Poland.

In contrast, the problems encountered by the Gdansk Cooperative after 1990 were due to an internal structure that was no longer appropriate when market conditions changed. The cooperative lost the alignment between structure and strategy that had been crucial to its early success. Initially, there was a problem as a direct result of the tight financial squeeze on the state sector. Gdansk Cooperative's industrial maintenance and high-rise construction clients were large state-owned enterprises, as well as government-funded administrative and infrastructure institutions. Private sector companies owned few large-scale buildings, factories, or other industrial assets that could be serviced by the cooperative and its new subsidiaries. About 80 percent of the cooperative's customers were state firms, and the remaining 20 percent were government organizations, such as highway administration authorities and historical monument preservation societies.

As a result of the Balcerowicz Plan, government subsidies were withdrawn from state-owned enterprises; and as state sector companies were forced to exert tighter control over costs, demand for high-rise industrial maintenance services plummeted. In 1991, 20 percent of the cooperative's sales had been made to a nitrogen plant and two coal factories in southern Poland, all three of which had been steady customers since 1985. By mid-1992, however, these clients had been stripped of financial support from Warsaw, and they disappeared entirely from the Gdansk Cooperative's order book. Under similar circumstances, the Gdansk Oil Refinery, which had provided the cooperative with its most lucrative contracts since 1983, placed only a meager 200 million zloty ($12,500) order for minor repairs on a leaky oil tank in 1992. As state-owned enterprises were forced to cut back on high-altitude maintenance and industrial chimney construction, business prospects for the Gdansk Cooperative's private sector subsidiaries soured.

Difficulties quickly surfaced at Oliwia, a joint venture that had been established for industrial chimney production and maintenance. The company received no new orders after mid-1992. Among destitute state-owned enterprises, there simply was no demand for industrial chimney construction. Oliwia was forced to abandon its fashionable downtown headquarters and relocate its offices to a small, low-cost apartment on the periphery of Gdansk. By early 1993, the company, unable to collect payment from its state-owned clients, was struggling to complete jobs for which it had been contracted in the past. Oliwia had accumulated a debt of 500 million zloty ($32,000) in overdue payments to various equipment suppliers, and bankruptcy appeared imminent.

Another joint venture, Kominbud, was also no longer able to find state industrial clients for its chimney montage operations. As business deteriorated, Kominbud management shocked the Gdansk Cooperative by deserting the joint venture and creating a new firm called Kominbud, Ltd. Piotr Chmielewski, a member of the cooperative's executive committee, was outraged by the defection of Kominbud managers: "These people were not connected with the Gdansk Cooperative in the past," he said. "They had no loyalty. They had their own ideas for Kominbud." The internal structure of the cooperative was no longer sufficient to hold its portfolio of activities and its people together.

Trade

The Balcerowicz Plan legalized almost all private imports. It also made the Polish currency convertible for current account transactions, so that anyone who wanted to import goods could obtain foreign exchange without a problem. This combination of changes meant that importing goods into Poland suddenly became relatively easy and extremely profitable.

A Polish citizen who had a small amount of capital, perhaps even a hundred dollars, could travel to the West and bring back goods to sell. In all the major cities, stalls sprang up on street corners. Some observers claimed that this small-scale trade was a sign that the microeconomic transformation was not deep. In fact, the transformation of trade was only one small but obvious symptom of a much deeper process of change under way in other sectors.

According to official statistics, the proportionate increase in trade companies was greater than the increase in almost any other category.[7] Table 6-1 shows the surge in wholesale trade in and after 1990, using data from our surveys. Over 80 percent of wholesale trade firms were founded from 1990 on, and this statistic fits with evidence, from anecdotes and official statistics, of rapid growth in trade from early 1990.

But how exactly did private trade rise? What happened to firms that were initially successful when others entered and competition became much more intense? Once again, our cases provide considerable insight.

Doradca

Doradca was one of the first companies to seize new trading opportunities created by the rapidly changing conditions. One component of the second round of economic reforms introduced in 1988 by the Rakowski government was the partial liberalization, under clearly defined conditions, of hard currency trade between state enterprises. A firm that earned foreign currency from its exports now had the right to sell some of this currency directly to a firm that had permission to import. In principle at least, the price of this foreign exchange could be freely determined.

Doradca quickly opened a foreign exchange business separate from its consulting business. In early 1989, it established agents around the country to identify state enterprises in need of dollars for foreign trade. Doradca would pool the orders and buy dollars for zloty from the Export Development Bank, a state bank that had the authority to provide hard currency to importers. Doradca profited from a spread on the rates of exchange between the state enterprises and the Development Bank. Later in 1989, Doradca extended its foreign exchange business to private businesses and cooperatives. The network of agents, who were neither employees nor members, was the critical asset in the business, because it was the agents' contacts with managers in need of dollars that generated transactions.

Yet even more quickly than this opportunity had developed, it disappeared. The introduction of the Balcerowicz Plan in January 1990 further liberalized state enterprises' access to hard currency and created an essentially free market in foreign currency, at least for trade transactions. This development effectively eliminated Doradca's competitive advantage in the foreign exchange business.

Table 6-1 Crosstabulation of Sector and Period When Firm Was Founded

Sector of Activity	Before 1980		1980–1987		1988–1989		1990 and After		All	
	N	PCT	N	PCT	N	PCT	N	PCT	N	PCT
Traditional Services	72	25.0%	66	22.9%	43	14.9%	107	37.2%	288	100.0%
Modern Services	5	5.0	14	13.9	331	30.7	51	50.5	101	100.0
Transport	1	4.3	8	34.8	5	21.7	9	39.1	23	100.0
Restaurant	1	3.8	2	7.7	5	19.2	18	69.2	26	100.0
Retail Trade	14	7.0	16	8.0	25	12.6	144	72.4	199	100.0
Wholesale Trade	5	4.2	5	4.2	12	10.2	96	81.4	118	100.0
Production	82	44.1	38	20.4	23	12.4	43	23.1	186	100.0
All Firms	180	19.1	149	15.8	144	15.3	468	49.7	941	100.0

Note: N is the number of firms. *PCT* is the percentage of firms in a sector that was founded in a particular year.

Doradca, however, still had its network of agents, and one manager thought he could see a way to use the network effectively in the
new free trade environment of 1990. Boguslaw Brzuchalski, who had
joined Doradca in 1986 after having been with a state-owned foreign
trade organization, started a foreign trade practice that quickly grew
to replace the foreign exchange business. Brzuchalski's experience
with a state foreign trade enterprise had impressed on him the gross
inefficiency of state firms' foreign trade activities. He recalled, for
example, instances of ordering electrical goods and discovering that
as much as half of the shipment had been stolen by handlers before
reaching him. Security workers hired to protect the shipments soon
became part of the theft problem.

Brzuchalski and Bielecki recognized that their network of agents
could also coordinate orders for imports, so that, collectively, Doradca could generate orders of sufficient size to justify seeking out
suppliers in the West and organizing transportation and distribution.
Doradca's competition was centralized state trading companies, which
were widely and for the most part correctly viewed as ineffective
in finding new trading partners abroad. Brzuchalski and Regina
Chrapun, another of Doradca's three foreign trade employees, described one of their larger import transactions:

A Polish firm contacted us to help them find a new supplier of high-quality
sausage casings, which are not made in Poland. We searched for addresses
in the West of firms that might make casings. We sent out many telexes,
but got only a few answers. Finally, we found a small German firm in
Hamburg [only two employees] that was interested in exporting.

It took a month to receive and test samples and negotiate a price. Then
we sent telexes to thirty Polish firms proposing that they buy these casings,
because we needed more than one buyer to have enough volume to make
the transaction attractive. We got no answers. Then we called to big meat-
processing plants, and had great difficulty finding out who was responsible for purchasing casings. So, Brzuchalski drove to plants in Krakow,
Szczecin, and other towns to try to meet face-to-face and tell people that
other firms, too, would buy the casings. Our advantages, other than quality,
were that we would organize delivery to the factory, which the state trade
service would not do, and we had a better price.

This initial breakthrough into trade generated substantial income for
Doradca after 1990. Income from trade financed the firm's development of other service sector activities, particularly consulting and
computer-aided design. Doradca is an excellent example of how profit

opportunities in trade formed the essential basis of a process of wealth creation that also helped consumers. The wealth generated then fueled other activities.

Citrus Wholesale

The arbitrage opportunities created by the Balcerowicz Plan, and their importance in several dimensions, are illustrated by the case of Citrus Wholesale, a fruit import business founded by Jarek Poloczanski in 1990. A good example of the connections between the people in our study, Jarek worked for the Gdansk Cooperative during the 1980s.

The loose organizational structure of the Gdansk Cooperative was well suited to Jarek's entrepreneurial style. Workers were assembled into brigades to complete a job, and ambitious employees who showed managerial talent became brigade leaders. In this environment, competence was more important than personal connections or party membership, and Jarek excelled. He quickly rose to the position of brigade leader and proved adept at locating clients, organizing and motivating workers, and ensuring that supplies were delivered on time. Jarek was a key employee at the Gdansk Cooperative until 1990, when political and economic changes in Poland allowed him to take further advantage of his entrepreneurial talent.

The start of Jarek's independent business career began with a foreign contact. A former Gdansk Cooperative member who in 1988 had emigrated to Austria recommended Jarek as a reliable person to an Austrian company, Rehmann. Rehmann had been trading with Poland since 1988 and in the wake of the Balcerowicz Plan wanted to expand its activities. Rehmann's owner was impressed with Jarek's potential and quickly proposed a deal: Rehmann, which had access to a modern banking system as well as assets that could serve as loan collateral, would provide financing from Austria, and Jarek would handle the operating side of the business in Poland. The only issue to be resolved was the product that the new partners would import.

In a country where severe shortages of basic foodstuffs had been commonplace, supplies of "exotic" fruits such as bananas and citrus fruits were virtually nonexistent. Bananas had not appeared in significant quantities in Poland since the 1970s. Realizing that bananas could be a profitable market, Jarek and his Austrian partners began to study the banana industry. Jarek stayed awake nights reading textbooks on the ripening process, filled notebooks with information on prices and suppliers, and spoke with port employees who had handled banana imports to Poland in the 1960s and 1970s. He made phone calls to fruit warehouses all over Europe and learned about the industry's pricing structure, delivery schedules, and transport requirements.

Despite economic reforms, bananas still had not reached the Polish market by early 1990, for a number of reasons. First, there was a lack of "banana knowledge." Bananas were a very fragile fruit that needed to be transported and stored at low temperatures. If exposed to hot weather or if handled improperly, they spoiled quickly. Another obstacle for would-be importers was Poland's rudimentary financial system. It was virtually impossible to arrange timely international payments for the import of Western goods. Finally, there were many other opportunities available in Poland to attract entrepreneurs. Jarek, therefore, seemed to be in an ideal situation. As a result of his extensive research, he had developed a certain level of expertise. He had studied the market thoroughly, competition was nonexistent, and financing would be arranged through his partners in Austria. By being a first mover, he could choose from a number of Gdansk cold storage facilities and establish business relationships with food wholesalers.

Jarek's experience as a brigade leader at the Gdansk Cooperative proved to be valuable as he organized the new operation. His organizational ability gave the new venture its competitive edge. Jarek's principles were to focus on one market, to have an informal and flexible structure, and to pay people only according to their actual performance.

Starting with a phone book and making calls to every listed company that looked as if it might be affiliated with the fruit business, he located a ripening facility in Gdansk that was part of an immense state-run food-processing concern. Built in the 1960s in Gdansk's Baltic port, this was the largest cold storage and fruit-ripening facility in Central Europe. It would be able to accommodate weekly banana shipments of 500 tons. In April 1990, Jarek visited the facility and found that it was virtually inactive. Aside from limited trade activity in tea and coffee, most of the building's capacity remained idle, and there was no work to occupy the facility's state-paid employees. Sensing an opportunity, Jarek proposed a deal. If the facility managers would rent him the idle ripening rooms, he would pay workers several times their state salaries to help him unload bananas and oversee the ripening process. After a series of negotiations, which lasted several days, Jarek persuaded the company's management to rent him cold storage rooms, a warehouse, and an office. Thus, the state sector provided the physical capital for his new private business.

Jarek arranged his payments to the state enterprise carefully. For the ripening rooms, where gas heaters would accelerate the ripening process, he would pay per kilo of bananas rather than for the actual space occupied. The more bananas he ripened, the more he would pay. The ripening fee was initially set at 1,000 zlotys ($0.10) per kilogram.

Jarek hired three administrative workers, ten people to unload banana shipments, and three people to oversee the ripening process. Most of these people had previously worked in this same state enterprise. The state enterprise itself could have imported bananas, using its facility and its people. But the managers of this enterprise did not recognize the opportunity, did not have the competitive drive, and did not have the ability to organize work in this new way. Thus, directly from the state sector, Jarek was also able to obtain the labor he needed for his new private business.

By May, Jarek had made all the preparations necessary to receive his first shipment. Eighteen tons of bananas, packed in a thousand standard 18-kilogram cartons, were to be transported by refrigerated truck from Vienna. Jarek had called virtually every local food shop to announce that he was expecting the bananas, and by the time the delivery truck arrived at his warehouse, a long queue of excited shop owners had already formed outside his door. The novelty of bananas in Poland is best illustrated by the question of a young child who turned to his father and asked, "What are these yellow sausages?"

Jarek's relationship with Rehmann did not last long. Dissatisfied with supply decisions made by Rehmann and uncomfortable in his relationship with other parts of the Rehmann business in Poland, Jarek decided to go into business for himself. In August 1990, he left his Austrian partners and formed his own company, Citrus Wholesale. By that time, he knew the market well and was able to contact European suppliers on his own. His agreement with the state-run ripening rooms remained intact, and he continued to use the building.

The foreigners had been a catalyst, and they had provided the essential initial capital. But within a year of starting up, Jarek was capable of running this business without them. In fact, because of his understanding of local market conditions, he could do a better job on his own, free from the need to consult with his partners in Austria.

His early results operating by himself were excellent. Citrus Wholesale became well known among retail fruit vendors in northern Poland, and the company soon became the major supplier of bananas
in a 250-kilometer region around Gdansk.

As a result, 1990 was a phenomenal year for Jarek in the banana
trade. Citrus Wholesale finished the year with sales of 40 billion zloty
($4 million) and a profit of 4 billion zloty ($400,000), a fortune for an
industrial worker who for years had eked out a living on a state-
administered wage. Furthermore, at a time when the average monthly
wage in Poland was approximately 800,000 zloty ($82), Jarek was
paying his own employees "bonuses" of up to 10 million zloty ($1,000)
per month. "For the people I employed, I was a salvation," he said.
For himself, Jarek was able to buy a new BMW, imported from
Germany, a Peugeot for his wife, a large-screen Mitsubishi television
set, and a VCR. Within a year of Poland's economic reforms, Jarek
was at the forefront of Poland's dynamic new class of entrepreneurs.

This was the first stage of dramatic economic transformation—
a surge of imports from which people with some capital, contacts,
and the ability to organize could rapidly make a fortune. However,
the success of traders like Jarek did not go unnoticed by other ambitious Poles. With few barriers to prevent them from entering the
market, other fruit wholesale companies began to emerge all over
Poland. Jarek was unable to build a sustainable competitive advantage
to keep him ahead of new entrants. "I thought I would be able to
create a network of warehouses in Poland," he said. "I was naive.
Others are not blind. They moved into the banana business very
quickly. Suddenly, there were a lot of importers, and competition
became very tough." Whereas in 1990, Jarek had been virtually the
only banana supplier within a 250-kilometer region around Gdansk,
by 1991, one or two fruit importers comparable in size to Citrus
Wholesale had appeared in every major city in northern Poland.

Jarek learned quickly that customer loyalty did not exist in the
banana business. Bananas were a standard commodity, and vendors'
purchasing decisions were based exclusively on price. Jarek's distant
customers turned to new local suppliers in order to reduce transport
costs. Within a short time, instead of supplying all of northern Poland, Citrus Wholesale was supplying only a small section of the city
of Gdansk.

As the number of competitors increased, price competition became intense. In early 1992, Citrus Wholesale's average import price

for an 18-kilogram carton of bananas was about 160,000 zloty ($12), and the retail price in Poland could range from 50,000 ($3.50) to 230,000 zloty ($16), depending on market conditions. Increasingly, oversupply was forcing Citrus Wholesale to sell below cost.

With a shrinking customer base and lower turnover, Jarek found that the ripening facilities he was renting in the Gdansk port were too extensive. To cut costs, in May 1992 he moved to a smaller facility in another section of Gdansk. Whereas the old facility could accommodate thirty thousand 18-kilogram cartons of bananas, the new facility could accommodate only five thousand cartons. Jarek also reduced the size of his work force. When he moved to the new building, he retained only six of the workers he had employed at the state-run ripening facility.

Citrus Wholesale, which had earned profits of as much as $50,000 per month in 1990, suffered losses totaling 300 million zloty ($22,200) for the period from June to September 1992. Citrus Wholesale's monthly banana turnover fell from over 23,000 cartons in January 1991 to just under 3,000 cartons by June 1992. The company ceased earning a profit in May 1992. By mid-October, Citrus Wholesale had not ordered, or sold, any bananas for three weeks.

What conclusions can we draw from Citrus Wholesale's experience? Despite its short life, Citrus Wholesale generated wealth and helped transform the organization of work in the fruit business in Poland. It also generated human capital that survived the demise of one particular line of business and lived longer than the firm itself.

More generally, the opening up of the Polish economy to imports induced private individuals to engage in trading activities and helped many of them to earn a great deal of money in 1990 (a small amount of capital and foreign contacts could take an entrepreneur a long way in 1990). The flood of entrepreneurs into trade was just the beginning of the transformation of Poland's economy. The high profits to be made from trade swelled entry into the sector and increased competition. One outcome was that a competitive advantage that made a firm successful in 1990 might prove inadequate in 1991; and unless an entrepreneur could continue to build and develop, particularly by improving quality and providing more value for customers, competitors would take away his or her market share and greatly reduce his or her profit.[8] This shrinking of any one firm's market, however, is perfectly consistent with the increase in the number of private firms shown in the statistics. Another outcome was that imports continued, providing previously unavailable goods. The return of bananas to grocery stores is just one example of the broadening of consumer choices made possible by the Balcerowicz Plan.

Not every firm suffered the fate of Citrus Wholesale. Semeco, the next trade company we will examine in detail, had much more success, at least at first, both in trade and using trade as a basis for developing other activities. The Semeco case provides an excellent example of how the growth of trade directly supported the development of private services and manufacturing.

Semeco

The case of Semeco shows the important role of state enterprises, first as suppliers or customers and later as competitors. It also illustrates that many of the "foreigners" who helped the private sector develop actually had very strong ties to Poland.

There were three important figures in Semeco. All of them were Poles. Two of them, Bogdan Barczyk and Jerry Mallenberg, had emigrated to Sweden in the 1970s. The third, Waldemar Staszak, had turned from political to business activity during the 1980s. Barczyk knew Staszak through Solidarity-related activities, and this personal contact was the basis of the subsequent business development.

In 1988, Poland's parliament passed the Law on Joint Ventures. This law allowed Polish state-owned enterprises to establish a joint stock company with a foreign firm or with Polish expatriates, subject to a permit issued by the Ministry of Foreign Trade. Polish equity was required to be at least 51 percent, and the company manager was required to be a resident Polish citizen. Joint ventures were allowed a two-year tax exemption, after which profits would be taxed at a rate of 50 percent rather than the standard 65 percent. Reinvested profits would remain tax exempt.

The Law on Joint Ventures created opportunities for Svenska Corab AB, the Swedish agricultural trading firm that Barczyk and Mallenberg owned and operated. As native Poles, albeit expatriates, Barczyk and Mallenberg were in a unique position to take advantage of the new law, and they quickly set about creating a joint venture that would allow them to exploit unprecedented access to the Polish market. Most of Svenska Corab's business involved trade in food products, and the Polish countryside was rich in produce, particularly apples, cucumbers, and tomatoes. Barczyk and Mallenberg were confident that they would be able to find buyers for Polish produce in Sweden. They planned to create in Poland a joint venture that they could use as a supply base for their overseas trade operations.

When Barczyk and Mallenberg contacted Waldemar Staszak and revealed their plans, the Gdansk entrepreneur was eager to serve as a liaison between Svenska Corab and the Polish market. He agreed to play a major role in the establishment of the joint venture. Staszak would be responsible for locating state-owned joint venture partners who would be willing to contribute the required Polish capital, and he himself would serve as general director of the venture. Thus, shortly after his initial discussions with Barczyk and Mallenberg, Staszak approached the management of two local, state-run firms in which he had high-level contacts. Both companies proved eager to sign onto a joint venture and develop business relationships with a Western firm. Servomotor, a state-run cooperative that performed ship repairs and sold nautical equipment in the port of Gdansk, contributed $24,000 of the joint venture's initial capital in exchange for a 48 percent ownership stake. Metal, another Gdansk state-run cooperative involved in ship repairs, provided $1,500 for a 3 percent stake. Semeco was therefore founded, in part, in cooperation with what were effectively state enterprises. Svenska Corab received the remaining 49 percent, the maximum ownership share allowed a foreign partner, in exchange for transportation equipment that could be used to deliver Polish produce to the Baltic coast. Combining the first two letters of "Servomotor" and "Metal," the partners dubbed their venture "Semeco."

In July 1988, Semeco Co. Ltd. commenced operations in Gdynia, a port city near Gdansk on Poland's Baltic coast. As required by the Law on Joint Ventures, the company was established with the equivalent of $50,000 in equity capital. The company's board consisted of Waldemar Staszak, who was named general director although he did not have an ownership stake; Barczyk, who was named president and reestablished permanent residence in Poland to help direct the company's activities; and Mallenberg, who remained in Sweden to oversee the activities of Svenska Corab.

Barczyk and Mallenberg were primarily interested in importing agricultural products and flowers from Poland. The Semeco joint venture provided the Swedish-based traders with the means to export these goods from Poland, and Staszak, with his entrepreneurial background and extensive Polish contacts, proved to be an ideal partner.

He quickly set about locating private farmers who had not already contracted their produce for sale to the central government and who would be willing to sell to the joint venture on credit, to be reimbursed only after Svenska Corab was able to distribute their produce in Sweden. Polish farmers were generally conservative and suspicious of new proposals, but Staszak proved to be an excellent salesman for the company, and he soon created a 200-kilometer-wide network of private produce suppliers in northern and central Poland. Staszak began buying up large stocks of apples, onions, cucumbers, tomatoes, and flowers and exporting them to Svenska Corab. Income from the sale of these products in the West was then channeled back to Staszak, who paid off the Polish farmers and placed orders for ever larger shipments of Polish produce.

By the end of 1989, Semeco's Polish-Swedish produce trade had become profitable enough that the company was able to purchase a large amount of Swedish chocolate and sell it to a national food distributor in Poland shortly before the start of the Christmas season. This chocolate transaction signaled the beginning of a new era for Semeco. Within a short time, importing Swedish grocery items for resale in Poland would become a major business for the company. Semeco's exports from Poland and imports into Poland were integrally related.

Semeco's partners decided to develop the grocery import business that they had begun with the shipment of Christmas chocolates in 1989. By mid-1990, their grocery imports from Sweden were sizable enough that retail distribution in Poland made sense, and it was a business that could easily be shifted to one of Semeco's subsidiaries: Semeco-Okmess. Furthermore, the Semeco partners were convinced that Western-style supermarkets would be a welcome alternative to traditional Polish food stores, which were renowned for their low-quality service and meager product selections. Semeco's managers had figured out that Polish retail trade needed to be completely reorganized. The same conclusion was being reached by entrepreneurs all over Poland at this time.

Shopping in Poland's state-run food shops was an unpleasant experience. Goods were often stacked on shelves located behind service counters that were operated by brusque, middle-aged women wearing food-stained smocks. Customers formed queues at the service counters and ordered their groceries from the women at the registers, who in turn retrieved the items from the shelves. Because all groceries were stored behind the counters, shoppers had no opportunity to inspect products before making a purchase and often felt required to know exactly what they wanted to buy before entering the store. Furthermore, food stores did not provide bags for carrying groceries; customers were expected to bring their own.

With the Western supermarket concept in mind, Semeco-Okmess began to open a chain of grocery stores in Gdansk. Management secured leases for large commercial buildings in colossal, block-style apartment districts—locations that assured the company of a steady supply of shoppers. In less than two years, Semeco-Okmess opened five Western-style supermarkets in the Gdansk region. All interior furnishings for the stores, including modern shelving, promotion racks, and conveyor-belt-driven checkout counters, were purchased in Sweden. Over 80 percent of the food items sold in the stores were Western products shipped from Sweden by Svenska Corab. Successful wholesale trade supported and even drove the development of retail space.

The Semeco-Okmess stores were much more attractive and convenient than Poland's state-run alternatives. In Semeco's supermarkets, customers could leisurely walk through grocery-stocked aisles, where they were able to inspect products and make their own selections. By allowing customers to select their own groceries, Semeco eliminated the service counters that separated clients from products, and queues were kept to a minimum. The predominance of Western foods, still something of a novelty in Poland, was an additional attraction for Gdansk shoppers. Furthermore, Semeco-Okmess supermarkets remained open twenty-four hours a day, a service concept that was new to Poland's food-retailing industry.

Semeco-Okmess supermarkets were enormously successful. As a result of the stores' favorable locations and high visibility, the company logo became one of the most well recognized in Gdansk. Customers flocked to the stores to take advantage of a leisurely shopping style, convenient hours, and Western groceries. Semeco-Okmess quickly grew into Semeco's largest company, accounting for 35 percent of the organization's $25 million in turnover in 1991. The company profit margin was approximately 30 percent, well above the national average for the high-volume grocery business. Encouraged by its early success, Semeco-Okmess planned to add new stores at a rate of one every six months. The new stores were to be opened without loans or external financing; each new supermarket would be funded solely by Semeco-Okmess profits.

What was the key to this success? Semeco fundamentally reorganized the way groceries were sold, following the model of Western countries. This reorganization was made possible by the macroeconomic changes in the Polish economy; it would have made no sense in a shortage economy and would have been difficult without access to imported products.

Semeco, just like Citrus Wholesale, seized the profit opportunities made possible by the reorganization of trade. Semeco's relationship with the state sector was both important and ironic. Beginning with capital from state enterprises, it was able to develop a successful private business that could take advantage of opportunities much faster than could the state sector. There certainly are circumstances under which state enterprises can change the way work is organized, but—at least in the Polish case—private businesses have proved able to make those changes much more quickly.

Assessment

There is a perception among many Western observers that trading activities generate jobs that are in some sense inferior to jobs in manufacturing or in better parts of the service sector. Is there any evidence to support this position?

At least for the variables that we can measure, our survey evidence finds no evidence to support the view that trade provides jobs that are less desirable than jobs in other parts of the private sector. Our second Krakow sample focused particularly on employment conditions in private sector firms. In that sample there is substantial variation in average wages within the private sector, including a strong sectoral pattern. Restaurants pay the lowest wages, $120; traditional services pay the second lowest, $123; transport pays the second highest, $259; and retail pays the highest, $281. The finding that wages are relatively high in retail is surprising but not completely implausible. Retail opportunities have expanded very rapidly in the private sector and have been extremely profitable over the past three years. Manufacturing has average wages just above the mean for the whole sample, at $184.[9]

Within each sector there are high-paying and low-paying jobs. We find the highest proportion of high-paying jobs in retail trade, where 86 percent of firms pay average earnings of over $200 per month. At the same time, 63 percent of firms in wholesale trade pay more than $200 per month on average, and 50 percent pay more than

$250 per month. In short, our research indicates that trade jobs are valuable by themselves, and there is no reason to think that these jobs are "less good" than jobs created elsewhere in the economy.

The Doradca, Citrus Wholesale, and Semeco cases bring out two points that apply generally to private sector activities other than trade. First, interactions with foreigners played an important role in private sector development. Foreigners were more than trade partners; they were also sources of capital, contacts, and managerial knowledge. Our surveys confirm the finding in most of our cases that the Polish private sector is primarily based on domestic initiative and resources. Nevertheless, foreigners often played an important role as catalysts, particularly through offering ready distribution channels.

Second, once the economic system changed dramatically at the start of 1990, success came to those who could change the way work was organized. What did this mean in concrete terms? If an entrepreneur could produce a product in a way that no state sector firm did, 1990 was a good year for that person. Trade was a sector in which the advantages of superior organization could make a person successful very quickly.

Many people who had never worked in the private sector before were engaged in small-scale trade activities. Those who were prepared, financially and psychologically, expanded rapidly. Although only a small amount of human and financial capital was necessary to enter this sector, those who did best started with a large amount of capital and considerable work experience.

Skeptical observers of the Polish reform have argued that an expansion of private trade is not a sufficient basis for a modern economy. In our view, this position is only partially correct, because the development of private trade was integrally linked to the development of other forms of private business. Moreover, in Poland, it was logical that trade should be the first sector to change.[10] And the trade boom benefited other sectors of the economy. Firms that made money on trade in 1990 were able to invest part of the proceeds in other activities. Some firms that did well in wholesale trade moved rapidly into retail or production or various forms of service. Individuals learned about business and about how to operate on their own in a market economy. This knowledge had an important direct effect on their ability to work better either for themselves or for someone else. Furthermore, the private sector's ability to import quickly became an ability to export.

The ability to import freely made exporting much easier. Imported inputs could provide the necessary high-quality materials. These materials could then be sourced domestically later. The liberalization of trade therefore directly stimulated the growth of private manufacturing and services. In the following sections of this chapter we explain how this happened.

Manufacturing

It was evident from the launching of the Balcerowicz Plan in 1990 that if Polish economic reform was going to lead to a sustainable increase in living standards, significant private sector development in other parts of the economy, including manufacturing, would be needed. It is in manufacturing that Western economists and businesspeople usually look for the answer to whether the Polish economic reform has been successful, and it is in this sector that some observers have deemed the effects of the Balcerowicz Plan to have been insufficient (Webster 1992; Berg and Blanchard 1994). The reasons cited for this shortfall include lack of outside capital, high minimum required scale of operation, and lack of appropriate skills and technology. The decline of state industry has also seemingly strengthened this argument. Our analysis of what has happened so far, however, is much more positive.

Manufacturing provides many examples of the process that we call "starting over"—the reorganization of work through the creation of new private sector firms. Starting fresh offers clear advantages. Any new private sector firm has a chance to create from scratch a business strategy, a consistent internal organizational structure, and an appropriate system of compensation.

In an economy making the transition from plans to markets, almost every manufacturing process needs to be fundamentally reorganized. Organizations that can institute such a change will make larger profits and will grow. Organizations that cannot make the necessary adjustments will contract and eventually die. Starting over has therefore proved to be the fundamental mechanism for the reorganization of industrial production. Our surveys indicate that some private sector manufacturing firms are small and weak and have trouble growing. Many of those firms, however, were formed before 1980 and engage in small-scale, traditional activities, such as the making of handicrafts, small-scale textiles, and souvenirs of various kinds— minor activities in most European countries.

At the end of the 1980s, a significant part of the private manufacturing sector in Poland consisted of firms that were based on the old set of relative prices and had no chance for survival after price liberalization. Under the communist system, some small private manufacturing companies had prospered by taking advantage of the economy of shortage, the supplier's market, and the lack of foreign competition. These companies were in the enviable position of being able both to use subsidized raw materials and to set their own prices freely. Though often primitively equipped, these businesses had enjoyed profit-to-sales ratios in the range of 50 to 100 percent.

A major advantage of the Balcerowicz Plan was its recognition that input prices had to be put on a sustainable basis. Cheap energy, which the Soviet Union had provided, was one element of a trade structure and an underlying political order that no longer existed. From 1990, energy prices moved much closer to sustainable levels, setting the right incentives for future investment decisions. Because the old prices had been so distorted, however, there was a substantial negative effect on some businesses, even those in the private sector. Under the stabilization program, these businesses suddenly faced foreign competition and limited demand. Thus, paradoxically, the arrival of a free market brought an end to the prosperity of many established small private family businesses, and the number of private companies in the industry and construction sectors actually fell during the first quarter of 1990.

Nevertheless, while the Balcerowicz Plan was curtailing the profitability of some activities, it was creating new opportunities. Firms with the right combination of product strategy and internal structure were able to reposition themselves quickly to take advantage of the change in macroeconomic conditions.

Many casual observers of Poland have suggested that manufacturing has struggled to develop in the private sector. Our research indicates otherwise. Right from the beginning of the Balcerowicz Plan there have been notable successes in private manufacturing, and the sector as a whole has expanded steadily.

Some observers have confused the problems in "old" private manufacturing firms with the true situation in firms founded more recently. For example, in our large sample, the production sector contains a high proportion of relatively old firms—nearly 45 percent were started before 1980. But production firms continued to be founded during the 1980s, and over 20 percent of this sector started in or after 1990. (All these numbers are drawn from Table 6-1).

Some established manufacturing firms failed because, although they had prospered under the communists, they could not adapt to the completely new economic conditions in 1990. For example, the category of "handicrafts" represents mostly traditional private sector activities, which were allowed to operate under the communists. The "net balance" of firm creation in this sector—start-ups minus suspensions and liquidations—was negative in the first three quarters of 1990. The most striking contrast is with the trade sector, which consists largely of entrepreneurs who entered this activity in 1989 and 1990. Even in the first quarter of 1990, there was a positive net balance of firm creation for this sector, and this net balance rose rapidly during 1990.

However, just as in other parts of the private sector, new entrepreneurs did well when they identified a viable market segment, entered early, and steadily improved their quality and value. Successful entrepreneurs were those who were able to update and improve their product strategy over time and who developed organizational structures that could handle expansion. Starting over has been just as crucial in manufacturing as in other sectors. Several cases illustrate this point well.

Semeco

We have argued that the rapid growth of private sector trade had a positive effect on other sectors. The best examples are cases in which people who made money in trade subsequently moved into manufacturing, usually making products related to what they were trading. This movement was already happening at Semeco early in 1990.

After their initial trading success, the partners in Semeco agreed that the best way to capitalize on new business opportunities in Poland was to establish a foothold in as many of the country's underdeveloped markets as possible. They planned to convert Semeco from an agricultural trading company into a major Polish conglomerate. Semeco would become a holding company, establishing subsidiaries that would become early leaders in a broad spectrum of consumer markets. The holding company strategy was to be based on rapid development and extensive diversification, with business activities ranging from meat processing to newspaper publishing. After creating each new company, Semeco's directors would install a management team. The management team would be required to submit monthly performance reports to Semeco, and, once the new company became profitable, its managers would be expected to repay the start-up capital provided by Semeco. Aside from reviewing monthly progress reports and providing occasional financial assistance, Barczyk, Staszak, and Mallenberg would have limited involvement in the activities of Semeco subsidiaries once they had become well established. This arrangement would free up Semeco's managerial resources to pursue new markets and continually create new companies. Initially financing its expansion strategy with profit earned through its trade activity with Svenska Corab, Semeco created subsidiaries and entered new industries at a dizzying pace.

Some of these changes occurred before the Balcerowicz Plan but when it was already clear that the communist economy would be dismantled at least to some extent. Nevertheless, finding a partnership with the state sector was still important. In June 1989, Semeco established a meat-processing company called SGS Co. Ltd. in partnership with Spolem, a state-run food store chain that operated a nationwide monopoly. Semeco was a 68 percent shareholder in the partnership; Spolem owned 32 percent. SGS, which was located in Gdynia and employed thirty workers, was designed exclusively to serve Spolem, and every week the government-operated food store chain purchased the entire output of its meat-processing subsidiary.

Three months later, in September 1989, Semeco created its second subsidiary, a wood-processing company called Semex Production Co. Ltd. Semex had a work force of 250 and specialized in the manufacture of simple wood products such as industrial pallets and fence posts. These products were designed for export, and the company focused its marketing efforts in Sweden and Germany. Semeco therefore survived and even prospered at the beginning of the Balcerowicz Plan. Because of its product strategy, the organization could adapt to cope with the new macroeconomic situation. With an effective internal structure at this time, Semeco was able to develop a large number of new opportunities, including in manufacturing. Private sector manufacturing was beginning to take off.

SeCeS-Pol

In the development of private manufacturing, the link between state enterprises and newly emergent private businesses has proved to be very important. The story of SeCeS-Pol illustrates the helpful role of the state sector as an essential customer and as a weak competitor. In addition, however, the continuing decline of the state sector after 1990 posed problems for SeCeS-Pol, which could be resolved only through a change in product strategy. The liberalization of trade made this change possible.

Jerzy Siemienczuk was a brilliant engineer who finished university in the early 1980s and became chief engineer at a state-owned, steel-based manufacturing company called Budimor. He designed industrial steel products and quickly became the company's most prized employee. Within a year of starting work, he was awarded a new car, virtually unprecedented material wealth for a recent university graduate.

In 1984, Jerzy left Budimor to become the director of production at Gdansk Panstwowy Instytut Sanitarny (the Gdansk Sanitary Installation Institute, which we will refer to by its Polish initials, GPIS), which produced a wide variety of steel-based heating and plumbing equipment. It was at GPIS, where he managed a department of 120 workers, that Jerzy first worked on heat exchangers—devices that convert very hot high-pressure water supplied by power stations into water of a temperature and pressure that can be tolerated by commercial and residential heating systems.[11] Jerzy believed that the existing product was poorly designed, and he introduced a number of modifications, including a revolutionary interior pipe design, that significantly enhanced the device's performance.

Part of the communists' reform legislation introduced in early 1988 was a law that permitted the development of private sector firms making high-technology or innovative products. Under the right conditions, these firms could also receive some tax breaks. This change in the legal environment sparked Jerzy's sense of entrepreneurship, and he immediately initiated efforts to privatize his department at GPIS because privatization seemed the most feasible strategy for establishing his own firm. He was familiar with the business, he was respected by his colleagues, and, most important, his department at GPIS already had a manufacturing process in place. However, internal jealousies and fears that he and his coworkers would earn too much money too quickly led state-appointed managers at the firm to reject his idea. Jerzy decided to leave his secure, state-sponsored engineering post and strike out on his own. With no assets to his name, the resourceful engineer was confident that he would find the means to create a private manufacturing company.

After some difficulties, including dealings with an Austrian businessman who proved less than honest, Jerzy was confronted by a new obstacle: he had no manufacturing machinery and no capital to continue development. By early 1988, he had exhausted his personal financing sources while renovating the building he wanted to use, and he could begin manufacturing only if he could sell heat exchangers by advance order for payment in cash.

Most companies, particularly those that did not own production equipment, would be unable to market an unseen, untested product. Jerzy, however, had earned a reputation as an outstanding heat engineer and was highly regarded in Poland's heat exchange industry. In September 1988, in the nearby town of Ciechanow, he approached a power company for which he had designed heat exchangers in the past. The state-owned power company had been pleased with Jerzy's work, and the power company's management agreed to purchase SeCeS-Pol's first heat exchange system for 330 million zloty ($110,000). The power company paid 60 percent, or 200 million zloty, in advance but demanded that the product be delivered within one month.

With his fresh capital of 200 million zloty ($67,000), Jerzy purchased a turning lathe, industrial steel presses, a drilling machine, and other equipment necessary for the manufacture of heat exchangers. He also bought raw materials from Polish steel mills, including sheet metal, raw steel, and stainless steel pipe, all of which would be forged into heat exchanger components on Jerzy's new machinery. Jerzy hired six employees away from his old department at GPIS and assumed his familiar management role as they installed the new equipment. The crew worked at a furious pace, and, after assembling an entire manufacturing system within one month, was able to produce SeCeS-Pol's first heat exchanger on November 30, 1988.

Starting with nothing more than an empty building, Jerzy and his colleagues miraculously managed to fill the Ciechanow power company's order only four days behind schedule. Jerzy delivered the product personally in order to make amends for the delay. This was the only time that SeCeS-Pol would ever deliver a product behind schedule.

New orders soon followed, and SeCeS-Pol quickly earned a reputation for producing among the highest-quality heat exchangers in Poland. Jerzy and his crew worked intensely for up to eighteen hours a day, perfecting the manufacturing process and improving productivity as the new orders flowed in. By the end of the year, after less than two months of operation, SeCeS-Pol had paid for all of its new machinery and had earned a profit of 11 million zloty ($3,670).

What gave SeCeS-Pol its edge? Jerzy was able to organize work quite differently from the usual case in state enterprises. His work force was highly motivated, he managed the work process closely, and he watched market conditions very carefully. But a large part of his success was due to the fact that he had to compete primarily with state enterprises.

In the late 1980s, approximately eight state-owned, steel-based manufacturing firms dominated Poland's heat exchanger industry. These companies primarily served local markets, although the two largest firms, both of which were located in southern Poland, served a national clientele. These state-run companies were generally poorly managed and overstaffed and had high overhead costs. Supply shortages, particularly of steel inputs, continually interrupted production. During Poland's communist era, however, the central government subsidized these companies, and they were able to survive despite low productivity. Furthermore, Poland's heat exchanger producers monopolized local markets and were able to develop solid, long-standing relationships with state-owned clients who were not cost conscious. The major customer for heat exchangers in Poland was OPEC—the acronym for a nationwide monopoly that managed Poland's energy and power network and that alone accounted for over 80 percent of heat exchanger purchases in Poland (not to be confused with the international oil cartel). The remaining customers were primarily housing cooperatives and construction companies that were required to provide heat exchangers for newly built homes and apartment complexes.

The heat exchanger industry was characterized by significant entry barriers. Production of the exchangers required highly specialized technical knowledge, as well as a large investment in manufacturing equipment. As a result, SeCeS-Pol was the only new entrant to the industry when legal changes in 1988 permitted the establishment of private, high-tech firms. Jerzy recalled that when SeCeS-Pol began manufacturing heat exchangers, producers competed not for customers but for inputs:

When I started the company, I could sell everything I produced. The problem was obtaining materials. Everything was allocated by the central government, and of the nation's limited pool of stainless steel, only 2 percent or 3 percent was set aside for sale to private firms. This was virtually nothing. I was often forced to buy my steel at high cost from state-owned manufacturing firms that had received large allocations.

Limits on steel sales to private companies were removed in mid-1989, and in 1990, after implementation of the Balcerowicz Plan, supply shortages ceased to be a major problem. This provided a major immediate boost to successful private producers such as SeCeS-Pol.

A second direct benefit of the Balcerowicz Plan was that trade liberalization and currency convertibility made it possible to import capital equipment for the private sector. This equipment permitted both a greater volume of production and higher quality, which in turn made possible an increase in private sector exports.

In January 1991, Jerzy imported from Germany a steel pipe production line that cost 1.5 million DM ($1 million). The automated line embodied the latest in Western pipe production technology and was much more sophisticated than the equipment used in Polish steel plants. Soon after purchasing the line, Jerzy hired a team of six engineers to design modifications that would enhance its performance. The engineers, all recent graduates of the Gdansk Polytechnic Institute, were young and highly talented. Jerzy had discovered them through the typical combination of luck and informal connections that characterized the Polish labor market.

In January 1991, a young Polytechnic graduate in need of pocket money had turned up at the SeCeS-Pol plant when he heard that one of Jerzy's machining lathes was in need of repair. Jerzy allowed him to try his hand at the lathe and, impressed by the speed and quality of the young engineer's work, offered him full-time employment as a technician on the pipe production line. Pleased with the new technician and eager to perfect the production process, Jerzy decided that the company would benefit from the input of more engineers. His new employee recommended a colleague from the Polytechnic, whom Jerzy immediately hired and who, in turn, recommended another recent graduate. In this fashion, other mechanical experts followed, until Jerzy had assembled a team of six smart and successful Polytechnic engineers who had worked together through five years of university studies. Within four months, the new line was able to produce 14 meters of 8-millimeter-diameter steel pipe per minute, and Jerzy claimed that it was the fastest line in the world.

Despite a high level of manual labor in the final assembly process, fewer than 3 percent of SeCeS-Pol's heat exchangers were rejected for unsatisfactory performance at the quality control station. The low percentage of defective exchangers despite primitive assembly conditions resulted largely from Jerzy's practice of compensating workers on a performance basis rather than an hourly basis. With this manufacturing system, SeCeS-Pol had the capacity to produce over ten thousand heat exchangers per year.

SeCeS-Pol was able to achieve rapid growth because it produced higher-quality heat exchangers at lower cost than its state-run competitors. SeCeS-Pol's cost advantages resulted from three factors. First, state-owned companies, which were often overstaffed, were burdened by high administrative costs that SeCeS-Pol was able to avoid. Second, even though some managers in state enterprises realized they were at a competitive disadvantage, they found it very difficult to reorganize work to keep up with the pace of change in the private sector. They faced too many constraints and restrictions, most of them due to the attitudes of managers and workers. Third, SeCeS-Pol was the only Polish heat exchanger manufacturer that was able to produce its own stainless steel pipe. SeCeS-Pol managers estimated that because of that capability the company's costs were between 5 and 20 percent lower than competitors'. In fact, SeCeS-Pol's competitors in the heat exchanger industry had begun buying 8-millimeter steel pipe produced by Jerzy's company. SeCeS-Pol's pipe was more reliable and less expensive than pipe produced by state-run steel mills. For those reasons, SeCeS-Pol was able to gain market share despite long-standing relationships between more established producers and their customers. In December 1992, the company's trade director estimated that SeCeS-Pol was supplying approximately two-thirds of Poland's heat exchanger market.

Yet, while SeCeS-Pol had been growing, domestic demand for heat exchangers had been steadily declining. Poland's major purchasers of heat exchangers were the government-funded OPEC companies, and OPEC companies constituted 70 percent of SeCeS-Pol's customer base. Poland's cash-starved reform government, however, was unable to provide adequate financing for its national network of power suppliers and, under financial pressure, the OPEC companies began to scale back on purchases of heat exchangers. As a result, growth in sales of SeCeS-Pol's heat exchangers slowed and then stagnated. In 1992, total sales of heat exchangers remained at their 1991 level of approximately 10,000 units: for the first time in company history, SeCeS-Pol did not achieve an increase in annual sales volume.

The financial squeeze in the state sector increased difficulties for many private sector companies, limiting their growth and even causing some to fail. SeCeS-Pol, however, was able to adjust its product strategy to fit changing market conditions. Jerzy's response was to manufacture other steel-based products in order to achieve further growth. He already owned the appropriate technology and was well connected in the steel industry. Producing other steel-based goods was a simple matter of adding capacity.

While Jerzy changed the product mix, he also oriented output more toward exports. On special order for a French transportation firm, SeCeS-Pol began to produce large, rectangular steel containers and reinforced steel platforms that were to be used for industrial transport and storage. The same plant, separate from SeCes-Pol's main facility, employed fifteen production workers and also produced a limited number of excavator shovels for export to Germany. Eventually, this plant housed the manufacturing operations for a joint venture partnership that SeCeS-Pol had established with a Danish company to produce plate-type heat exchangers.

As his company expanded, Jerzy changed his style of management and the internal structure of his company. In the early days, he had personally overseen every aspect of the company's operations. He had been responsible for all hiring, purchasing, and investment decisions. As the company acquired new plants that were spread over a wide geographic area and produced a wide assortment of products, Jerzy realized that he could no longer control all of SeCeS-Pol's daily operations. So he selected a manager for each location, and the factories operated as distinct companies. Each plant kept its own books, handled its own finances, and set its own production schedules. Plant directors were responsible for all internal management decisions. Managers were held directly responsible for factory performance, and a large portion of their compensation was performance based. In January 1992, a plant manager earned 38 million zloty ($3,230), of which only 2 million zloty ($170) was base pay and the rest was various forms of incentive.

Jerzy's efforts to introduce new products and enter new markets had a significant impact on the size of the firm. By 1992, SeCeS-Pol was employing 200 workers and had achieved sales of 42.2 billion zloty ($3.1 million) for the first ten months of the year. Of this amount, sales of heat exchangers and stainless steel pipe accounted for 33.5 billion zloty ($2.5 million). The company owned three production facilities in Gdansk, operated between 15 and 20 sales outlets in Poland, and was a partner in three joint ventures that would soon begin marketing heat exchangers abroad. The company had become one of the largest producers of heat exchangers in Poland.

What explains SeCeS-Pol's success? The initial concentration of economic activity in large state enterprises meant there existed important market niches that had the potential to be profitable. The partial liberalization of private business at the end of the 1980s made entry into these new niches possible, but shortages of inputs constrained operations. The change in macroeconomic conditions brought by the Balcerowicz Plan removed that constraint. The state sector was not able to respond. State enterprises' internal structures were too cumbersome to alter quickly, and the people working in these firms were not ready for rapid change. State firms retained some advantages in the form of capital equipment, but in businesses where economies of scale did not prevent new entry—such as heat exchangers—private firms could and did enter manufacturing.

By liberalizing trade, the Balcerowicz Plan made it possible to import capital equipment. This equipment was used effectively by private firms, and—as in the case of SeCeS-Pol—it helped them to increase their exports. Here was a direct link between the development of imports, manufacturing, and exports.

Jerzy Siemienczuk built SeCeS-Pol with well-managed technological innovation. He not only introduced new high-quality products but also managed to stay ahead of rapidly developing market conditions. Jerzy delegated effectively and changed the company's internal organization to better support its larger scale of operation. Overall, SeCeS-Pol is an outstanding example of private sector manufacturing success.

Styl France

The case of Styl France illustrates additional important aspects of private sector development in manufacturing. The story of this company demonstrates the importance of links with foreigners and how the liberalization of imports led directly to higher exports.

Czeslaw Bereza, whose family had emigrated from Poland to France when he was young but who had remained in contact with Poland and its economic conditions, founded Styl France to produce low-cost furniture. While in France, Czelaw had had a number of occupations, including furniture repair and carpentry instructor. His partner in Styl France was one of his former furniture customers, August Royet. Royet had immigrated to France from Italy twenty years earlier and had been operating an antique furniture dealership outside Lyons ever since. Each partner agreed to contribute the equivalent of $25,000 to the venture. Czeslaw provided his share in the form of machinery from his antique repair shop in Lyons. Royet's $25,000 contribution was a mix of used machinery and operating capital. The new company, which would specialize in the production of imitation antique furniture for export to Lyons, was named Styl France.

With the help of a local Pole, Andrzej Magielka, Czeslaw located a former poultry facility in a small town called Kartuzy. He gutted the building's interior, which was still outfitted with breeding hutches, and quickly installed the electric saws, sanders, and other pieces of carpentry equipment, a total of eight machines, that he and Royet had transported from France. As soon as the machinery was installed, he placed an employment announcement in the local newspaper. From among the throng of local farmers who responded, all of whom wished to abandon a difficult agricultural life for work at a "French" company, Czeslaw hired five workers, none of whom had experience in furniture manufacturing. In May 1990, equipped with a production facility, imported machinery, and a newly hired work force, Styl France was ready to begin its manufacturing operations.

At first, Czeslaw devoted almost all of his time to training his inexperienced workers. "When I worked as an instructor in France," he said, "I had to start from nothing and create professional-level carpenters in 500 hours. This turned out to be ideal preparation for what I was to face in Poland." For almost two months, Styl France operated with virtually no output as Czeslaw schooled his farmers in the art of furniture manufacturing. With no product on the market, however, Styl France was unable to generate turnover to cover operating expenses, which included salaries, factory overhead, and wood imports from France. To keep the company afloat, Royet was forced to borrow 180,000 francs (about $36,000) from a French bank. But Czeslaw was an expert trainer, and by August, Styl France had managed to produce its first eighty pieces of furniture, all of which were exported to Royet in Lyons.

Czeslaw and Royet had decided to focus their sales efforts on the French market for two reasons. First, both partners were well connected in the antique furniture business in southern France, and they felt that demand from this market alone would be sufficient to keep Styl France producing at capacity. Second, the company gained a substantial tax advantage by selling its products in France rather than Poland. To protect domestic wood-based industries, the Polish government levied a 30 percent duty on imported lumber and a 20 percent duty on imports of finished wood products. These taxes, however, were not binding if the imported wood was used to manufacture a product that was then exported. From the beginning, Styl France imported a substantial portion of its wood supplies from France.

In Kartuzy, Styl France produced high-quality, imitation antique furniture in a style called Louis Philippe. The company's products included desks, wardrobes, tables, chairs, and cabinets. Styl France's most popular piece was a walnut jamcase; by 1992, the company was producing between 400 and 500 of these small chests per year. All products were made entirely of wood, and, because labor was inexpensive in Poland, much of the production work was performed by hand.

Czeslaw was a self-trained master carpenter, and his manufacturing methods were based largely on intuition and experience. Under his guidance, the factory assumed a workshop-like character. Furniture was produced in small batches—ten to twenty pieces of a single type were produced at once—and workers were expected to do whatever was necessary to complete each piece. "There was no specialization in the factory," said Czeslaw. "Often a small group of two or three workers would manufacture a batch of furniture from start to finish."

The key to Styl France's competitive advantage was the effective organization of low-cost labor, resulting in very high quality at relatively low prices. In Poland, where Styl France paid workers 11,000 zloty ($1) per hour, labor was inexpensive. According to Czeslaw, the total hourly operating cost per worker at Styl France's factory was 30 francs ($6); in France, the same hourly measure was approximately 150 francs ($30).

The high labor content of Styl France's prodution process gave the company's furniture a significant advantage on the French market, where handcrafted furniture was highly valued. Although several companies in France were producing similar furniture, their manufacturing processes were entirely machine based. French labor was too expensive to allow for handwork. As a result, the French furniture did not have the curves or the natural appearance of Styl France's products.

The total cost of producing and exporting a single Duc Saint Julien buffet was 1,950 French francs ($390). Of the total cost, Styl France paid 650 francs ($130) for labor and factory overhead and another 100 francs ($20) for the Polish alder wood purchased from a local supplier. The remaining 1,200 francs ($240) for materials and transport were provided by Diffusion, which shipped French walnut wood, varnish, glue, and all furniture fittings to Styl France from Lyons. Styl France sold the Duc Saint Julien buffet to Diffusion for 750 francs ($150), which was just enough to cover its costs. In France, Diffusion sold the Duc Saint Julien buffet for 5,500 francs ($1,100). Clearly, Styl France was sufficiently labor intensive that the low wages of Poland gave it a significant cost advantage.

Styl France is a case in which the liberalization of trade was necessary for the development of a manufacturing enterprise, but trade liberalization was not sufficient for Styl France to succeed. Also needed was an entrepreneur able to train and organize Polish workers effectively, in order to take advantage of Poland's relatively low wage costs while producing a high-quality product. A foreign partner played an important strategic role, but the most important factor was the ability to organize work from scratch and in a way not seen in Poland since the communists came to power. Indeed, it was the thoughtful combination of local craft skill, low relative wages, and a very effective foreign distribution channel that distinguished Styl France from less successful ventures.

Assessment

The key elements demonstrated by the Semeco, SeCeS-Pol, and Styl France cases are the need to find a product for which there was a sustainable demand and the importance of aligning internal structure appropriately. In these firms there was a tension between focusing sufficiently on successful products, continually improving production or distribution, and remaining sufficiently flexible so that the fortune of the firm was not too closely tied to one product for which demand might decline or competition intensify too much.

Our research indicates that Polish private sector manufacturing has developed rapidly. The unsettled macroeconomic environment of 1990–1992 made life difficult, because production has a relatively long time horizon and a long payback period for investment. But since then the environment has calmed considerably.

Allowing the import of goods was essential for the development of exports. Foreign observers often miss this crucial point. Styl France began with imported materials, although it reduced its reliance on them over time. From Germany, SeCeS-Pol imported capital equipment, which it used to make pipe for sale in Denmark, among other places.

Under Polish conditions we would expect that many firms failed to grow while a few grew rapidly. This is exactly what we find. The key question is the proportion of successful firms. How many success stories are enough? Answering this question empirically or theoretically is hard, but evidence from the comprehensive databases of the "yellow pages" directories indicates a great deal of manufacturing growth.

Problems associated with raising external finance are definitely important. The relatively large amount of capital investment in manufacturing and the longer payback period probably mean that the manufacturing sector is more constrained by the availability of credit than is trade or modern services. As our cases indicate, and as Chapter 7 on finance will indicate in greater detail, an important constraint on the taking of credit in Poland has been high nominal interest rates.

Nevertheless, we find that the capital necessary for manufacturing development has been available in the private sector, though generally not through credit. Table 6-2 shows that almost 60 percent of production firms started out with less than $100, and overall the Polish manufacturing sector does not indicate higher initial capital requirements than other sectors. Skilled workers are scarce but can be trained. The most important constraint is the availability of entrepreneurs with the knowledge and managerial ability necessary to run a manufacturing firm. Such people are emerging in substantial numbers, and four years of reform is a relatively brief period within which to expect dramatic development of a new industrial sector based on entrepreneurial companies.

Although the growth of manufacturing is clearly important for the post-communist reform process, the evidence from our surveys suggests that manufacturing does not have distinct advantages over other sectors in terms of wages and employment. In particular, the modern services sector appears to have played an important role in pulling up private sector wages.

Table 6-2 Crosstabulation of Initial Capital and Sector of Activity

Initial Capital	Traditional Services		Modern Services		Transport		Restaurant		Retail		Wholesale		Production		All	
	N	PCT	N	PCT	N	PCT	N	PCT	N	PCT	N	PCT	N	PCT	N	PCT
Less than $100	76	32.9%	40	51.3%	3	23.1%	1	6.7%	28	15.7%	45	47.4%	59	58.4%	252	35.4%
$101–$500	53	22.9	11	14.1	3	23.1	2	13.3	25	14.0	11	11.6	11	10.9	116	16.3
$501–$1,000	22	9.5	6	7.7	1	7.7	3	20.0	22	12.4	2	2.1	6	5.9	62	8.7
$1,001–$5,000	28	12.1	10	12.8	3	23.1	5	33.3	38	21.3	13	13.7	9	8.9	106	14.9
$5,001–$10,000	27	11.7	5	6.4	1	7.7	1	6.7	20	11.2	8	8.4	10	9.9	72	10.1
$10,001–$20,000	14	6.1	1	1.3	—	—	2	13.3	19	10.7	6	7.3	3	3.0	45	6.3
$20,001–$50,000	5	2.2	3	3.8	2	15.4	—	—	18	10.1	9	9.5	1	1.0	38	5.3
More than $50,000	6	2.6	2	2.6	—	—	1	6.7	8	4.5	1	1.1	2	2.0	20	1.8
All	231	100.0	78	100.0	13	100.0	15	100.0	178	100.0	95	100.0	101	100.0	711	100.0

Note: N is the number of firms. *PCT* is the percentage of entrepreneurs in a sector that started with a given level of capital.

Modern Services

Poland, like other communist countries, was overindustrialized. Successful reform will necessarily mean a decline in manufacturing's share of GDP and employment. The sector that needs to grow the most, in relative and absolute terms, is services. At the same time, much of what we classify as the service sector is closely connected to manufacturing and appears to have played the leading role in pulling up wages. Although this sector does not lead in exports, there is considerable potential for trade development, particularly through substituting for imported services.

In analyzing the service sector, it is helpful to distinguish between what happened in "traditional" and "modern" services. Traditional services are service activities such as shoe repair and laundry, which do not make use of modern technologies. Examples of modern services are printing, publishing, and consulting. Most but not all modern services are sold to other businesses.

Table 6-1 shows that for the 941 firms in our large samples for which we have relevant data, 25 percent of traditional services firms were formed before 1980 and over 45 percent were founded before the beginning of 1988. As Table 6-1 indicates, many but by no means all traditional services firms were founded before the acceleration of reforms in the late 1980s. In 1988 and later, many new firms entered activities that should be considered traditional services, particularly construction. There is a clear contrast with modern services firms. Table 6.1 indicates that less than 20 percent were founded before 1988. For a precise understanding of why private sector activity in modern services has boomed, we turn to our case studies.

Phantom Press

Phantom Press is a publishing company that grew from nothing at the end of the 1980s and then encountered problems when competition intensified. Just as in our other cases, the relationships of this firm to state enterprises and to foreigners were crucial.

Having witnessed the immense popularity of underground publications in the early 1980s, Tadeusz Adamski was convinced that the literature market was one of the most underdeveloped markets in Poland. In the past, the state had run all publishing enterprises in Poland, and very little Western literature was allowed to filter through to Polish consumers. Most items in Polish bookstores had a socialist bent, and political, science fiction, and romance works from the West were unavailable. In an effort to prevent Western literature from reaching the market, government officials consistently denied operating licenses to prospective private publishers. Western literature, often referred to as "forbidden fruit," could be obtained only in limited quantity and in poorly printed editions from illegal underground publishers.

In the immediate aftermath of political liberalization in 1989, Tadeusz, conscious of the pent-up demand for previously "forbidden fruit," decided to start a publishing company that would translate and distribute Western books. In August 1989, having gathered 10 million zloty (about $1500) in loans from family and friends, he rented a small office in a Gdansk suburb, bought a telephone, and went into business as an independent publisher. He called his new company Phantom Press.

Tadeusz began by purchasing the Polish rights to a science fiction novel by an unacclaimed British author. In Gdansk, he hired an independent translator to create a Polish manuscript from the English version, and then he contracted a local state-owned publishing company to print several thousand copies. Phantom Press's first science fiction novel reached the Polish market in early September, and, though far from being a best-seller, the project was modestly profitable. Tadeusz immediately invested his earnings in a second science fiction novel, which he published a month later. The company continued to take on one project at a time, financing each new publication with previous profits.

Growth at Phantom Press was slow but steady. By November 1989, the company had five employees and had published three science fiction novels. Tadeusz, however, longed to publish popular Western authors and well-known titles, but capital constraints at Phantom Press limited his options. Furthermore, he had run into difficulties with the firm that was printing Phantom Press's books. The printer was a sluggishly operated state-owned company that often missed publication deadlines and had even sold a Phantom Press manuscript to a competitor—Tadeusz was shocked to find his book in retail stores "before" it had been published. The books that Tadeusz received from his Polish printer were generally of poor quality. Often, the embossing on the book covers was severely marred, or pages fell out because the wrong glue was used in the binding. Burdened by slow growth and an incompetent printer, Tadeusz resolved to find a foreign partner who could provide fresh capital, as well as access to a respectable foreign printer.

As in several of our other cases, a Polish private businessman sought to use foreigners to take advantage of the opportunities presented by the state sector's inability to respond to new markets, while circumventing the problems inherent in obtaining supplies from the state sector. Tadeusz also wanted to take advantage of the Law on Joint Ventures, which had benefited Semeco in its early days. The law exempted a joint venture from all taxes during its first three years of operation. If Tadeusz could find a foreign partner, the joint venture "tax holiday" would enable Phantom Press to achieve faster growth.

He found Richard Wojtak, a British citizen of Polish descent who was willing to contribute 475 million zloty ($50,000) for a 90 percent stake in the company. Tadeusz would contribute 10 million zloty ($1,050) for the remaining 10 percent. The joint venture would take over Phantom Press operations in Gdansk, and the new company would be called Phantom Press International.

Although the joint venture law provided Phantom Press International with tax advantages, it limited opportunities for profit distribution. Ten percent of after-tax profits had to be reinvested in the company, and cross-border profit transfers to the foreign partner were severely restricted. Furthermore, reinvested profits remained tax-exempt after the expiration of the tax holiday. This provision of the law provided a strong incentive for joint venture partners to reinvest rather than distribute profits.

Wojtak, however, was wary of Poland's unstable political and economic environment, and he insisted on access to earnings from his 475 million zloty investment. After consulting with Tadeusz, he devised a clever mechanism for indirect distribution of the joint venture's profits. He created a "partner" company in England called Phantom Press Ltd. Phantom Press Ltd. had no formal ties to Phantom Press International, but the partners agreed that Wojtak's company would serve as an agent for the joint venture. For a fee, Phantom Press Ltd. would negotiate all copyright agreements, manage relationships with British publishing houses, and purchase Western paper and other supplies necessary for the joint venture's publishing needs. This dual company structure would allow Wojtak to profit from Phantom Press activities without drawing directly from the firm's earnings.

Tadeusz's partnership with Wojtak paid handsome dividends. Wojtak's investment capital enabled Phantom Press International to acquire translation rights to popular titles by Salman Rushdie and well-known science fiction works by Ursula LeGuin. Wojtak also managed to purchase the rights to a series of forty British horror titles, many of which became top sellers in Poland. Buoyed by a fresh supply of foreign capital and a new repertoire of high-quality translation rights, business began to flourish at Phantom Press International.

Just as we saw with wholesale trade in the case of Citrus Wholesale, when the publishing industry was opened to competition, growth in the number of private firms was explosive. Tadeusz was not alone in perceiving pent-up demand among Poland's 40 million literature-starved consumers. Hundreds of independent publishing companies were established, and the market quickly became saturated. Competition and confusion in the industry was increased by the large number of newly formed, small-scale wholesalers, which became the main source of demand for new fiction. These wholesalers operated independently—there were no buyers' networks or clearinghouses—and the small, irregular orders that they placed with publishers were accompanied by high administrative costs. Tadeusz realized that in some Western countries, there were only two or three major book distributors. But in Poland there were two hundred. In the city of Wroclaw alone, forty-two distributors serviced seventy-three retail shops.

The high-risk, unstable environment of Poland's private publishing industry is well illustrated by an experience that Phantom Press had with one of its Krakow wholesale customers in 1991. Several weeks after placing an order worth 800 million zloty ($72,730), the unprofitable wholesaler still had not managed to pay Phantom Press. When Tadeusz traveled to Krakow to collect, the desperate wholesaler suggested that they play roulette for the balance of his debt. Tadeusz agreed and won the bet, and Phantom Press assumed ownership of the customer's assets in Krakow. Tadeusz soon converted the wholesaler's facility into Phantom Press's Krakow trade office.

Unlike the overly decentralized book wholesalers' market, the market for copyright licenses, which publishers were required to obtain before printing a book, was highly concentrated. During communist times in Eastern Europe, almost all of the region's foreign copyrights were supplied to state-owned publishers by two copyright brokers: Gerd Plessl Agency (GPA) in Germany and Prava i Prevodi in Yugoslavia. These brokers had signed representation agreements with the agents of many Western authors, and they had become well known in world publishing circles. GPA and Prava i Prevodi had even acquired publishing rights to Western works that were banned behind the Iron Curtain. These rights, which had been obtained at low cost, proved highly profitable once Eastern European publishing markets were opened. Because literary agents preferred to conduct business with a single broker rather than with a large number of smaller publishers, GPA and Prava i Prevodi remained Eastern Europe's principal providers of foreign copyrights even after the region's communist regimes were ousted in 1989 and 1990.

As a result of these developments, Poland's new generation of publishers, including Phantom Press, acquired almost all copyright licenses indirectly through GPA and Prava i Prevodi. In many cases, overly eager small-scale publishers purchased the rights to popular titles, only to find that they were unable to finance publication. Ironically, because these copyrights were unexploited by their owners and were unavailable to more able publishers, many popular Western books remained beyond the reach of Polish consumers. This situation was particularly frustrating for Tadeusz, whose company had the resources to publish but was unable to secure the rights to many widely recognized titles.

By 1992, it was difficult for companies to turn a profit in Poland's saturated publishing industry, and a shakeout had become inevitable. "We are one of two profitable publishing companies in Poland," said Tadeusz. "We have low costs, as well as a tax holiday because our company is a joint venture." As financially troubled publishers went bankrupt, Phantom Press was able to acquire unexploited copyright licenses at low prices. In the fall of 1991, Phantom Press acquired all of the copyrights of a failed state publishing company called ALFA in Wroclaw, whose unpublished titles included works by Stephen King and Agatha Christie. "In the last month alone," said Tadeusz, "four other publishing companies have offered to sell us all of their copyrights. Two months ago I would have called these companies competition."

Phantom Press was in many ways a linchpin in the system of private book production in Poland because it acted as an effective coordinating mechanism. Its connections to other parts of the industry illustrate some of the ways in which the private sector grows.

After securing the rights to a book, Phantom Press subcontracted an independent translator to produce a Polish-language manuscript. The company worked closely with approximately four hundred local translators, who were paid between 5 and 50 million zloty ($500–$5000) per book, depending on the length and difficulty of the work. Thus, for example, the company paid 45 million zloty ($4,500) for translation of a single volume of Winston Churchill's history of World War II but generally paid only 5 million zloty ($500) for translation of a romance novel. Translation of each new book required between eight and eighteen months. Once the Polish-language manuscript was completed, it was delivered to Phantom Press's computerized design office, where the text was laid out in publishable format. Many independent publishing companies subcontracted design work to outside specialists, but Tadeusz had determined that Phantom Press could do the same work in-house at 25 percent of the cost. The Phantom Press design office was well organized; a staff of thirty had the capacity to lay out up to fifty books per month.

Phantom Press's book design was then sent to HarperCollins, a well-known publisher in Great Britain. Phantom Press had been using HarperCollins's publishing services since early 1991, and Tadeusz and Wojtak were pleased with the quality and pricing of the publisher's work. HarperCollins not only produced higher-quality publications than Polish state-owned publishers but managed to do so at lower cost. HarperCollins had more advanced technology, a faster printing process, and a smaller work force than the Polish companies. And, unlike Polish printers seeking to produce high-quality books, HarperCollins did not have to import high-grade paper, inks, and other materials at high cost. Because HarperCollins met deadlines and proved to be such a reliable partner, Phantom Press reduced its costs by publishing abroad. Publishing prices varied with design complexity and the number of books printed, and HarperCollins generally completed orders within two weeks. In early 1992, when Phantom Press was ordering approximately forty thousand copies per title, the company's unit publishing cost for a standard romance novel was approximately 2,000 zloty ($0.17).

HarperCollins delivered each shipment of completed books to the Phantom Press warehouse in Gdansk. Phantom Press was capable of distributing all new books to 130 independent fiction wholesalers throughout Poland within twenty-four hours. At a time when most Polish publishers allowed wholesalers to achieve profit margins of approximately 20 percent, Phantom Press allowed margins of between 30 and 40 percent. Thus, for a typical science fiction work with a market price of 16,000 zloty ($1.35), Phantom Press charged wholesalers 12,000 zloty ($1.00). Phantom Press's unit profit was generally between 1,000 and 4,000 zloty ($0.08–$0.34). "Furthermore," said Tadeusz, "our company is strong enough that we are able to sell 20 percent of our books for up-front cash payments. No other publisher in Poland can do this."

Phantom Press experienced phenomenal growth. In January 1991, the company published only a single book. One year later, Phantom Press was publishing at a rate of forty books per month. Its success was based on the elements that we have identified in other sectors: capable management, implementing a focused strategy; close contact with the market to anticipate future demand; effective work incentives, in this case through a mix of in-house work and subcontracting outsiders; access to sufficient capital from outside but especially from retained earnings; and judicious use of foreign contacts, particularly in production. Phantom Press stayed ahead of the market and was better organized than its competitors.

Profilm

Profilm is a film-making company that further illustrates the ways in which creative entrepreneurs were able to take advantage of new opportunities. The original Profilm was founded in 1988 as a cooperative and had the same legal form as the Gdansk Cooperative and Doradca. Its goal was to make films, but at first it did not do well. The primary problem was that before 1989, independent Polish film producers had a very limited customer base. Most of Poland's films were made on a not-for-profit basis by artistic and political groups, and companies such as Profilm were limited to largely unprofitable niche markets, such as scientific documentaries for research institutes.

Polish television was the largest user of Polish-produced films. The television industry was controlled by a government monopoly called Television of Poland (TVP), which operated two national networks, TV1 and TV2. In addition to the national networks, TVP operated nine regional affiliates throughout Poland. TVP was a colossal organization, employing over four thousand workers in Warsaw and over two thousand at the nine local affiliates. Almost all programming was shown nationally, although the local networks were allotted a half-hour of programming time six days a week and four hours on Fridays. TVP employed a large number of directors and equipment crews, and during communist times, the networks produced virtually all television material in their own studios.

In 1989, after the change in government, Solidarity representatives were appointed to important government posts. The appointments had significant implications for Poland's television industry. When Andrzej Drawicz, a close ally of Lech Walesa, was appointed director of TVP, he announced that the networks would begin purchasing films created by independent producers. Almost overnight, a major market became accessible to companies like Profilm.

By early 1990, regulations for the establishment of private firms had been relaxed, and in April, Maciej Grzywaczewski created (or, more accurately, registered for tax purposes) an independent, privately owned film production company. He had no partners, no assets, and no employees. His only connection to his previous activities in the film industry was the name of his firm, Profilm, which he inherited from the cooperative. From Maciej's perspective, the private company had two distinct advantages over the cooperative. First, as the sole owner, he could expend his energies on making important management decisions rather than building consensus among a group of his strong-willed partners. Second, salaries in Polish state-owned companies and cooperatives were constrained by the new excess wage tax, and Maciej realized that in order to produce high-quality films he would be required to subcontract independent directors who commanded exorbitant fees. As a result of the wage tax, the original cooperative had become a high-cost organizational structure for film producers. Thus, with virtually no capital, Maciej had abandoned the cooperative, rented a small office in a Gdansk suburb, and gone into business for himself.

Eager to begin his operations, Maciej felt that the most expeditious way for Profilm to place a product on the market would be to complete a project that he had already begun. After some negotiation, TV2 agreed to purchase a film about an expatriate Polish singer based in Munich. At the same time, Maciej offered to shoot a two-piece series on the history and political activities of Radio Free Europe, an organization that had widespread appeal in Eastern Europe and, rather conveniently, had significant operations in Munich. Envisioning a large audience for a Radio Free Europe documentary, TV2 agreed to buy both segments. Buoyed by the success of his negotiations with TV2, Maciej rushed back to Gdansk with Profilm's first three production contracts.

With no capital to fund his operations, Maciej had to find outside financing. He had agreed to hire Beata Postnikoff, a highly respected TV2 film director, to direct the Munich projects for a salary of 7 million zloty ($737). He also had to rent equipment and hire crew members, as well as cover all editing and production costs. Polish banks charged annual interest rates of from 60 to 80 percent on commercial loans, so Maciej did not see bank financing as a viable option. Fortunately, he had an acquaintance who operated a chain of retail shops in Gdansk and was willing to provide funding in return for 50 percent of the profits generated by the Munich films. Maciej accepted the offer, and soon Beata Postnikoff assembled a crew of coworkers and set off for Munich. In May, the crew returned from Munich with raw film clips, which were edited in Profilm's Gdansk office and then delivered to TV2 in Warsaw. Over the course of the next several weeks, Profilm's first three products were aired on national television. The films were profitable for Profilm, and Maciej continued to use informal financing arrangements until his company was able to generate enough turnover to fund its own operations.

For the remainder of 1990, Profilm based its operations on documentary films preordered by the television networks. Among the films the company created in 1990 were *Voice of America*, on the radio network's operation in Poland; *Small Poland*, on the experiences of Poles living in emigration camps in Great Britain; and *Fragments of Hope*, on the lives of autistic children. Contracts for documentary films were signed for single projects only, and there were no guarantees of future business. Each film required a new idea, a new contract, and a new crew. Maciej, who spent most of his time on the telephone piecing together projects and negotiating with clients, felt that the business was in a constant state of flux. By the end of the year, although Profilm had begun to establish a name for itself as a producer of high-quality documentaries, Maciej was considering going into advertising as a way to obtain stability.

Television advertising, which was at odds with communist doctrine, did not exist in Poland before 1990. Profilm became the first private company to sign an advertising representation agreement with a national network. In its dual role as producer and network representative, Profilm would be able to earn a production fee for the commercials that it filmed for corporate clients, as well as a sales commission from the fee that clients paid to TV2 for airtime.

Profilm rapidly developed its advertising business. The company produced commercials for a large number of local firms, including Heweliusz, the city's top hotel; Elkor, a large producer of telephone exchanges; and Agros, a state-owned food-processing company. Profilm even developed an international clientele when British Airways hired the company to produce its Polish-market advertisements. Profilm charged customers between 3 and 30 million zloty for creating a commercial, depending on production costs. In addition, customers paid TV2 a fee of 200 million zloty ($18,200) per minute of airtime, of which Profilm received 10 percent, or 20 million zloty ($182). Television advertising was lucrative, and it soon became Profilm's major business activity, accounting for over 80 percent of revenue during the first half of 1991.

However, just as quickly as it had sparked expansion at Profilm, the advertising industry collapsed. By the end of 1991, financial pressure on the state sector meant that Polish companies were no longer able to afford television advertising, and demand for Profilm's production services disappeared. Western companies, which relied almost exclusively on Western firms to handle their advertising needs, replaced Polish companies as the major purchasers of TVP advertising time. By the end of 1991, Western products accounted for over 90 percent of the advertisements on Polish television, and Profilm's participation in the industry had become negligible.

Maciej, however, had already found a new product: a political talk show. Each week, prominent politicians with opposing views on a pressing national issue were to be invited to a Warsaw studio, where they would conduct an hour-long debate to be moderated by a popular and photogenic journalist, Wieslaw Walendziak. Anticipating lively, heated exchanges, Maciej and Walendziak decided to call the show *Without Anaesthesia* (*Bez Znieczulenia*). *Without Anaesthesia* could be prerecorded in Warsaw, sent to Profilm in Gdansk for editing, and then returned to Warsaw to be aired by one of the national networks. They rented studio space in the basement of a national museum in Warsaw, hired camera crews, and rented filming equipment. Within two weeks, they were prepared to begin filming, and within a month, they had completed the first episode. The adversarial format of *Without Anaesthesia* was a novelty on Polish television, which in communist times had opted for consensus. One particularly stormy episode pitted President Lech Walesa against Prime Minister Jan Olszewski shortly before Walesa forced Olszewski's resignation. Another matched two former prime ministers at opposing ends of the political spectrum: Jan Krzysztof Bielecki, a liberal reformer, and Waldemar Pawlak, leader of a peasant party that had emerged from Poland's communist ranks.

Without Anaesthesia became enormously popular. In the politically charged environment of reformist Poland, 26 percent of television viewers (8 million Poles) tuned into the program every week. TV2 extended Profilm's contract to sixty episodes, positioning the company to become a major supplier of serial television shows.

Profilm continued to produce several other serials and was able to build a stable base of revenues for the company.[12] In 1992 turnover was approximately 7 billion zloty ($500,000), with a profit margin close to 10 percent. Profilm had moved its operations into a high-rise office building in downtown Gdansk, and its work force had expanded to five employees. Because all film crews and equipment were contracted on a project-by-project basis, the company's investment expenditures were minimal. These costs were included in a film's budget and billed directly to customers. For the production of its films, Profilm subcontracted approximately thirty freelance workers on a regular basis.

Profilm's primary business had become nationally televised serial shows, which by late 1992 accounted for over 85 percent of the company's revenue. The company's success as a producer of serial shows was sealed in late 1991, when *Without Anaesthesia* was awarded the television industry's most prestigious artistic prize, the Wiktor, the Polish equivalent of an Oscar or an Emmy in the United States. On the strength of *Without Anaesthesia*, Profilm was able to sell five more shows to the national networks, and by November, Profilm had more serials on the air than any other private producer in Poland.

Profilm's success demonstrates the need to innovate and continually stay ahead of market development in a situation such as Poland's. Profilm was able to grow while remaining extremely flexible, particularly through careful use of subcontracting. Market opportunities have arisen and disappeared very quickly in Poland over the past four years, but well-organized service sector firms like Profilm have managed to expand steadily.

Semeco

Semeco, the diversified conglomerate based on trade and the food business, also expanded into modern services. Its first venture of this kind began in February 1990, when the company invested 2.5 billion zloty ($263,000) in the establishment of *Gazeta Gdanska* (literally, *Gdansk Newspaper*), the first private newspaper in the Baltic coast region. The paper was to be a fresh alternative to the traditional communist-style newspapers that had been published in the region for forty years. "The situation in Poland simply demanded a new newspaper," said Semeco partner Bogdan Barczyk.

Gazeta Gdanska had a liberal orientation that appealed primarily to Gdansk's intelligentsia and to an emerging class of young entrepreneurs. Managers at *Gazeta Gdanska* made special efforts to employ journalists who had never worked for the communist press. In fact, of the forty employees first hired by the company, most had been affiliated with the illegal trade union Solidarity and had worked for underground press and radio organizations throughout the 1980s. Prominent among *Gazeta Gdanska*'s original journalists were Donald Tusk, assistant editor-in-chief until he was elected to the national parliament in 1991; Andrzej Zarebski, who was appointed spokesman for the prime minister in 1991 and was eventually elected to parliament; and Krzysztof Wyszkowski, who became mass media adviser for Prime Minister Jan Olszewski in mid-1991. Prominent liberals Janusz Lewandowski, who would eventually be named minister of privatization, and Jan Krzysztof Bielecki, who was appointed prime minister in 1991, were frequent contributors to the paper.

At the beginning there were numerous problems. The state-owned printing presses gave the lowest priority to the printing of *Gazeta Gdanska*. This meant delays and difficult communications with the printer. RSW, the state-run organization that still controlled the kiosks in which many newspapers were sold, either failed to deliver *Gazeta Gdanska* on time or did not display the paper in a prominent position. Nevertheless, like other successful private firms, the newspaper company survived because it was well organized and provided particularly good service to advertisers. *Gazeta Gdanska* had better advertisements, including attractive graphics, than the established newspapers. The newspaper also targeted emerging entrepreneurs with relevant stories and sparked readers' interest by pioneering the use of color pictures and special insert sections.

By the end of 1990, the paper's daily circulation reached 60,000, significant in a region with a total population of approximately 700,000. *Gazeta Gdanska* was doing well because it had more than good journalists. It also developed well-organized marketing, sales, and production departments. Above all, it had strong and effective coordination by management. In November 1991, the newspaper expanded its operations, developing into a full-fledged publishing house called Wydawnictwo Gazeta Gdanska (Gazeta Gdanska Publishers).

However, Wydawnictwo Gazeta Gdanska's outside publishing interests were limited; the company's primary focus remained the daily newspaper.

In March 1990, Semeco moved further into modern services by opening the Semeco Art Agency in Warsaw. This subsidiary was intended to become a central dealer in Poland's infant contemporary art industry. Prominent artists were invited to the agency's gallery to display and discuss their work. Although at first the Semeco Art Agency was not profitable, Waldemar Staszak and his Semeco partners expected art markets to become popular once economic development in Poland made possible the development of a well-established middle class.

With the introduction of economic reforms in January 1990, the process of establishing a private business was simplified and made available to all prospective Polish entrepreneurs. As a result, thousands of new businesses were opened by inexperienced managers. Recognizing a need for business consulting services, in August Semeco established Consulting ABC Co. Ltd., a subsidiary that would provide accounting, auditing, business development, and management consulting services to Polish firms. In addition, Consulting ABC's ten-member staff would be able to provide consulting services to Semeco's other subsidiaries at favorable rates.

Although Consulting ABC was established to meet perceived demand in the private sector, the firm's major clients were foreign companies interested in investing in Poland and Polish state-owned enterprises that were undergoing privatization. For foreign clients, Consulting ABC often performed industry studies and provided Polish contacts. For state-owned clients undergoing privatization, the company usually performed feasibility studies and asset valuation. Consulting ABC's work with private firms primarily involved the development of business plans, a prerequisite for bank loans.

In October, several months after establishing Consulting ABC, Semeco created its second publishing subsidiary. The company, called ABC Book-Press-TV Co. Ltd., was actually a partnership with Adam Kinaszewski, the chief reporter for *Gazeta Gdanska*. Semeco and Kinaszewski each controlled a 50 percent stake in the Gdansk-based venture, which employed fifteen workers. ABC Book-Press-TV Co.'s major product was a business telephone book, but the company also published a number of advertisements for local firms.

In May 1991, Semeco established Security Gdansk Co. Ltd., a 150-employee company that provided security and protection services for businesses in the Gdansk-Sopot-Gdynia region. One of its major clients was Gdansk's Manhattan Business Center, an agglomeration of private shops and offices (much like a Western shopping mall) located a block away from Semeco's main office. Security Gdansk Co. also provided security services for all of the Semeco-Okmess supermarkets.

Semeco's aggressive expansion into the service sector demonstrates the growth and profit potential that existed in 1990–1991. Semeco's competitive advantage derived from its management's ability to reorganize work effectively. The way in which Semeco changed the organization of shopping is a striking case in point. Semeco managers mastered the principles of reorganization and expanded their lines of business very rapidly. As we will soon discuss, their early success and overdiversification later caused significant problems.

Assessment

The service sector was underdeveloped during the communist period, and it was obvious after the introduction of the Balcerowicz Plan that this sector would expand in absolute and relative terms. Table 6-1 shows that over half of the modern services firms and 37 percent of the traditional services firms were formed in or after 1990. As in other sectors, a certain amount of expansion was easy and obvious. Many people could enter small-scale activities with a little capital (see Table 6-2), earning more than they could make in the state sector and employing a few people. As in other sectors, people who set up services firms were primarily operating in the private sector before 1990.

The service sector has generated high-paying jobs, particularly in activities that we call "modern services." Some but by no means the majority of these jobs involve working with foreigners—for example, in consulting or law firms. More generally, there has been a vast wave of new firms dealing with all aspects of media and information. Our second Krakow survey established that not all of the jobs in these firms pay well, and their average wages are lower than in the trade sector, but these firms do typically pay employees with higher education very well.

The principles underlying the successful development of this sector are the same as those in trade and manufacturing. Firms have done well when top management has focused on underserved product markets, designed well-aligned organizational structures and compensation systems, and found suitable people to employ. In many cases employees needed to receive a substantial amount of on-the-job training but thereafter became extremely productive.

Phantom Press demonstrates the value of focusing on a particular set of activities. The opposite strategy, engaging in a diverse range of unconnected activities, was demonstrated by another firm in our sample, which not only has published books but has printed business cards, brochures, and labels for cans, sold laundry detergents, run calisthenics classes, and organized museum exhibitions. The owners told us they would also like to trade with Russia "in any goods which seem appropriate." In the post-reform operating environment of Poland, entering simple service activities was easy. This company quickly reached fifteen full-time employees and another fifteen part-time, in large part because its printing was of relatively high quality. But its management has followed too many diverse issues and has not concentrated on developing what the organization does best—printing. Being so spread out makes it hard to outperform increasingly high-quality competition in each market.

The Polish service sector has grown rapidly, and this growth is an important part of the overall reorganization of work in the Polish economy. Strikingly, most of the growth in services has been the result of starting over rather than the restructuring of state enterprises. In the service sector, as in private business more generally, private entrepreneurs have emerged who are able to organize work effectively and to make people productive. This has happened quickly and in a way that has benefited both people able to obtain the new jobs and consumers of the new services.

Some entrepreneurs have been able to build substantial service firms, employing several hundred people. Where did they and other successful entrepreneurs find the capital to finance this development? To what extent has the availability of external finance constrained private sector development? And did the provision of external finance itself constitute a significant entrepreneurial opportunity? We address these issues in the next chapter.

CHAPTER 7

The Limits of
Private Sector Development

A Financial Constraint Appears

The Balcerowicz Plan created the basis for sustained growth in private sector activity. In 1993, Poland's GDP grew 4 percent. Growth for 1994 is expected to be 5 percent, a remarkably high rate due primarily to the continued growth of the private sector. This sector employed less than 20 percent of the urban work force in 1989 but now probably employs close to 50 percent. Such rapid growth in the number of jobs, most of which pay wages as high as or higher than jobs in the state sector, is unprecedented.

Private sector development remains the main mechanism for transformation of the micro economy in Poland. Private firms have developed in all parts of the economy, including manufacturing. It is private entrepreneurs—not state enterprise managers—who are able to rapidly and effectively reorganize work. And it is the reorganization of work that raises productivity, makes Poland competitive in world markets, and will continue to allow rapid economic growth.

Overall, the 1980s should be characterized as a period in which entrepreneurial potential developed and both human and financial capital accumulated in the private sector. The prolonged economic crisis and the aftermath of the political confrontation in 1980–1981 encouraged entrepreneurial people to seek opportunities outside the state sector. The development of managerial skills was particularly important during the period of partial communist reform, 1988–1989. But despite all the rapid development that we have documented, the private sector in the 1980s remained stymied by economic shortages, restrictions on trade, and a multitude of government regulations.

At a stroke, the Balcerowicz Plan removed the constraints on the Polish private sector and made possible a period of remarkably rapid growth. It is true that the trade sector initially grew fastest; but, as we have argued, the development of trade had immediate positive effects on both private manufacturing and services. Through eliminating shortages and opening the economy, the Balcerowicz Plan effectively unleashed the potential of the private sector.

While the private sector as a whole was expanding rapidly, however, some new private firms were encountering difficulties. At first, state enterprises left a lot of unfilled niches, which permitted easy entry. But as more private businesses entered, and as state firms began to respond, it became harder for private entrepreneurs to provide a differentiated product and to make a profit. The continued squeeze on state enterprises meant that they steadily reduced their orders, and this reduction had a significant negative effect on some private enterprises.

The most important constraint on private sector development, however, was due to the difficulties in raising outside capital. The financial sector changed more slowly than was desirable. The state banks were slow to change in part because of their links to state firms. Some private banks emerged with the express intention of lending to private business. But, unfortunately, in the first two or three years after the introduction of the Balcerowicz Plan, these private banks found that private firms did not yet have credit histories and sufficient reputations, so that lending to them was an extremely risky proposition—in contrast, for example, to lending to consumers.

Moreover, Polish nominal interest rates remained relatively high. At these rates entrepreneurs were unwilling to borrow and preferred to rely on retained earnings to finance their activities. Initially, the private sector probably could not have borrowed more because firms did not yet have sufficient track records to show lenders. But by 1993, if inflation had been lower, interest rates would also have been lower, and, in all likelihood, private firms could have borrowed more, and private sector development would have been even more rapid.

Finance and Banking

Table 6-2 shows that many entrepreneurs began with a small amount of capital. Over 50 percent began with less than $500, and 74 percent started out with less than $5,000. Over 50 percent of modern services firms and nearly 50 percent of wholesale trade firms were started with less than $100. Strikingly, nearly 60 percent of production firms began with less than $100. For most Polish entrepreneurs this initial capital consisted of their own savings together with, less often, money from family and friends. Given that most of these entrepreneurs started in business before 1989, when their activities were tolerated but only barely by the communist regime, this lack of outside capital is not surprising.

There was no way of knowing how long these firms would remain in business. There was political risk, because the private sector could have closed down at any time, and the economic environment was unstable. It was also extremely hard to enforce any contracts—for example, for credit. These firms also had almost no collateral, particularly because they were not allowed to pledge real estate. The lack of outside financing was not necessarily a major constraint because the initial capital requirement in the Polish private sector was low. However, there were definite advantages to starting out with more capital.

Table 7-1 shows a strong link between initial capital and estimated value of the company at the time of our interview. Over three-quarters of people starting with capital under $100 and over half of those starting with from $101 to $500 have companies that are now worth under $10,000. Less than 5 percent of people starting with under $1,000 and only 9 percent of those starting with from $1,001 to $5,000 now have companies worth more than $100,000. The proportion of people with higher-valued companies now is generally higher for groups with larger amounts of initial capital. Having access to outside credit has definitely helped some firms develop. There is some evidence that firms that have received credit tend to employ more people. In our employment regression, which we use as the basic indicator of firm performance, we always find a dummy variable for having successfully obtained credit to be significant and to have a positive sign.[1]

In short, a large amount of capital was never necessary to enter the Polish private sector, at least until 1991. But having more than $5,000 initially may have helped subsequent performance. Obtaining

Table 7-1 Crosstabulation of Initial Capital and Estimated Value of Firm Now

Initial Capital	N/A		Less Than $1,000		$10,000–$49,000		$50,000–$99,999		$100,000–$249,999		$250,000–$499,999		More Than $500,000		All	
	N	PCT	N	PCT	N	PCT	N	PCT	N	PCT	N	PCT	N	PCT	N	PCT
N/A	14	15.7%	59	66.3%	12	13.5%	1	1.1%	1	1.1%	—	—	2	2.2%	89	100.0%
Less than $100	9	3.6	194	77.6	34	13.6	8	3.2	2	0.8	1	0.4%	2	0.8	250	100.0
$101–$500	3	2.6	63	54.8	41	35.7	2	1.7	2	1.7	3	2.6	1	0.9	115	100.0
$501–$1,000	4	6.5	25	40.3	25	40.3	6	9.7	1	1.6	1	1.6	—	—	62	100.0
$1,001–$5,000	7	6.7	42	40.4	40	38.5	6	5.8	8	7.7	—	—	1	1.0	104	100.0
$5,001–$10,000	4	5.6	13	18.1	35	48.6	10	13.9	5	6.9	4	5.6	1	1.4	72	100.0
$10,001–$20,000	—	—	1	2.3	31	70.5	9	20.5	2	4.5	—	—	1	2.3	44	100.0
$20,001–$50,000	—	—	1	2.6	19	50.0	8	21.1	7	18.4	3	7.9	—	—	38	100.0
More than $50,000	1	5.0	1	5.0	4	20.0	1	5.0	4	20.0	4	20.0	5	25.0	20	100.0
All	42	5.3	399	50.3	241	30.4	51	6.4	32	4.0	16	2.0	13	1.6	794	100.0

Note: N is the number of firms. *PCT* is the percentage of firms with the indicated level of initial capital that now have an estimated value in the given range.

access to bank credit may also have been helpful, although borrowing under Polish conditions can be rather risky.

Financing Firms

There are two important points about the financing of Polish private sector firms. First, companies were deterred from borrowing by high nominal interest rates after 1990, even though real interest rates were quite low. Second, new private businesses often lack sufficient collateral to be able to borrow. The latter problem declines in importance as the private sector develops and its own capital accumulates, but this process takes several years. In Polish circumstances, we should not presume that companies that borrow necessarily show better performance than others either before or after they get a loan. We encountered numerous cases in which entrepreneurs attributed their successes to the fact that they did not borrow from a bank and others' failure to the fact that they did.

As Polish entrepreneurs are well aware, taking on debt can reduce a firm's options. If market conditions turn against the company or if internal organization problems appear, having debt can reduce a company's ability to make necessary changes. Instead of having time and being able to make adjustments, the entrepreneur may be driven by the short-term consideration of servicing existing debt. A business error may result in bankruptcy for a highly leveraged firm, but the same firm with less debt may just suffer lower earnings.

Nevertheless, we found many cases in which entrepreneurs said they would have borrowed had it not been for the level of nominal interest rates (in the 50–80 percent range for loans in 1990–1993). Note that this was true even though real interest rates—the nominal rate minus inflation—were not particularly high. What was the problem with this configuration of interest rates?

Higher nominal interest rates, for a given real rate, skew repayments toward the beginning of the loan, so that borrowers have to repay a larger amount in real terms more quickly. Compare what happens if a firm borrows $100 at 10 percent nominal or at 100 percent nominal per year. In the first case, the inflation rate is 10 percent; in the second, it is 100 percent per year. In the first case, the borrower has to repay $10, which is 10 percent of $100, after one year, but the price level has gone up by 10 percent. So, in initial dollars, the borrower actually has to repay $9.09. In the second case, the borrower repays $100, which is worth $50 in terms of initial dollars. Thus, although the real interest rate in both cases is the same, when inflation and the nominal interest rate are higher, borrowers have to repay a larger amount in real terms sooner. High nominal interest rates also mean that temporarily declining sales sufficiently reduce cash flow so that a firm cannot make the required debt payments and may fail, even though its business remains sound. This is less of a problem if the loan is longer term or if short-term loans can be rolled over. But if loans are evaluated every three months and the solvency of borrowers is judged anew by the lender, then this problem is potentially very large.

High nominal interest rates deterred many of our interviewees from borrowing, even though they needed the working capital to finance their inventories. Of course, the reason that managers gave was not the technical one. Instead, they simply said that interest rates were too high. One manager at the Gdansk Cooperative pointed out an irony in Polish credit allocation. Until 1989, credit was de facto limited to state enterprises, and the cooperative could see no point in even applying for it. Since 1989, anyone has been entitled to apply for credit, but interest rates have been so high that borrowing does not make sense for the cooperative.

There has also frequently been a problem with insufficient collateral in the private sector. For example, a retail/wholesale paint distributor had sales in 1990 of over $100,000 and sales in 1991 of over $500,000. Nevertheless, this company was turned down twice for bank credit that it would have used to install computers and buy forklifts for its warehouses. The reason given for the refusal was that the firm had only a small amount of its own fixed capital and most of its money was tied up as working capital. The paint company, like many firms, financed its remarkable growth primarily from retained earnings. However, during the seasonal slowdown in construction it delayed payments to its state supplier. It had to pay a high interest rate on such money—100 percent a year in 1992—but said there was no alternative.

Why did private banking not develop to finance private enterprises? To understand the issues involved, we studied in detail one of the new private banks that had been founded since 1989. What made this bank particularly interesting was the fact that its founders originally had the explicit goal of financing the private sector. The history of this bank and the issues that it currently faces reveal a great deal about the problems of providing adequate financing for new firms. It also extends our analysis of strategy and structure in private sector firms to include banking.

Banking

By the time Poland elected a Solidarity government in mid-1989 and replaced the central planning system with a free market in January 1990, major reforms in the country's banking industry had already begun. In 1982, the National Bank of Poland (NBP) was separated from the Ministry of Finance and given the ability to operate as an independent commercial bank. During the 1980s, NBP dominated Polish banking, because in addition to serving as the country's central bank, it conducted nationwide commercial activities through its nine regional offices.

Private banks were not permitted in communist Poland, and under communist regimes the NBP functioned as a monopoly. However, in January 1989, as a result of the New Banking Law and Act on the National Bank of Poland, the NBP monopoly was broken apart, and independent commercial banks were created from its nine regional offices. The NBP retained central banking responsibilities but was required to withdraw from all but a few commercial activities. The nine new banks, which remained state owned, inherited all assets and liabilities of the depositors and borrowers in their respective regions.

As Poland's banking monopoly was being dismantled, the requirements for establishing a new bank were liberalized. Qualified Polish citizens with adequate funding could finally become private bankers. Specifically, permission from the NBP for the establishment of a new bank required that three conditions be met: (1) the bank's sponsors were required to contribute capital of 5 billion zloty ($500,000 in 1990) in the case of Polish ownership, and 70 billion zloty ($7 million in 1990) in the case of foreign ownership; (2) premises had to be suitable for banking operations; and (3) senior banking officials were required to have adequate experience and training.

In 1991, the National Bank of Poland imposed more demanding entry requirements—including an increase in minimum start-up capital for Polish owners from 5 billion to 70 billion zloty—and tightened supervision in an effort to foster the entry of fewer banks with better long-term prospects and to reduce the likelihood of banking scandals.

By the end of 1991, over one hundred licenses had been granted for the establishment of new commercial banks, the majority of which were private (some were cooperatives). However, despite the proliferation of new private banks in Poland, banking activity remained highly concentrated: in 1992, the nine state-owned banks still held over 80 percent of the economy's entire loan portfolio.

In Poland's rudimentary market economy, most entrepreneurs lacked capital, connections, and well-established plans and were thus ineligible for foreign loans. According to one entrepreneur in the banking sector, "Many people here have ideas and want loans, but they have no collateral. There is no way for them to get Western credit, probably not even Polish credit."

Poland's antiquated banking system also initially posed a serious operating problem for many trade enterprises. For example, in the case of Citrus Wholesale, Western European fruit distributors required that all orders be covered by advance cash payment. To maintain a steady supply of bananas, Jarek Poloczanski had to repatriate earnings to his Austrian partners as soon as each shipment of bananas was sold so that the Austrian partners could pay for the next shipment. Poland's banking system, however, was not equipped to make rapid international transactions, and a transfer of funds between Poland and Austria required from one to two months. Thus, Jarek was forced to make frequent flights to Vienna carrying up to $200,000 in cash. Fortunately, some modernization of the payments system took place in 1990, and international fund transfers became much easier within several months.

Banking reform had a profound effect on a small group of finance professors at the University of Gdansk. For over fifteen years Marian Lukaszewski, Edmund Tolwinski, and Wojciech Zurawik had tried to reconcile their finance courses with Poland's Marxist agenda, and they were well aware of the shortcomings of the national banking system.

At the end of the communist period, the strongest bank in the Gdansk region was Bank Gdanski, formerly an integral part of the NBP, which received a forty-nine-branch banking operation when it and other commercial banks were legally separated from the central bank at the beginning of 1989. In the past, when private enterprise was strongly discouraged, all of the National Bank of Poland's (and subsequently Bank Gdanski's) clients had been state-run firms. With the loosening of the communist system during the 1980s, and particularly with the new communist legislation in 1989, many new private companies were created in the Gdansk region. Although these compa-

nies needed fresh capital, Bank Gdanski showed little interest in providing loans to the private sector. The bank, which inherited comfortable, long-standing relationships with its state-operated clients, had
never aggressively pursued new business. Furthermore, large state
enterprises had much more significant financial requirements than the
new private firms had. By restricting its clientele to the state sector,
Bank Gdanski could extend larger loans and limit its transaction costs.
Thus, despite the recent reforms in the banking sector, bank financing
was virtually unavailable to the rapidly increasing number of entrepreneurs in the Gdansk-Sopot-Gdynia region and to an evolving class
of local consumers. The finance professors at the University of
Gdansk noted these developments with interest. They realized that
local conditions were ideal for the establishment of a private bank, and
they felt that they were well qualified to become financial managers.
Inspired by Poland's "leap" to a free market, the three academics
were ready for a taste of the private business world. "After all," said
Zurawik, "sitting in an office surrounded by books is not enough in
life."

Thus, Lukaszewski, Tolwinski, and Zurawik drew up ambitious
plans for the creation of a local bank, which they called Sopot Bank.
To receive an operating license from the NBP, they had to meet the
central bank's three requirements. First, they needed to raise 5 billion
zloty in start-up capital. Lukaszewski and his colleagues embarked
on an aggressive campaign to assemble a group of investors. They
advertised Sopot Bank's initial stock offering on local television and
printed broadsides in the regional press. They turned to professional
colleagues, local acquaintances, the city of Sopot, and even several
large state firms, including the local shipyards. Within four months,
the entrepreneurial professors managed to attract 5.008 billion zloty
(approximately $526,000) in capital contributions from 342 sharehold-
ers. The largest contributors were the Maritime Agency of Gdynia,
the city of Sopot, and the Vistula Shipyard, which purchased, respectively, 20, 15, and 10 percent of Sopot Bank's initial stock issue.
Some local private enterprises also bought shares.

Having raised the capital required by the NBP, the bank's management team signed a lease with the city of Sopot for 140 square
meters of office space in the basement of a small building on Freedom
Avenue, the most heavily traveled street in Sopot. Shortly afterward,
citing their academic expertise, the NBP declared the University of
Gdansk finance professors well qualified to manage a bank. Lukaszewski and his colleagues thus managed to fulfill all three of the central

bank's requirements, and the NBP issued an operating license to Sopot Bank in early March 1990. In May, shareholders elected a board
of directors, and in July, the first private bank in the tri-city region
began its commercial activities.

During its first two years, the bank collected 90 billion zloty in
deposits and sold a second issue of stock for 5 billion zloty, raising
total share capital to 10 billion zloty. Although Sopot Bank offered a
range of services, its primary commercial activities were taking deposits and lending. The company had forty employees and seven hundred shareholders. Major shareholders at this time were the city of
Sopot (29.5 percent), the Maritime Agency of Gdynia (10.2 percent),
and Denmark's DiskontoBanken Bank (7.6 percent).[2]

Sopot Bank targeted private households rather than commercial
depositors because Polish households tended to be much more stable
depositors than Polish firms. The country's undercapitalized companies were often forced to rapidly withdraw deposits in order to cover
expenses that could not be met by unstable earnings. "Consider the
case of one of the large shipyards in the coastal area," said Lukaszewski. "It may be wealthy in terms of assets, but it also has debts and
virtually no cash flow. The shipyard has to pay salaries and operating
costs even though its customers have virtually disappeared. It cannot
afford to keep money in the bank."

High interest rates in Poland made savings deposits an attractive
investment for private households, earning approximately 50 percent
in 1992. In addition, interest earned on savings deposits was tax free.
Lukaszewski and his colleagues noticed that even Western Europe-
ans—particularly Germans with Polish family ties—were opening
zloty-denominated savings accounts in Poland because large interest
rate differentials more than compensated for expected depreciation of
the zloty.

By the fall of 1992, Sopot Bank had accumulated deposits of
approximately 90 billion zloty ($6.5 million). Because the penalty for
premature withdrawal of a time deposit was forfeiture of all interest
payments, customers rarely withdrew deposit funds ahead of schedule. Sopot Bank's 39 percent annual interest rate on four-month deposits ranked highest among banks headquartered in the tri-city region and fifteenth among all Polish banks.

Sopot Bank's loan customers were primarily private households
and small businesses. Households accounted for 70 percent of the
value of the bank's outstanding loans, a situation that Lukaszewski
attributed to the plight of Polish companies. The bank's loans were

spread over a large customer base; no single borrower accounted for a significant percentage of the total loan portfolio. Sopot Bank's loans were usually for modest amounts. In September 1992, the bank's largest outstanding loan amounted to approximately 500 million zloty ($35,000).

Households generally took out loans from Sopot Bank in order to purchase durable goods such as automobiles, refrigerators, and television sets. For big-ticket consumer purchases, the bank had begun a popular installment plan. Under the plan, a creditworthy client who wished to buy a new car, for example, could visit a dealer and make an initial payment, which often amounted to approximately 30 percent of the automobile's value. With appropriate documentation, the client could then register the automobile with Sopot Bank, which would forward the dealer the unpaid portion of the purchase price. The client would then repay the bank's loan, plus interest, in monthly installments. By insuring its installment plan with a local state insurance company, Sopot Bank eliminated the risk of default on consumer loans.

Although Sopot Bank had an effective consumer lending program, the bank was unable to attract large commercial clients, in part because it lacked the capital to make sizable loans. Polish banking law required that banks maintain a ratio of total share capital to the value of outstanding loans of at least 8 percent. The NBP called this ratio the coefficient of financial solvency. Because a high coefficient of financial solvency was an indication that a bank was not using its loan funds efficiently, Sopot Bank sought to keep this ratio between 8 and 10 percent.

Polish law also limited the amount that a bank could lend to a single customer to 10 percent of the bank's share capital. With a capital endowment of 10 billion zloty, Sopot Bank was not permitted to make loans of more than 1 billion zloty ($70,000).

In mid-1992, 92 percent of Sopot Bank's commercial loans were administered to small, private companies. Servicing smaller clients had distinct advantages. Sopot Bank had come to know many of its clients personally, and these informal contacts often eased banking relationships. For example, as a result of Poland's difficult business environment, many small companies were unable to collect customer payments. These companies, in turn, were often forced to delay loan payments to banks, which led many banks to levy stiff penalties or implement costly court proceedings. Sopot Bank, however, had a different approach. According to Lukaszewski:

Last year, we lent 100 million zloty to an entrepreneur who opened a cafe in Gdansk. The loan was due in June, but this was before the summer season, and he was unable to earn enough money to pay us back by the deadline. Most banks would not have tried to understand his situation. We did, because we had come to know him personally. We waited, and eventually he paid. How much sense would it have made to levy fines and high interest charges against him? He would not have been able to pay these fines, anyway. Banking in Poland is an art.

By basing much of its lending activity on personal relationships and customer contact, Sopot Bank was able to achieve a high collection rate despite frequent payment delays. In December 1991, nonperforming loans accounted for only 2.6 billion zloty, or 4.4 percent of Sopot Bank's credit portfolio of 58.6 billion zloty. At the same time, two other local banks, Bank Gdanski and Bank Kommunalny of Gdynia, suffered nonperforming loan ratios of 23.8 and 41.7 percent, respectively.

The majority of Sopot Bank's commercial borrowers were involved in trade rather than manufacturing. Turnover in the trade sector was rapid—Sopot Bank assumed that on average trade companies rotated inventories twice a month—and loans to traders were short-term. Since trade credits were retired by the proceeds of the transaction, these loans were referred to as "self-liquidating."

Manufacturing companies, in contrast, borrowed for long-term investment and repaid the loans from general funds that may have been unrelated to the purpose for which the loan was made. Because investment in production facilities did not produce a payoff in the near term, industrial firms that relied on credit often became victims of Poland's high interest rates. By 1992, expensive loans—meaning high nominal interest rates—were a primary cause of industrial bankruptcies. Sopot Bank preferred to lend to companies in the trade sector as a result of the higher likelihood of repayment.

Sopot Bank required that each borrower secure a loan with at least one of three forms of collateral: (1) a property mortgage, (2) a notarized promissory note for cash or personal property equal to the value of the loan, or (3) valuables—such as jewelry—that could be deposited with the bank for the duration of the loan. Because documentation was often unreliable, lending department employees frequently visited customers to inspect collateral. Sopot Bank did not have a fixed set of lending criteria but evaluated each loan on an individual basis. All final lending decisions were made jointly by any two members of the bank's three-person management board.

The bank did not suffer for a lack of prospective borrowers. According to Lukaszewski, "Customers are queuing up for credits. People in the credit department don't have to go out and look for borrowers. This is a luxury. Between eighty and ninety percent of credit applicants are turned away. The bank simply does not have enough money to service all of these clients."

The Sopot Bank case demonstrates that there was a considerable amount of money to be made by lending to consumers. Loan rates were sufficiently high relative to deposit rates, and consumers could provide adequate collateral (usually the goods that they were borrowing money to buy). The experience of Sopot Bank also shows that in the early years of the Balcerowicz Plan it was difficult to justify lending to entrepreneurs bcause they lacked track records and because the overall business environment remained turbulent. Over time, however, as private firms better establish themselves, lending for working capital and investment should develop.

The Financing of Firms

Despite the problems with lending to the private sector, by 1992 there were several private banks in the Gdansk region, and even Bank Gdanski had become more oriented toward private sector lending. What then were the financial constraints as seen by private entrepreneurs?

There certainly have been financial constraints on private sector development in Poland, but the most important constraint does not appear to have been reluctance by commercial banks to lend. Since 1989, the most important problem in the financial market, as seen by entrepreneurs, has been the high level of nominal interest rates. This point comes through in five of our cases: SeCeS-Pol, Styl France, Profilm, Gdansk Cooperative, and Semeco.

SeCeS-Pol. In 1992 credit was an important issue for SeCeS-Pol, the successful manufacturer of heat exchange systems. As a result of excessive inflation, annual interest rates on commercial loans were often as high as 80 percent. This made bank financing uneconomical for long-term manufacturing investment of the type that SeCeS-Pol

needed for continued expansion. Thus, all growth at SeCeS-Pol had
to be funded internally. Unable to rely on outside financing, SeCeS-
Pol often had to turn down large orders if materials or manufacturing
costs were too high. Jerzy Siemienczuk recalled:

In early 1992, I received a $10 million order from a German company for
steel containers of unusual dimensions. To fill the order, I needed steel
components of nonstandard lengths. I approached a local steel company that
I thought would be able to supply me with the parts, but I learned that in
order to produce steel of the proper dimensions, the company would have
had to retool its entire manufacturing process. They therefore demanded a
$2 million advance payment. I did not have $2 million in reserve. I could
have produced the steel myself, but it would have taken six months to tool
up for production. This was far too long. Thus, I lost a big order. I am
forced to accept smaller orders that require lower materials costs.

Why did SeCeS-Pol not borrow from a source such as Sopot Bank?
According to the entrepreneur himself, interest rates were simply too
high.

Styl France. The lack of external finance was also a constraint on
Styl France, the furniture maker. Czeslaw Bereza realized that the
real competitive advantage of the company lay in the Kartuzy manufacturing operation, not in the distribution operation in France. Dissatisfied with his partner and aware that his furniture could be sold
successfully in markets other than Lyons, he began to entertain
thoughts of running a furniture production company on his own.
However, he lacked capital. Virtually all of the machinery in Styl
France's plant was owned by his French partner. In September 1992,
Czeslaw assessed his situation:

I would prefer to run this business alone. If I did not have my French
partner, I could make profits of 100 to 200 percent! Unfortunately, I don't
have the capital. It is possible to find a partner with capital, but difficult to
find a partner who is responsible. And Polish bank credits are far too expensive to even be considered.

This was said at a time when annual interest rates on loans from
Polish banks were approximately 70 percent.

Profilm. In the battle for TVP funds, Profilm's competitive position was weakened by the firm's inability to purchase its own equipment. High rental fees inflated Profilm's production costs and in turn

forced the company to charge higher prices for its films. Producers who were able to acquire their own equipment enjoyed greater flexibility in negotiating with the networks. "Unfortunately, I don't have enough money to buy equipment, and Polish bank loans are too expensive," Maciej Grzywaczewski stated. "I spend about 1.5 or 2 billion zloty per year on equipment rental. If I were to borrow money to buy equipment, I could very well spend the same amount on interest payments alone. It just does not make sense to borrow money to buy equipment."

Gdansk Cooperative. Even more serious financial problems arose for other private sector firms that were unable to finance their work-in-progress. A good example is the experience of the Gdansk Cooperative in 1992–1993. Beginning in 1992, the cooperative was unable to collect a growing number of overdue payments that had accrued from work the company had performed for state-owned clients. In June 1992, the cooperative finished rebuilding the base of a historical bridge in a northern Polish town called Elk, a 3 billion zloty ($200,000) job that had taken six months to complete. By March 1993, Elk authorities still owed the cooperative 300 million zloty ($20,000). Meanwhile, the cooperative was performing similar construction work on a bridge in the nearby town of Girzystko, a project that was begun in May 1992. By early 1993, Girzystko had not produced any of the payments it had been contracted to make on its 3 billion zloty ($200,000) order. In March 1993, the Gdansk Cooperative was owed a total of over 2.5 billion zloty ($157,000) in overdue payments.

Unable to collect payments from its state sector clients, the Gdansk Cooperative became deeply indebted to suppliers and government tax authorities. In March 1993, the cooperative's largest creditor was the state treasury, to which the company owed 200 million zloty ($12,500) in overdue turnover taxes. Other significant creditors included the national social insurance fund, to which the cooperative owed 100 million zloty ($6,250), and an industrial lumber supplier in southern Poland, to which the cooperative owed 80 million zloty ($5,000).

Semeco. An even more dramatic example of problems with external finance is provided by the case of Semeco, which actually borrowed substantial amounts from banks. Of the three owners, only one—Waldemar Staszak—was a strong proponent of bank financing. When the partners converted Semeco into a holding company in 1989, they agreed that all growth would be funded internally, with no outside financing. At a time when inflation was rampant in Poland, Polish banks charged high nominal interest rates on commercial loans in an effort to maintain positive real rates. In 1990 and 1991, annual interest rates on commercial credit ranged from 60 to 80 percent, and many companies were unable to repay loans taken from Polish banks. Yet Staszak had absolute confidence in Semeco's potential, and, without his partners' knowledge, he began to enter formal inquiries at commercial banks for loans that could be used to fuel the company's growth. "Unfortunately," said Bogdan Barczyk, "all of our agreements that concerned Semeco's finances were gentlemen's agreements. Nothing was put into writing."

By mid-1991, Staszak had located two banks where Semeco qualified for dollar-denominated loans. Dollar-denominated loans were especially attractive because the U.S. dollar was a much more stable currency than the zloty. As a result, annual interest rates on dollar-based loans were approximately 10 percent, significantly lower than the 60 percent rates charged for zloty-based loans. Between March and November 1991, with his mind set on expansion and willing to skirt the oral agreement he had made with his partners in order to achieve expansion, Staszak took out Semeco development loans totaling $1.5 million from Poland's Export Development Bank and $1.0 million from PeKaO SA in Paris. The funds were used to establish two new subsidiaries, Security Gdansk and Broimpex, as well as to finance trade turnover at Semeco-Okmess and at Corab-System Co. Ltd., a food and grocery wholesale trading company.

Unfortunately, the cost of the dollar-based loans that Staszak optimistically acquired in 1991 escalated dramatically. The loans had been obtained at a time when the Polish zloty was stable against the U.S. currency at a rate of 9,500 zloty per U.S. dollar, but by March 1992 the zloty had lost value and stood at 13,500 zloty per dollar. Although Semeco conducted its business in zloty, the loans had to be repaid in dollars. As a result of zloty devaluation, the advantages that Staszak had perceived in interest rate differentials disappeared, and, in zloty terms, Semeco had to repay significantly more than it had borrowed one year earlier.

In early 1992, Semeco managed to meet interest payments on its loans but was unable to make payments on the principal. The Export Development Bank and PeKaO SA of Paris, worried by Semeco's requests to reschedule payments, wanted to sell the holding company's loans to other banks. These problems, though difficult, were not insurmountable. Unfortunately for Semeco, their onset occurred simultaneously with continued overall economic hard times in Poland and a series of management errors.

Assessment

Our extensive work with the emerging financial sector in Poland suggests three conclusions. First, it takes several years for a market-oriented banking system to develop. New banks have to raise capital and develop financial expertise, which was entirely lacking under the communist system. Existing state banks have to reorient their activities toward the private sector, and they will do so only when they have proper, profit-driven incentives to do so and when the problems in the state sector become completely apparent. Under these circumstances, it is unrealistic to expect rapid change in the banking system. If the regulatory environment is reformed and effective governance structures are imposed on state banks, then the system will move in the right direction. But what is really needed is for private sector firms to develop collateral, establish business plans, introduce cash management techniques, and, gradually, develop good credit histories.

Second, when the banking system is ready to lend to the private sector, it is essential that nominal interest rates be reduced to reasonable levels—below 20 percent per year and preferably below 10 percent. Even if real rates are zero or only slightly positive, nominal rates of 50 or 70 percent per year will discourage many firms from borrowing. Even worse, many of those who do borrow will not manage their cash flow sufficiently well to ensure repayment. In Poland, high nominal interest rates are the primary reason why the private sector finds it difficult to attract external finance.

Third, our work suggests that the nature of, and way to deal with, debt between firms is not as commonly believed. It is frequently claimed that interenterprise debt is a big problem for state enterprises during economic reform. The argument is that state enterprises are convinced that they do not need to worry if they do not pay each other, because there will be a general bailout by the government. Our experience with the Polish private sector, however, suggests a different model. At the beginning, even the most hard-headed private entrepreneur does not understand that customers may not be able to pay as promised. We have encountered such misperceptions in almost every company with which we dealt, even firms—such as Citrus Wholesale and SeCeS-Pol—in which management generally impressed us with their business acumen. Over time, managers learn that the combination of macro environment and legal situation means that people may not pay or may pay slowly and erratically. They start checking creditworthiness more carefully. They set tougher terms for credit and look for alternative ways to get their money back in the case of a default—for example, by seizing finished goods directly. In almost all cases they continue to extend credit. Doing so constitutes a risk, but to deny credit often means handing over customers to competitors.

The Shake-out

The story that we have told so far about the Polish private sector has been a positive one. There were, however, growing pains. Some companies failed early in the adjustment process, and almost none could maintain the rapid growth rates of 1990–1991. For some firms, the problems developed rapidly and had spectacular effects. No firm better exemplifies the issues and problems than Semeco.

The Fall of Semeco

Semeco had grown through a policy of aggressive diversification, including branching out into newspapers, consulting, publishing, art, and other activities. By the end of 1990, Semeco's second full year of operation, the company had created a total of eight subsidiaries. The ninth was added in February 1991. Corab-System Co. Ltd., the food and grocery wholesale trading company, was opened in Gdansk with 1 million zloty ($88,000) in equity capital. The company employed thirty traders, and, with Barczyk serving as president, Corab-System was the first Semeco subsidiary to be managed by a Semeco board member.

Through Corab-System's wholesale grocery trade, Semeco established a number of food and produce contacts in Lithuania. In October 1991, Semeco created a joint venture called Broimpex Co. Ltd. with one of Corab-System's major Lithuanian trading partners. Broimpex, which traded in agricultural products and fertilizers, focused its efforts on eastern markets. Semeco contributed 30 percent of the venture's equity capital and provided office space for the company's ten traders in Gdansk.

In the early years of Polish reform, Semeco's operating strategy proved enormously effective. The company was creating subsidiaries and entering new industries as quickly as its profits would allow. Poland's underdeveloped markets seemed able to support unlimited growth. Total turnover at Semeco companies expanded from $5 million in 1989 to $25 million in 1991, while employment grew from 200 to 650. The outlook was bright, and it seemed that the rate at which the company could expand was limited only by the amount of capital that it could obtain to invest in new businesses. The Semeco strategy seemed guaranteed to succeed, and it seemed that the capital that Staszak borrowed would allow the company to achieve successes at a faster pace.

Unfortunately, one by one Semeco's activities ran into trouble. Problems first surfaced at SGS Co. Ltd., Semeco's meat-processing subsidiary. Spolem, Semeco's state-owned partner in SGS, had purchased all of SGS's output on credit from the time the meat company began its operations in 1989. One year later, when its total debts to SGS amounted to 2 billion zloty ($211,000), Spolem announced that it would be unable to pay and immediately filed for bankruptcy protection. SGS, though never formally dissolved, was forced to shut down its operations in 1990, and by late 1992, the company was continuing its debt collection efforts in court.

Semex Production Co. Ltd., the wood-processing company, was the next Semeco subsidiary to be affected adversely by the continued decline of Poland's state sector. As a result of decreases in government subsidies to the lumber industry, prices for timber and other wood-based raw materials skyrocketed. The outcome was significant increases in Semex's production costs. In addition, the company's industrial pallets and wood fences were designed for export to Sweden and Germany, but high duties on imported wood products in those countries drove up the prices of Semex's products even further. Under these conditions, Semex was unable to compete with domestic producers, and the company was driven to insolvency in 1991.

ABC Press-Book-TV Co. Ltd. was carelessly managed and was never able to produce a significantly profitable product. Adam Kinaszewski, the 50 percent owner who was responsible for running the company, had other pressing obligations as chief reporter at *Gazeta Gdanska*. Furthermore, in 1991, he took a leave of absence from Gdansk in order to go to Warsaw to write a book on President Lech

Walesa. In his absence, the company floundered and was forced to declare bankruptcy in July 1992.

The Semeco Art Agency in Warsaw was expected to weather economic difficulties in Poland and blossom once the recession subsided. However, significant demand for modern art never materialized, and Semeco was forced to close the gallery in early 1992.

Gazeta Gdanska, the liberal newspaper published by Wydawnictwo Gazeta Gdanska, seemed to be a necessity at a time when Poland was in the midst of its transition to a free market. The paper, however, never produced a profit. "People in the Baltic coast region have been reading *Dziennik Baltycki* (*The Baltic Daily*) for forty years. It is difficult to change people's reading habits," complained the editor-in-chief of *Gazeta Gdanska*. "Additionally, as real take-home pay continues to decrease, Poles are buying fewer newspapers. *Gazeta Gdanska*'s daily circulation has fallen from 60,000 in 1991 to between 35,000 and 40,000 today." As a result, after absorbing 15 billion zloty in investment capital from Semeco over its three-year life span, *Gazeta Gdanska* was losing approximately 200 million zloty ($13,000) per month in late 1992, and the paper was on the verge of collapse.

Corab-System, the Polish-Lithuanian agricultural trade subsidiary, was buffeted by economic difficulties in both of its base markets. In a desperate effort to prop up the company, Staszak took out a zloty-denominated loan equivalent to $400,000 in May 1992, at an annual interest rate of 60 percent. The funds were intended to finance Corab-System's trade turnover. At the time, Barczyk was managing the trade subsidiary, but he became infuriated when he discovered that Staszak had saddled his company with bank debt of $400,000, and he resigned his position as president of Corab-System in June.

Semeco-Okmess, Semeco's flagship supermarket chain, had run deeply into debt. The company had begun taking bank loans in 1991, once again at the behest of Waldemar Staszak, who had installed a close friend as company president and his brother as marketing director. Staszak was confident that Semeco-Okmess could accumulate profits at a faster rate than the 60 percent annual interest charge levied on commercial loans. The company's first credit, equivalent to $80,000, was used to purchase grocery stock in Sweden. Furthermore, Semeco-Okmess had provided guarantees for the $400,000 turnover credit acquired by Corab-System in May 1992. By late 1992, Corab-System was unable to make payments on the loan, and it appeared as if Semeco-Okmess would be held responsible for repayment. Also, as a result of zloty devaluation, imported groceries had become much more expensive for Polish consumers. Whereas Semeco-Okmess had imported over 80 percent of its grocery stock from Sweden in 1990, by 1992 between 80 and 90 percent of the supermarkets' wares were supplied by Polish producers. The supermarket thus lost a significant amount of their Western-style appeal. Although Semeco-Okmess remained profitable, the company's profit margin declined from 30 percent in early 1991 to approximately 5 percent by mid-1992, and plans to add a new supermarket every six months were no longer feasible.

Semeco itself, the umbrella organization, was not able to escape the economic woes of its subsidiaries. While creating new companies over the previous three years, Semeco had extended development loans, which were to be repaid as the subsidiaries grew and became profitable. Once the loans were repaid, Semeco firms were expected to operate autonomously. By 1992, however, as the Semeco network was disintegrating, Semeco subsidiaries still owed the parent company approximately 15 billion zloty ($1 million) in unpaid loans. The primary debtors were Semeco-Okmess, which owed between 7 and 8 billion zloty; Corab-System, which owed 4 billion zloty; and SGS, which owed Semeco the entire 2 billion zloty that it was unable to collect from Spolem. At the same time that it was unable to collect debts owed by subsidiaries, Semeco was being pressured to repay the $2.5 million in dollar-denominated loans that it had acquired in 1991.

In quick succession, before creditors had an opportunity to intervene, Semeco's ownership stakes in the subsidiaries were signed over to Barczyk, Staszak, and Jerry Mallenberg. Barczyk assumed control of Security Gdansk and Wydawnictwo Gazeta Gdanska. Ownership of Sakko (a producer of baby hygiene items) and Corab-System was transferred to Staszak, and, in a related transaction, Corab-System took over Semeco's 30 percent stake in Broimpex. Consulting ABC was awarded to a group of shareholders led by Waldemar Staszak and his brother Zbigniew, who managed the firm. Finally, ownership of the lead company, Semeco-Okmess, was transferred to Mallenberg. Although Semeco-Okmess was the most profitable of Semeco's companies, it was also heavily indebted. To protect the supermarket chain's assets from creditors, Mallenberg created a new firm called Grosz and transferred all Semeco-Okmess assets to the new firm. Wherever the "Semeco-Okmess" name had appeared on Gdansk supermarkets in the past, it was suddenly replaced by "Grosz." Thus, much like the parent company Semeco, Semeco-Okmess became an empty shell.

The breakup of Semeco was a bitter affair. The downfall of one of the largest and most widely recognized private companies in the Baltic coast region was discussed repeatedly in the local press. Internal management disputes had driven a permanent wedge between the three owners, who had been the best of friends when they started the company four years earlier. With Semeco's affairs in the hands of creditors and the local courts, the three went their separate ways.

The story of Semeco is a salutary lesson in the pitfalls as well as the benefits of an emerging post-communist economy. A company needs to stay focused and make effective use of its most scarce resource—good managers. If these managers' time is spread too thinly, the result will be a failure to keep ahead of market developments, an ineffective internal structure, or even a loss of control over cash flow. These mistakes bring companies down in Poland just as they do in the United States.

Assessment

Many of the problems that have developed within private firms can be traced to the lack of professional management skills. The same people who successfully started companies as entrepreneurs proved unable to manage and sustain growth. In particular, there was a failure to manage the internal and external finances of the firm. We have seen numerous cases in which a basically sound company was brought down by errors in cash-flow management.

Many companies also failed to adapt as their markets changed. Given the nature of the transformation in Poland, particularly the extensive import of new goods and the rapid development of import substitutes, market conditions have altered very quickly. Unless a company has stayed in front of these developments by improving its product—particularly in terms of quality—and controlling its costs, then it is unlikely to have done well. An activity that was enormously profitable in 1990 or 1991 can easily have become inviable one year later.

Diversification by firms—being involved in more than one activity—has often proved to be a curse rather than a cure. Doing too many things at once stretches the capabilities of management and prevents managers from focusing on what they do best. Some diversification in the early turbulent stages may make sense, but among the companies we have studied, the key to enduring success has been a focus on improving quality and moving to higher-value-added market segments, particularly to exports.

Dramatic stories of mismanagement and failure in the private sector, however, need to be kept in perspective. They illustrate the ways in which the boom of the private sector quickly, for some, turned to bust. But the overall picture of private sector development is overwhelmingly favorable. Almost all of the respondents in our large samples are still operating the first private firm they founded. Consistent with these results is the fact that less than 5 percent of respondents said they previously ran a private sector firm that failed.

Why have so few entrepreneurs experienced any form of failure? There are two plausible answers. First, we are sampling only firms that have survived to 1993. Entrepreneurs who fail may not restart a business. Second, a line of business may "fail" without bankruptcy of the firm—particularly given the low levels of outside financing that these entrepreneurs have. The entrepreneur may change activities, fire workers, or even effectively stop operating while still formally continuing in business. In any case, our evidence suggests that most people who entered the Polish private sector—at any time—did well enough to remain there, at least up to the beginning of 1993.

Managerial Implications

Many entrepreneurs benefited from the change in macroeconomic and trade conditions, but some have done much less well or have been driven out of business. Our analysis of reasons for the successes and failures of private sector firms emphasizes three key factors.

First, the product strategy of the firm is clearly of paramount importance. There has to be a market, and the firm has to position itself in such a way that it either offers a unique product or has a cost advantage. We frequently find a commitment to service, and willingness to take actions that build reputation characterizes the most successful private sector firms. Successful private sector firms have first and foremost proven themselves able to become market oriented: willing to seek out customers, concerned with delivering a high-quality product, and always trying to improve themselves.

The importance of specialization and focus on core activities may seem obvious to outside observers. But to the entrepreneurs involved, it is often far from clear where they should concentrate their efforts. The economic turbulence creates new opportunities. If they have contacts or an initial edge in a new market, shouldn't they enter it and at least make some easy money? This logic is hard to resist.

Just as compelling is the argument that the overall "recession" in Poland—the word that many entrepreneurs use to refer to macroeconomic conditions after 1990—makes it dangerous or impossible to specialize. A firm might focus on one activity only to see that activity disappear without warning.

As persuasive as these arguments may seem, particularly to the entrepreneurs, there is an unmistakable danger that managers will spread themselves too thin and be unable to build a sustainable competitive advantage in any one activity. Our discussion of particular cases demonstrates this experience repeatedly. Successful companies are those that focus early on products for which demand is steady or rising. Making the right choice usually involves a combination of luck and managerial ability.

Second, successful firms are those that have effectively used and further developed the available human capital. The 1980s provided an important training period for private entrepreneurs. The experience that many of them obtained during this period was essential to them later. The 1980s also were a time during which employees could be educated to work more effectively.

The story of the Polish private sector is one of human capital development: people realizing their dreams, developing their potential, or just finding work. An important aspect of the transition process is that many of the best people—the most highly skilled workers and the best managers—voluntarily left the state sector to start their own companies or to work for someone else. The role of foreigners in human capital development should also be stressed. Our large sample work shows that around 20 percent of Polish entrepreneurs earned their initial start-up capital by working abroad. Anecdotal evidence, including many of our cases, indicates a much wider role for economic relationships with foreigners. Working with foreign businesspeople taught many Polish entrepreneurs how to work more effectively. The transfer and adaptation of skills, particularly in management, began with the partial opening of the Polish economy in the mid-1980s and took a massive leap forward in 1990.

Third, Polish private sector firms have succeeded only when they have the right alignment of internal structure and external strategy. The same point has been made by other authors in various contexts, from the development of the M-form corporation (Chandler 1962) to the introduction of "modern" manufacturing techniques (Milgrom and Roberts 1990 and 1992). An important part of our contribution is to identify precisely what matters in the alignment of strategy and structure in a post-communist economy. The external environment in Poland has changed repeatedly and in unique ways not seen in developed market economies.

We stress that in the post-communist environment, management is an essential and scarce resource because it is of paramount importance to effectively organize and coordinate efforts. Firms that diversify have the advantage of spreading their risks to some extent, but they run the danger of becoming unfocused. The right strategy is to focus on a particular part of the product market and make sure the internal structure and compensation system in the firm are appropriate. On the whole, this is what the private sector has been able to do and what the state sector has failed to do.

Overall Conclusions

Starting over has proven to be the key mechanism for effecting economic reform at the firm level. Private sector firms have proven much more able to reorganize work than have state firms. As a consequence, the new private sector will continue to lead the Polish economic recovery from the consequences of communism.

The communists prepared the ground for successful economic reform—probably inadvertently—by allowing several years of private sector development in a partially liberalized economy. But the timing and content of the Balcerowicz Plan were crucial in many ways. The plan unleashed the potential of the private sector in a direction that was consistent with world prices and with macroeconomic stability. Some private firms were hurt by this change in policy, either because they could not make the necessary changes or because they were unlucky. But on the whole the private sector surged forward and created the basis for a remarkable economic miracle.

Within the context of the Polish economic reform, we have identified some management strategies that are better than others. Successful entrepreneurs are typically those who have focused on a particular product or niche market and developed a strong competitive advantage there, rather than spreading themselves too thin by over-diversifying. Offering higher quality and better service has frequently been the key to rapid growth. Companies that have grown almost always exhibit a sensible alignment of strategy, structure, and compensation system.

Although both the economic and the managerial findings of our work are based on close examination of the Polish experience, we think the same results are likely to apply to other post-communist countries. In all of these countries, the reorganization of work is the key underlying microeconomic process. State enterprises always face the difficulty of dealing with inherited constraints and the need to make a large number of changes more or less simultaneously in order to benefit from complementarities. In contrast, complementarities come naturally and almost automatically to the private sector.

Across countries we would expect state enterprise restructuring to be more important where there is a faster pace of privatization than in Poland. We would also expect that greater legal or regulatory constraints on new businesses would slow private sector development below the Polish rate. Macroeconomic problems, particularly high inflation, probably hold back both the private and the state sectors. Nevertheless, as long as the issue is the reorganization of work and the main processes are state enterprise restructuring and starting over, we are likely to find that private sector development is a critical element of the overall economic and managerial transformation. An important economic policy issue for governments is therefore finding how best to support starting over. Many governments in post-communist countries would do well to follow the example of the Balcerowicz Plan.

PART III

Starting Over: The Lessons from Poland

CHAPTER 8

A Reinterpretation of Economic Reform
After Communism

IN Part I we argued that the problems apparent in restructuring state enterprises are due to the necessity of completely reorganizing work in a post-communist country. State enterprises have struggled because successful reorganization requires a remarkably challenging combination of good management, leadership, access to capital, favorable external conditions, and worker cooperation. In Part II we established that the Polish private sector has been most successful where the state sector has had greatest difficulties—in fundamentally reorganizing work. Although individual firms have fallen as well as risen, the private sector as a whole has demonstrated remarkable and robust growth over the past five years. Nevertheless, important constraints and problems remain.

Our analysis so far raises two sets of questions. First, to what extent has Polish private sector development been similar to the pattern in other post-communist countries? What parts of the Polish experience can be considered unusual or exceptional, and to what extent do our conclusions, based on the Polish experience, apply more broadly to other post-communist economies? Obviously, an answer to these questions requires a comparison of Poland with similar post-communist countries.

Second, what relationships exist between Polish private sector development and policies pursued first by communist and then by democratic governments? What does our microeconomic research imply about the appropriateness of the macroeconomic policies that were pursued? Is there any evidence to suggest that slower, more gradual policies would have had on balance a positive effect on economic performance? What other policies could have been or could still be altered to improve prospects in the private sector?

Cross-Country Comparison

To understand the emergence of the private sector in Poland, it is necessary to consider cross-country developments at the end of the 1980s and the early 1990s as communism crumbled across the region.[1] The issue of which countries to compare with Poland is a difficult one. The former Soviet Union has followed a unique pattern of private sector development, due to its particular legal and political history, and is not readily comparable with Poland.[2] Bulgaria, Romania, and Albania all continue to have very weak private sectors primarily because these activities were tightly controlled under the old regimes and because the new economic policies have not clearly encouraged private sector development. Our comparison, therefore, focuses on Poland, Hungary, and Czechoslovakia before its division into two sovereign republics and before its large-scale privatization took effect.[3]

Unfortunately, there has been little empirical work based on interviews with entrepreneurs that can be compared directly with the results that we present in Part II. Several surveys of private firms have been conducted by a team based in Gdansk (Grabowski and Kulawczuk 1991b, Wyznikiewicz, Pinto, and Grabowski 1993), and an analysis of rural entrepreneurship in Hungary is available, based on data from the 1970s and early 1980s (Szelenyi 1988). A World Bank comparative study of private manufacturing in the Czech and Slovak Federated Republic (CSFR), Hungary, and Poland is the most extensive to date and provides many interesting results (Webster 1992 and 1993, and Webster and Swanson 1993). Rather than review this work, we present evidence based on our own research, primarily consultants' reports commissioned from each country. To concentrate on early private sector development, we present figures through 1991.

To facilitate an evaluation of the relative importance of private sector activity, Table 8-1 gives data for estimated urban labor forces: 4 million in Hungary, 7 million CSFR, and 12 million in Poland.

We use this measure, rather than total population, as the basis for comparison because around one-fourth of the Polish work force is in agriculture. The average total employment in Poland in 1990 was 16.5 million, but employment in agriculture accounted for 4.4 million (*Rocznik Statystyczny* 1991, p. 93, Table 2 [174]). The fraction of labor working in Hungarian and CSFR agriculture is much lower.

In number of incorporated private businesses at the end of 1991, Hungary clearly had the lead with 1.3 incorporated businesses per 100 people in the urban labor force; Poland had 0.3, and CSFR had 0.1. But in relative number of unincorporated businesses, CSFR had the lead, with 16 such firms per 100; both Poland and Hungary had 13. However, there are good reasons to suspect that a large number of registered entrepreneurs in CSFR were actually working for other people and declaring themselves to be self-employed as a way to avoid the wage tax. Unfortunately, it is very hard to know how much these different private sectors contributed to national output. One set of low estimates for the share of the private sector in GDP in 1991 was 14.7 percent for Poland, 16.6 percent for Hungary, and 3.1 percent for CSFR (Brandsma 1991).[4] We estimate that by the end of 1991 the private sector provided from 20 to 25 percent of urban employment in both Poland and Hungary and in CSFR accounted for less than 5 percent.[5]

Our conclusion is that by the end of 1991 the private sector was relatively strong in both Hungary and Poland, compared to the private sector in CSFR and implicitly in other post-communist countries. This strength, however, was manifested differently in Hungary and Poland. We therefore have two phenomena to explain. First, why were Hungary and Poland ahead of CSFR in private sector development? Second, why has the private sector in Hungary developed in a corporate form, whereas in Poland a much larger part is unincorporated?

The answer to these questions does not seem to lie with government policy in 1991. Table 8-1 summarizes relevant measures of government policy. With regard to macroeconomic policy and basic legal framework, the countries were similar. For example, all had substantially liberalized trade while still having—at the end of 1991—some trade restrictions. In all three countries private business is now subject to a commercial code that draws heavily on the German-Austrian model and is related to the countries' prewar experiences.

Similarly, government tax policy cannot really explain the differences among these three countries. As Table 8-1 shows, corporate

Table 8-1 Comparison of Government Policies in CSFR, Hungary, and Poland at the End of 1991

	CSFR	Hungary	Poland
1. General Indicators			
Population	16 million	10 million	38 million
Labor Force (urban)	7 million	4 million	12 million
Numbers of Private Firms			
• Incorporated	5,000	50,000	40,000
• Unincorporated	1.1 million	400,000–500,000	1.5 million
Sectors of Private Activity (% of registered entrepreneurs in a sector)			
• Industry	2–28%	NA	26%
• Trade	17%	NA	38%
Equal Legal Treatment	Yes	Yes	Yes
Macroeconomic Situation			
• Substantial Convertibility	Yes	Yes	Yes
• Black-Market Premium	5%	5%	No
• Liberal Trade	Mostly	Mostly	Mostly
• Shortages	No	No	No
2. Taxes			
Tax Rates (%)			
• Corporate Income	20–55%	40%	40%
• Private Income	15% to $1,000, 55% top rate	4% to $1,000, 50% top rate	20% to $1,000, 80% top rate
Social Security Tax	8.7%	43%	45%
Wage Tax (per employee)	50%	—	20%
Excess Wage Tax	Yes; 200–750% (not if small)	No (Yes for SOEs)	No (Yes for SOEs)

	Col 1	Col 2	Col 3
Tax Advantages for Private Sector			
• Accelerated Depreciation	Yes (recent)	Yes	Yes (restricted)
• Carry-forward Losses	Yes (recent)	No	No
• Tax Credits	No	Yes	No
Tariffs	0–40% (usually)	Various	15% (many exceptions)
Capital Needed for Limited Liability	$1,000	$15,000	$3,000
Tax Advantages for Joint Ventures	Yes	Yes	Yes
Minimum Capital Required for Joint Ventures	($50,000) (Valued in dollars)	50 million forints ($650,000)	100,000 Crowns ($3,300)
3. Credit Situation			
Dominant state banks?	Yes	Yes	Yes
Preferential Interest Rates?	No	No	No
Nominal Interest Rates in 1991	40–70%	20–50%	20%
Inflation 1991	60%	35%	50%
Private Share of Total Credit	<21%	25%	<5%
Private Housing (% Share of Total)	40%	NA	45%
4. Privatization Progress			
Large Companies	Very Slow	Slow	Beginning
Percent Privatized at End of 1991	<10%	10% (fully) 25% (corporatized)	A few (foreign deals)
Shops and Restaurants Privatized (% of total numbers)	60–80%	10%	10%
Restitution			
• Laws Passed	No	Yes	Yes
• Politics Settled	No	No	Yes
• Claims Settled	No	No	No

Source: Johnson 1994a. © 1994. National Bureau of Economic Research. Reprinted with permission by University of Chicago Press.

Note: NA denotes not available.

income tax rates in all three were remarkably similar in 1991. A comparison of the rates of taxation on individual entrepreneurs— based on calculations of the tax rate that an individual must pay at various levels of income, converted into dollars—suggests that tax rates are highest at all income levels in Poland, lowest for low incomes in Hungary, and lowest for mid-range incomes ($3,000–$5,000) in CSFR. These estimates do not reflect other tax legislation, such as accelerated depreciation and the ability to deduct business expenses from taxable income. As documented elsewhere, at this time it was easiest to reduce taxable income in Poland and hardest in CSFR (Johnson 1994a). Nevertheless, registered entrepreneurs in Poland have prospered not because of favorable tax rates but despite very high rates.

In terms of credit conditions as measured by nominal and real rates of interest, it appears CSFR had an advantage in the form of low real interest rates during the first half of 1990, but in 1991 its real rates were very high. Unfortunately, it was not possible to obtain information about the extent of credit rationing to private firms, and this may be more important than the posted lending rate. Hungary may have had the best combination at this time—nominal interest rates roughly in line with inflation and an established pattern of lending by some state banks to private firms. The continued instability of real and nominal zloty interest rates in Poland should probably be considered a major disadvantage.

In light of these comparisons of conditions after liberalization, the explanation of differences among Poland, Hungary, and the CSFR appears to lie more with economic developments before the communists lost power in each country. Indeed, the history of economic reforms during the last ten or twenty years continues to shape the fortunes of the private sectors in these countries. At first this seems strange, because their communist regimes for the most part succeeded in imposing very similar economic structures in all three countries.[6] However, the communist economic reforms of the 1980s established—probably inadvertently—the basis for sustained Polish private sector development. Reforms conducted at the same time in Hungary had similar—probably more intentional—effects, but the forms taken by the private sector in Poland and Hungary were rather different.

In Poland there was much more liberalization of travel and informal importing. There was also, from the beginning of 1988, a much worse macroeconomic situation, in which the government lost control over the inflation rate. Permissive legislation was introduced at the same time as there were enormous discrepancies between prices inside and outside Poland. Under these conditions, individuals made money and gained experience. Corporate forms were sometimes convenient but were never essential to private sector development. Because the Hungarian economy remained more tightly controlled, similar "hothouse" conditions were never created, and private sector development was more even paced.

This helps explain why the unincorporated private sector is relatively stronger in Poland, whereas the private corporate sector is more developed in Hungary. Individual enterprise is stimulated more by the availability of foreign travel and small-scale import opportunities. The relatively stable macroeconomic environment of Hungary meant that more capital was needed to start a private firm, and this required the use of a corporate form. Moreover, as our survey research shows, Polish entrepreneurs live and grow on internally generated capital, partly because the capital market is not well developed. The capital market is better developed in Hungary and permits larger-scale private enterprise.

The private sector has done well in Hungary in part because there was a steady liberalization of the private sector over a long period. The Polish private sector has also done well, primarily because it was able to grow in the midst of an unstable macro economy. In CSFR, primarily because there was no meaningful economic reform during the communist period, new start-up private firms were less important in the early stages of reform.

Starting Over Across Countries

All post-communist countries face the same problem. The organization of work that was appropriate under the communist economic system is no longer sensible or functional. In every part of the economy, the organization of work needs to be fundamentally transformed.

The transformation of work is the essential counterpart to other economic changes, which are more commonly emphasized. Post-communist economies certainly do need the rapid development of trade and services, together with smaller-scale manufacturing. New, higher quality products must be introduced in all sectors. Firms have to compete with imports and learn how to export to other countries.

But all of these changes imply and require a complete transformation of how work is organized.

The combination varies between countries. With only a few exceptions, large-scale privatization and restructuring efforts have been disappointing almost everywhere. In Eastern Europe, Poland, Hungary, Romania, and Bulgaria have had to rely more on private sector development ("starting over"). The Czech Republic, and to a lesser extent Slovakia, have succeeded in implementing so-called mass privatization programs and will probably experience more state enterprise restructuring than countries that have privatized less.

Within the former Soviet Union, only Russia has succeeded in privatizing a large share of state industry. All other countries will experience microeconomic transformation only if new private firms are successful. Realistically, even Russia needs to have substantial new private sector growth if it is to transform its service and trade sectors and if it is to stimulate competition, and hence restructuring, in the manufacturing sector.

Of course, starting over and state enterprise restructuring are complementary rather than mutually exclusive. Given the experience of the past five years, a reforming government should attempt privatization if at all feasible. Privatized firms have more difficulty securing government subsidies, which helps consolidate effective corporate control and should lead to more effective state enterprise restructuring. Successful cases like Prochnik will, we contend, be relatively rare, but where they exist the revitalized enterprises contribute to the growth of new private businesses by serving as customers, distributors, and sources of equipment and technology. It is too early to be certain, but we believe that in five to ten years starting over will have emerged as the primary mechanism for microeconomic transformation, even in countries that had a large degree of privatization. It is simply much more difficult to change existing organizational structures than to develop new ones.

How then can a country promote more starting over? The answer lies in the Polish experience. Stabilizing the economy and liberalizing all aspects of internal and external trade is the most effective way of stimulating the creation of new private business. Poland had the advantage that many people had already entered the private sector prior to 1990. But even where that is not the case, the best policy to promote starting over is to create a stable, liberal environment in which entrepreneurs are willing to invest. Polish economic performance demonstrates that starting over by itself can generate rapid growth, even if there is not much privatization.

Policy Implications

Up to this point we have concentrated on the detailed microeconomics of what happened within the state and private sectors in Poland and the challenges facing entrepreneurs and enterprise managers. These developments are interesting not only in themselves but because of what they imply about overall policy. The argument presented so far has five steps.

First, the reorganization of work is a fundamental part of the post-communist transformation and is found in almost every aspect of economic life in Poland. If an enterprise does not reorganize substantially, then most likely it is not changing, and its problems will mount. A large firm that inherits a favorable market position may survive for some time, but the likelihood of decline and eventual collapse increases.

Second, starting over in the private sector is easier and quicker than restructuring state enterprises. Private firms can rapidly find an alignment between the right product strategy and a supportive internal structure—including marketing and sales, the organization of work, human resources, and decision-making processes. The private sector adapts quickly to changing economic conditions. State enterprises can change, but, because of their inherited organizational baggage, very outdated capital, limited resources and the rigors of competition, successful restructuring is difficult and requires a good deal of time. Restructuring state enterprises is so difficult because it requires the simultaneous change of almost all characteristics of a firm. The available evidence suggest that managers often fail to understand what needs to be done. But even if there is a clear strategy, implementation may fail for any number of reasons, especially a lack of support from managers and employees. Hannon and Freeman (1989) argue that there is compelling evidence that even in the United States new firms are continuously emerging and growing and replacing large, mature firms that decline and die because they are unable to meet changing circumstances. Thus the challenges facing large state enterprises in post-communist countries may be a much more severe manifestation of a general set of problems affecting large, mature firms elsewhere.

Third, the private sector develops despite difficulties, and many individual firms struggle or do not survive. Relative prices may vary considerably, particularly in the aftermath of price liberalization. Competition, partly from imports but increasingly from domestic firms, rises inexorably. Highly profitable sectors quickly attract new entrants.

Lack of professional management and adequate training is apparent in many of the mistakes made in the private sector, particularly mistakes concerning the control of accounts receivable and cash flow. There is a tendency to hold on to yesterday's growth strategy for too long. Being overly diversified is a problem because it can stretch the scarcest resource—managerial ability—too thin and lead to insufficient development of product quality, economies of scale, and marketing and sales proficiency for each line of business.

Fourth, many private sector firms have been constrained by their limited ability to bring in external financing at reasonable cost. Interest rates have remained high in nominal terms, and bank credit is viewed as expensive by the entrepreneurs. Of equal importance, however, is the fact that these firms lack collateral and for the most part do not have meaningful track records. Under these circumstances, it is unreasonable to expect private sector firms to quickly obtain access to external financing.

Fifth, the evidence shows that many private sector firms have business strategies that succeed domestically, internationally, and over many years when implemented competently. The key is to identify and focus on a market or a particular niche and to respond quickly and efficiently as the market changes. In other words, the essential requirements for business success are largely the same as in any Western economy. The differences, such as they are, are due primarily to the particular way in which the Polish macroeconomy has changed over the past five years.

The argument and evidence that we present in this book have important implications for reform policy in all post-communist countries. The problems facing these countries have many commonalities with those facing Polish policymakers. Hence, our interpretation of the Polish experiences provides a unique perspective on the Balcerowicz Plan and on the efficacy of similar policies for other post-communist countries. In the remainder of this section we analyze the Balcerowicz Plan and some of the criticisms commonly directed against it, and we offer suggestions for enhancement based on the microeconomic process of starting over.

Trade Policy

The Balcerowicz Plan involved a great deal of trade liberalization, through reducing effective tariffs and making the zloty almost completely convertible, and has been criticized by policymakers, analysts, and practitioners for opening the Polish economy too much. In our opinion, however, these external trade measures were essential for the positive development of private sector businesses.

Moving Poland close to world prices for most tradable goods removed a great many distortions and made it possible to trade sensibly. The import of Western consumer goods had an immediate and positive effect on many consumers' welfare. Furthermore, the import of capital equipment or raw materials was the necessary prerequisite of exports—recall, for example, the case of SeCeS-Pol or Styl France. The evidence shows clearly that foreigners frequently played an important role as catalysts in the reorganization of work, and as such were significant far beyond the scope of their direct capital investment. These foreigners usually transferred know-how, particularly management skills.

Did competition from imports unduly damage parts of the private sector? It is certainly true that an increase in imports can drive out private as well as state producers. Unfortunately, this effect seems unavoidable. But the failure of some private firms does not mean the economic reform process is flawed. Under the circumstances, rapid trade liberalization was undoubtedly the right policy because it created opportunities for the most effective private firms to avail themselves of international markets. Export performance will increase rapidly as private sector managers accumulate relevant experience and as the banking system improves its ability to finance trade.

Financial Sector Reform

The Polish banking system has not yet played a major role in private sector development. The monobank was broken up at the beginning of 1989 and was divided into nine commercial banks, each having a regional basis. There were also six specialist banks—for example, one for food processing and another for the financing of foreign trade. At least fifty private banks were created from 1989 to 1991, but they have remained very small, and perhaps a third of them have not yet raised enough capital to become viable.

In 1990 the state banks were extremely inefficient in their transfer of money, particularly in and out of Poland. Simple transactions
could take several weeks or even months. Many private importers
who relied on a rapid turnover of goods devised ways to send large
sums of cash out of the country. Initial regulation of banking activities
was also unsatisfactory. This was most evident in the ART-B scandal
of summer 1991, which resulted in the dismissal of the president of
the National Bank of Poland and the arrest of the senior vice president.[7] Since 1990, however, banks have been regulated more effectively, particularly under the supervision of a new department created
in the Ministry of Finance. Competition between banks for business
has also resulted in faster money transfer. The combination of regulation and the ending of subsidies to banks has forced the financial
system to improve.

In December 1990, state banks were responsible for at least 97
percent of all credits. Since then, this proportion has declined steadily, most notably with the privatization of two large former state
banks, Bank Slaski and Wielkopolski Bank Kredytowy. Under pressure from the Ministry of Finance and newly appointed corporate
boards, state banks' balance sheets have been cleaned up and their
lending practices made more transparent. State banks have gradually
reduced the proportion of their loans going to state enterprises. Credits for private firms and individuals were 17 percent of total bank
credits on March 31, 1991, and 21 percent on September 30, 1991.
Nevertheless, as our survey evidence showed, the growth of most
private sector firms is based primarily on their retained earnings.
Does this suggest that banking reform should have been handled differently? Our view is that although banking reform could have been
handled better, the major constraints on the development of credits
for the private sector are macroeconomic policy and the lack of sufficient collateral and credit histories to support lending.

In post-communist countries, the financial system cannot be re-
oriented quickly to serve the private sector. In particular, the information necessary to lend properly to private sector firms is not available
at the start of the reform process. Obtaining reliable information
about private firms is very hard, in part because there is almost no
supporting infrastructure in the form of firms that collect and process
information about financial risks. Moreover, existing information is
not meaningful because it does not provide a reliable indicator of
creditworthiness. Past track records and current repayments are not
good predictors of future ability to repay because market conditions

are still too unsettled. For these reasons it is unreasonable to consider the initial lack of credit for the private sector as a problem that can be easily fixed.

Polish experience suggests that banks become more private sector oriented quite rapidly, particularly as the problems in the state sector become apparent. Our work suggests that in the two to three years following the introduction of the Balcerowicz Plan, the most important constraint on private sector borrowing was nominal interest rates that remained too high. Unfortunately, faced with an inflation rate that has remained stubbornly high, the government has had to maintain quite high nominal interest rates. The benchmark National Bank of Poland refinance rate peaked at 432 percent per year in January 1990 and then fell steadily to 34 percent in June 1990. However, it rose again from October 1990 to February 1991, reaching 72 percent per year. By October 1991 it was down to 40 percent, about the level it has stayed, with only a slow, small decrease through 1994. Loan rates were usually about one-fifth higher than the refinance rate.

Calculating real interest rates when both nominal rates and inflation are high is difficult, but the following general conclusions are possible. Very high inflation meant negative real interest rates at the beginning of 1990, at the same time as nominal rates were shockingly high. In June 1990, monthly inflation was down to 3.4 percent (equivalent to 49 percent per year). Monthly inflation remained in the 2 to 6 percent range during 1990–1992 (annualized rates of 27 to 100 percent), which means that the real interest rate moved from being positive to negative from month to month.

There is also a problem with the availability of collateral. In Poland, as in most post-communist countries, there is a significant amount of unmortgaged private property. The private sector owns more than three-fourths of housing in the countryside, and over one-fourth in towns. It is possible to borrow against the security of a private apartment, but banks require that no one other than the owner is registered as living there. This form of credit is easier to obtain in the countryside, but it still requires a lot of administrative work, and the property must be properly evaluated. Poland is still waiting for legal changes that would allow an individual to sign away his or her protection from eviction, and earlier enactment of such changes would have facilitated the development of mortgage credit.

In sum, credit market institutions were understandably reluctant to support young private firms. More rapid restructuring of bank portfolios and bank privatization would probably have had a positive effect. What is likely, however, is that the amount of credit going to the private sector would have remained limited by high nominal interest rates. Effective intermediation for the private sector requires both more efficient banks and lower inflation.

Public Finance

Polish private sector growth was not the result of particularly favorable government tax policies. In fact, Polish tax policies have been very similar to those of other post-communist countries, such as the former Czechoslovakia, in which the private sector has been weaker. In Poland, private firms face the same turnover and social security taxes as state firms. During 1990–1991, spolki faced a corporate income tax of 40 percent, although the effective tax rate might have been much lower.[8] State firms also paid 40 percent corporate income tax, but they were liable for two important taxes from which the private sector was exempt. First, there was the excess wage tax, which penalized firms paying wages above a norm set by the government. In 1990, there were bitter complaints from the private sector when it was subject to the same excess wage tax as the state sector. Private firms were fully exempted from this tax only in 1991, but anecdotal evidence suggests they found ways to avoid it even in 1990. Second, state enterprises paid to the government a "dividend" based on the value of their fixed assets. The desire to reduce this effective tax is often an incentive to privatize—as we saw in the case of Prochnik, presented in Chapter 3.

Individuals operating as a business had to pay not only income tax but also a leveling tax. In 1991 an entrepreneur was liable for this second tax if his or her annual income exceeded 36 million zloty ($3,000). The Polish tax rates in 1991 were quite high, relative to both CSFR and Hungary and in absolute terms (Johnson 1994a). In addition, an entrepreneur had to pay a 20 percent wage tax and a social insurance contribution that was at least 238,000 zloty ($20) per month.[9]

In the second half of 1990, a one-year tax holiday was available to individuals in wholesale trade. Whether it increased the total number of firms is unknown, but there is strong anecdotal evidence that it induced the re-registration of already existing firms. Some individual firms created in September and October 1990 were able to avoid paying customs duty because of a complicated legal situation. As a result, advertisements like this one appeared in newspapers: "I have a company opened in September 1990, and I am looking for proposals."

Significant tax changes during 1991 included allowing losses from one year to be included in costs for up to three years. There was also an increase in amortization allowances. More important, it remained possible to include almost all investment as a cost of production, as long as it could be bought in units costing less than 1 million zloty (about $100). So, for example, if a business person wanted to buy a new set of office furniture, it was best to buy each chair separately. For this reason, leasing is currently a popular method of obtaining capital equipment.

The tax system could certainly have been made more favorable to the private sector. In particular, more tax breaks for investment could have encouraged growth and also prevented the hiding of investment as current spending. However, our overall assessment is that the tax system in 1990–1991 was just sufficiently lenient to allow private firms to develop. For example, the communists used tax inspectors to intimidate private businesses in the 1980s, and this practice was virtually discontinued after 1989. The tax system did not encourage but also did not prevent private sector growth.

Privatization

Privatization is obviously far from complete. We have argued that given the challenges facing state enterprises, requiring a total restructuring of the way work is organized, privatization neither guarantees nor is sufficient for competitive viability in the long run. But if privatization occurs efficiently and offers managers incentives to undertake massive change, then it can certainly help. Prochnik is an excellent case in support of this point. The comparison of the Szczecin and Gdansk shipyards (see Chapter 4) demonstrates that the most challenging issues involve management and leadership rather than ownership.

In our view privatization along the lines we have emphasized, which brings the state sector into line with the private sector in terms of strategy formulation and organizational and human resources practices, is essential. A great deal can be accomplished without it, but not enough.

Small privatization definitely helped to put physical capital in the hands of private business. By the end of 1990, private firms oper-

ated 65 percent of all shops but only 27 percent of total retail space—
some large cooperative and state stores remained. However, after the
first six months of 1991, 75 percent of shops, accounting for 80 percent of retail sales, were privately run. The total number of private
shops in mid-1991 was 456,000, up from 346,300 a year before.

Furthermore, following successes in selling off shops and restaurants, steps were taken to promote a separate track for the privatization of "small" industrial assets. The most important part of this
process was privatization by "liquidation." By December 1991 at least
875 firms had undergone this process, which usually means they end
up being owned by their employees. The employees have to provide
20 percent of the firm as a down payment and can buy the rest of
the firm from the state in installments. These firms, however, are
relatively small, and privatized firms so far probably account for no
more than 10 percent of the total assets of state firms.

The privatization of retail space has proceeded much more
smoothly. Under the communist regime, many shops were in principle privately owned but in practice were controlled by a state agency
of some kind. Early in 1990 private owners were able to regain this
property. In addition, after May 1990, newly elected noncommunist
municipalities had the right to dispose of shops that had been state
owned. Most of these municipalities were short of money, so they
moved quickly to auction off the movable property of shops, along
with fairly short-term leases for the building (usually the leases run
for a few years). This process seems to have gone quite smoothly,
although there have been complaints that municipal authorities raise
rents repeatedly even when doing so is not allowed by the lease.

In sum, the privatization policies pursued for large enterprises
did not contribute much to private sector development. There was
some spinoff of assets from the state sector, through the sale or lease
of equipment and premises, but there could have been much more.
In contrast, the privatization of smaller assets, both shops and firms,
proceeded much more smoothly and may be judged a success in terms
of helping private sector development.

The Legacy of Balcerowicz's Plan
for Economic Reform

Our analysis suggests that Leszek Balcerowicz's plan has had profound, positive effects on the Polish economy, even though by the

end of 1991 many key aspects of the plan seemed no longer to be in place: the effectively fixed exchange rate had been abandoned, the excess wage tax rules had been relaxed, and policymakers accepted the continuation of inflation as high as 50 percent per year. Despite such revisions, the Balcerowicz Plan remains very influential and intact in at least three forms: as a long list of irreversible achievements, as a set of priorities, and as a way of making economic policy.

The plan's major achievement was to destroy the final remnants of the old economic system. Shortages were eliminated, foreign trade was liberalized, the currency was made almost completely convertible, most retail trade was privatized, output prices were freed, and the cost of energy was raised to world levels. These were the prerequisites of a market economy. The last two communist governments took some steps in this direction, but it was Balcerowicz who struck the decisive blow. It is extremely unlikely that these policies can be undone, and they therefore will remain the basis for the development of a genuine market economy.

Balcerowicz's main macroeconomic priority was to bring inflation down to a low, West European level. This goal has not yet been achieved, but controlling inflation remained part of Polish government policy even after Balcerowicz's resignation in December 1991. Changes in supporting policies, such as those affecting the exchange rate, have signalled a weakening of the anti-inflation policies but not their complete abandonment. The main priority for microeconomic policy also remains to privatize most state industry, although the policies pursued have not yet been successful.

Balcerowicz's most influential legacy is the high professional standards that governed the preparation of his policies and the high level of support they received throughout the West, especially but not only from multilateral financial institutions. A new young technocratic elite emerged to occupy key positions, particularly in the Ministry of Finance and the Ministry of Privatization. Any successor to Balcerowicz who presents a policy in a way that does not match his high standards will face considerable criticism in the government, the national parliament, and the broader political debates of Poland.

Because of the Balcerowicz Plan, we can identify several constraints on the choices of subsequent governments. First, the policies of Balcerowicz irrevocably opened Poland to the West. To close the Polish economy again is unthinkable, and although some parties have proposed this idea, they have no real political credibility.

Second, although some social groups perceive the reform negatively, these groups do not agree on the requirements for an alternative set of policies. Furthermore, a significant number of people have directly benefited from the reforms. So even if there were a coherent alternative set of policies, it is far from clear that it would have strong support either in the country or in parliament.

Third, the executive remains weak. Under the configuration of parties in 1991–1993, the executive never had the ability to control the legislative process and timetable.[10] Deputies who identified weaknesses in the government's legislation could use their discovery to embarrass the government and obstruct its proposals almost without limit. As a result, the Bielecki government found it hard to speed up the reform process by introducing mass privatization or constitutional reform, but the Olszewski government found it difficult to loosen macroeconomic policy. Furthermore, on some economic issues Olszewski's team had to rely on the support of the Liberal Democratic Congress (KL-D) and the Democratic Union (UD), which were not part of the government coalition and were able to lobby in favor of tight monetary and fiscal policies.

Fourth and perhaps most important, a sustained phase of private business development has begun. Without the Balcerowicz reforms, this development either would not have taken place or would have happened much more slowly. As we indicated in Part II, private business has already transformed the functioning of a large part of the Polish economy. If the basic macroeconomic policies of the government remain unchanged, and even without substantial privatization, the private sector will rapidly grow to dominate and determine the course of the Polish economy.

Implications for Macroeconomic Policy

In Chapter 1 we posed a central question about the appropriateness of the Balcerowicz Plan. Was this set of policies suitable for controlling inflation but unsuitable for stimulating restructuring and private sector development? In other words, was the plan in any sense bad microeconomics? Our answer is that the plan was very good microeconomics. Its positive effects at the microeconomic level of the Polish economy are apparent from studying both state enterprise restructuring experiences and private sector development. To change the way both state and private enterprises operated, it was necessary to change macroeconomic conditions in an irreversible way. Gradual measures were tried in 1988 and 1989, and although they allowed easier entry into the private sector, a continuation of these policies would not have permitted sustainable development. Structures constructed during a period of very high inflation are unlikely to last, because they are established on the basis of the wrong relative prices and an unsustainable system of subsidies.

In a way, however, Balcerowicz and his colleagues were lucky that the communists tried gradual reform and created a "hothouse" that stimulated private sector development. But we must emphasize that the benefits of this policy were felt only *because* Balcerowicz then stabilized the economy. It was the stabilization and liberalization of the Polish economy that allowed the private sector to take off.

In terms of the microeconomic effects of macroeconomic policy after 1990, our evidence implies that the problem in Poland was not too much stabilization but rather too little. The reduction of inflation to 10 percent a year, instead of to 50 percent, would have made a fundamental difference in the availability of affordable credit to the private sector. Greater availability of cheap bank finance would have had and still could have a significant positive effect on private sector development.

For political reasons the Polish government backed off from its ambitious stabilization plans and did not fully follow through on the auspicious start of 1989–1990. Some commentators emphasized that although the pilot—Leszek Balcerowicz—was dropped, the course remained completely unchanged. This observation proved not entirely correct. There was a softening of the policies and a failure to reach the initial low-inflation goal.

A major problem was fallacious reasoning based on an incorrect analogy with the West. For example, in the United States it is widely believed, particularly by those in the Federal Reserve System and the financial markets, that toughening anti-inflation policy results in a contraction of the economy and, conversely, that if the Fed lets up against inflation, most usually through lowering interest rates, economic growth is likely to accelerate, at least in the short term.[11] Our evidence, however, suggests that not only does this mechanism *not* apply to Poland, but the converse was true, at least in the early 1990s.

In our view, a more vigorous anti-inflation policy from the second half of 1990 would have produced more rapid economic recovery. Moderately high inflation, between 30 and 50 percent per year, implies that nominal interest rates have to be kept at about the same high levels, in order to have real rates that are positive or close to positive. Positive real interest rates are required in order to rebuild the financial system and to eliminate the system of haphazard subsidies through the credit system. Lower inflation would have reduced interest rates and made external finance cheaper for private firms. In our assessment, cheaper loans would have had a significant positive effect on output and employment in the private sector.

A counterargument is that lower interest rates would have increased only the amount of capital going to the state sector. However, in the Polish operating environment, as we have seen, banks began to avoid lending to state firms when it became apparent that state firms would not be able to repay. There is no reason to believe the same assessment would not have been made at lower interest rates.

Furthermore, inflation means either continued currency depreciation or a real appreciation and a consequent loss of competitiveness. In the first case the inflation spiral continues, and in the second case the development of a sustainable export basis is undermined. Poland was probably hurt in both respects: there was a real overvaluation by early 1991, and the subsequent versions of a crawling peg (under which the exchange rate changes by small amounts at regular intervals) have helped build in inflation inertia.

Our analysis therefore suggests an unusual assessment of the Balcerowicz Plan and the macroeconomic policies that followed. In light of their effects of the microeconomy, our assessment is that the tough initial policies should have been sustained. Bringing inflation below 10 percent per year—one of Balcerowicz's original goals— would most likely have had significant positive effects on private sector development. Balcerowicz's macroeconomic policies were essential to restructuring and private sector growth, but the positive microeconomic effects would have been greater if his initial very tough anti-inflation policies had been continued.

Regional Development

Our assessment of Polish private sector development to date is rather positive, and we are optimistic about the future of these businesses. But an important caveat is in order. The process that we have described has taken place primarily in large cities. Small towns and rural areas have not benefited from private sector growth to anywhere near the same degree.

A major problem concerning the private sector is that its growth is uneven. New businesses have grown much more in big cities than elsewhere. What may be needed to spread the benefits or cushion the blows associated with economic reform is not a different macroeconomic policy but a well-targeted regional policy. Simply giving money to deprived areas is likely far from adequate or even sensible. Instead, local entities, including local governments, working with international lending agencies, need to facilitate the development of some competitive advantages in each region. Such advantages could be based on existing skills and firms or could develop around new foreign investment. But these policies need to be strategic—that is, they need to position a region of Poland firmly in the world economy. In these places it may be costly to wait for the market; thus, some explicit support for institutional development may be appropriate.

The market has worked wonders in places where private sector growth proved self-reinforcing and a virtuous circle of development has been established. But Poland is too fragmented, particularly because of the lack of labor mobility, for these benefits to reach everyone. Tough macro policies and market-led growth are leading Poland to overall prosperity, but some government intervention—preferably by local people aware of how to position themselves in the world market—is necessary to spread the benefits of growth.

Conclusion

Why has the Polish private sector done relatively well in its unusual, unincorporated form? In our opinion, the answer lies in the way the Polish economy was reformed. The Polish private sector is the product of a particular sequence of events, primarily due to changing government policy.

The Polish Private Sector

The relaxation of controls over the private sector came earlier in Poland than in other communist countries in Eastern Europe, with the exception of Hungary. The new wave of spolki creation in Poland did not really begin until 1988, but since the mid-1980s there had been gradual liberalization of private economic activity. For example, new cooperatives that were essentially private firms were created

(Johnson and Loveman 1992). There was a rapid growth in individual international trade by Poles. The Polish government did not impose any restrictions on people's travel, unless they were considered to be opponents of the regime. (Foreign travel was much harder for Hungarians and citizens of Czechoslovakia.) It was quite common for young Poles to work in Western Europe for a few months a year. Well-educated people, for example, often worked as manual laborers at harvest time in France or Sweden. These experiences matter, because it was in these small ways that Poles learned about private business, acquired modest amounts of capital, and made connections with the outside world.

Most important, it was possible to earn very high rates of return on some imports. The best example is computers. People could begin by buying computer equipment by mail order from abroad at a cost of a few hundred or thousand dollars and sell this equipment to state firms at prices that yielded a return of several hundred percent. Then, by reinvesting in other computer-related imports, they could accumulate—within a few years—hundreds of thousands of dollars. There was a rapid accumulation of capital, both financial and human, which was unique to Poland.

The communists also tried to rebuild some legitimacy by widening the scope of private sector activity. In particular, the last communist government—headed by Mieczyslaw Rakowski—passed legislation that by early 1989 had essentially removed all legal and most administrative barriers on the private sector. These changes, however, brought little in terms of visible benefits while the communists retained power. Their macroeconomic policy was very unsuccessful and caused rapid inflation despite partial price controls.[12] The result was terrible shortages and grossly distorted prices, a situation that worsened the supply problems of the private sector. Circumventing import controls helped private businesspeople to make money on semilegal trade, but the same controls constrained the speed with which this trade could develop.

We have explored the details of the political transformation and the construction of the economic reform of 1990 at length elsewhere (Johnson and Kowalska 1994), and the main results are clear. Almost overnight there was an end to shortages, and the zloty became convertible at a stable exchange rate.[13] It became possible to import freely, and private traders moved rapidly to do so.

Two points are important. The first is that the Balcerowicz Plan did not have to change much in terms of the legal treatment of the private sector. The most important steps had already been taken. Second, the stabilization of the economy and rapid liberalization of foreign trade had a major stimulative effect on the private sector. Not all of the private sector was favorably affected, and many firms that had prospered under the previous price system found themselves unable to survive at world prices. It is also true that the first quarter of 1990 showed only limited private sector growth. But this growth soon became apparent—the total net balance of individual firm creation improved every quarter in 1990.

The Nature of Economic Reform

Our empirical work in Poland over the past four years leads to six conclusions that individually and collectively add to what is known about the process of economic reform in post-communist economies and enhance our understanding of management practice under the turbulent conditions of reform.

First, management skill and leadership matter a great deal in post-communist countries. If state enterprises are to be restructured and private enterprises are to grow, managers have to redefine their business strategies and design their internal organizations appropriately, and they have to build support for such changes among crucial stakeholders. Post-communist countries need professional managers who understand, for example, the management of cash flow, who can adapt to changing market behavior, who can create effective marketing and sales operations, and who can provide leadership to their firms.

Our research suggests that managerial effectiveness is strongly affected by certain kinds of experience. In our opinion, working in the private sector is the best possible training for either restructuring a large state firm or running a new start-up. An implication, then, for government policy is the need not only to privatize state firms but also to bring in new top management, preferably with private sector experience. It is clearly important to create outside shareholders who are willing to put pressure on management for market-oriented strategies, provide sensible incentives, and hold management accountable for financial performance.

So far there has been a net flow of managers from the state to the private sector. Poland may finally be ready to implement a mass privatization program and should strongly consider mechanisms for attracting managerial talent, developed in private businesses, back into the state sector. Top managers in privatized enterprises can be offered generous compensation, contingent on performance, and should be replaced if their performance is ineffective.

Second, the incentives faced by managers are very important, but getting the incentives right is not enough. Managers remaining in the state sector have to seek fundamental reorganization of work within their enterprises. This reorganization will occur only if the old incentives, to lobby and feather their own nests at the expense of enterprise performance, disappear.

Incentives alone are not enough because managers also need to have strategic vision, leadership capabilities, and a wide range of management skills. The key policy issue is, again, where the necessary human capital comes from and how to encourage its formation. The Polish "hothouse" conditions of the late 1980s stimulated managerial development but could have led too far in the wrong direction. The Balcerowicz Plan was a masterstroke because, among its other achievements, it released the accumulated managerial ability to work freely at world prices and in a sustainable trade regime. This is the basis for lasting growth.

Third, faster or more complete restructuring does not lead to fewer jobs. Destruction is a crucial part of economic reform because of the need for a far-reaching reorganization of work at the enterprise and industry levels. Successful state enterprise restructuring, as the comparison of the Szczecin and Gdansk shipyards shows, *saves* jobs that otherwise would be lost and raises wages that otherwise would be lower. New private business development is the primary source of job growth, because it serves as the principal mechanism for reallocating labor and capital from state to private sector.

Fourth, not everyone benefits from the restructuring process. Some people lose their jobs and are not able to find other work. Some people become stuck in low-wage, low-skill jobs that will either disappear or for which the real compensation will fall. Private sector growth has tended to favor young, better-educated, and more highly skilled people in urban areas. It is an illusion to think that everyone benefits simultaneously.

Government needs to reach out to people *and regions* that are hard hit. Subsidies are not enough. Local governments should have the vision and resources necessary to encourage foreign investors who can build an export-oriented local economy. There is a need to retrain people and even to help domestic businesses move to low-wage, depressed areas. Investments in transport infrastructure should be made with this goal in mind.

In almost every country in Eastern Europe and the former Soviet Union there has been a political swing back to the left. People become dissatisfied and disillusioned. Even those who benefit from reform may not realize that they are benefiting or may not organize themselves to support the reform policies. The notable exception is the Czech Republic, where Prime Minister Vaclav Klaus has worked hard to explain how policies benefit people overall. In part this is a profound problem of communications and setting of expectations, but a privatization scheme that puts ownership of property in the hands of many people can only be helpful. Furthermore, even a modest social safety net that encourages mobility and transition but reduces hardship is well worth the cost.

Fifth, it is essential to get the macroeconomic policies right from the start. The Balcerowicz Plan contained the necessary elements for macroeconomic policy across a wide range of conditions, although for countries starting with lower inflation it is obviously not necessary to have such drastic initial anti-inflation policies. Under the circumstances of mid-1989, and considering the lack of experience with post-communist economic transformation, the Balcerowicz Plan was incredibly effective. If the Plan had not stabilized the macroeconomy, made the currency convertible, and opened the country to trade, private sector growth would not have been so rapid, pervasive, and sustainable.

Poland also began the Balcerowicz Plan with broad political support for reform. But even in Poland political support crumbled rapidly and much faster than anyone anticipated. In this context, the advantage of making an irreversible breakthrough is obvious. The breakthrough forces managers in state enterprises to come to grips with their problems and allows the private sector to grow. The Balcerowicz Plan achieved that breakthrough. Once the breakthrough was made, no one could credibly propose a return to the old system. The pace of further growth, however, still depends on policy. Inflation needs to be under 10 percent, and only if that rate is reached will the financial system really begin to work. Likewise, the economy should be opened as much as possible, because imports are needed to develop exports. Foreigners play key strategic roles in restructuring and transferring management skills, which may be much more important than the amount of their investment.

Sixth, the nature of restructuring and private sector growth has important implications for foreign firms making investments or otherwise becoming involved in post-communist countries. Good managers are available in post-communist countries, but they are often not at the top of existing state enterprises. Although there is an urgent need for additional training among entrepreneurs and private sector managers, these people can certainly play important roles in making joint ventures and foreign direct investment more successful.

In sum, the Polish experience demonstrates remarkable progress in one of the most difficult socioeconomic and managerial tasks undertaken in this century. Vibrant enterprises are emerging that will help Poland achieve its espoused goal of attaining a standard of living consistent with its Western European neighbors. As other post-communist countries watch Poland with great interest, they would be well served to see a process that succeeded, perhaps unconsciously, by starting over.

Notes

Chapter 2

1. For greater detail see Kornai (1992).
2. Lipton and Sachs (1990) discuss this issue both theoretically and for the particular conditions of Poland during this period.
3. The functioning of the credit system under communism is reviewed by Johnson, Kroll, and Horton (1993).
4. Polish agriculture was the only sector in which private activity remained important in the whole of communist Eastern Europe. However, state trading agencies always tightly controlled the flow of products to and from this sector. For this and other reasons, Polish agriculture has not prospered during the reforms of the 1990s. Its particular problems and current situation are beyond the scope of this book.
5. In this section we draw on the more detailed analysis of Johnson and Kowalska (1994).
6. There was some slippage in the second half of 1990, when Poland exceeded IMF requirements only for net foreign exchange reserves. Poland's hard currency reserves more than doubled during 1990, from $3.6 billion U.S. (end 1989) to $8 billion (December 31, 1990). Despite all the setbacks in 1991, reserves were still $6.4 billion on November 30, 1991. The enormous improvement in Poland's current account is an unmistakable success of the stabilization program.
7. Lipton and Sachs (1990) discuss these measurement problems at length.
8. See Goodman and Loveman (1991).
9. Workers' councils were introduced during the 1981 reforms but had little influence until the 1989 liberalization.

Chapter 3

1. Although shipbuilding, at first blush, may not seem to be a very attractive industry on world markets, recall that the communist countries had

specialized in heavy industries, few of which would seem appealing in the long term.

2. Of course, the political history of the Gdansk Shipyard cannot be divorced from its economic circumstances at the outset of reform, and we do not intend to argue that the differences between Gdansk and Szczecin are immaterial. Instead, we argue that the problems faced by the management of the two shipyards are sufficiently similar to provide an enlightening comparison.

3. "Cut-make-trim" refers to the process of manufacturing garments on a contract basis for other companies that typically supply the design and the materials and then sell the finished product under their own name.

4. The 12 percent margin applies to exports sewn with fabrics supplied by Prochnik. Cut-make-trim exports were much more profitable.

Chapter 4

1. The desire to minimize imports also led planners to prefer a comprehensive product mix.

2. The excess wage tax—the *popiwek*—placed a heavy tax on the total wage bill in excess of an agreed-on level. The tax, intended to restrict wage increases and reduce overall inflation, did not make allowances for changes in the number of employees.

3. Although the role of government subsidization is hotly contested, many shipbuilding companies, especially in Japan and Korea, have reported profitable operations in recent years.

4. European Community member countries subsidize their shipbuilding industries, and in 1993 the German government announced substantial subsidies for former East German shipyards.

5. In light of the poor condition of the Polish government budget, it was quite unlikely that resources would be available for subsidies even if a convincing case could be made to support them.

6. According to shipyard officials, the unions supported the changes in compensation because most of their members received more under the new system than they were earning previously.

7. Of the forty-three orders that the Szczecin Shipyard had on its books in 1990, these four were the only ones that were profitable.

8. Many of the seven hundred jobs were affiliated with the workers' hotels and other amenities that Piotrowski eliminated when he took over shipyard management. Since few production jobs were affected, and the unions recognized the need for cost control if the shipyard was to become a viable competitor, there was little organized resistance to the job cuts.

9. Banks were also more willing to provide guarantees for working capital

as a result of the shipyard's debt-restructuring agreement. The agreement significantly reduced the threat that the yard would use working capital to pay off creditors rather than to build ships.

10. In calculating cgt per worker, we adjusted the deadweight tonnage of each ship manufactured during a given year by a factor that reflected the number of labor hours required to produce the ship. The "corrected" deadweights were added together, and this sum was divided by the total number of shipyard employees.

Chapter 5

1. If anything, the inclusion of Lodz, which has the highest unemployment rate of any large Polish city, would tend to bias us toward more negative findings. Certainly there is a marked contrast between Krakow and Lodz on some important measures of private sector performance.

2. Unless otherwise indicated, all quotations in Chapters 5 through 8 are drawn from the case with the name of the firm, in Loveman, Johnson, and Kotchen (1994).

3. The information on ages and experience is from three of our samples, with a total of 545 observations. We did not ask these questions in the Warsaw and Monki surveys. Breaking down this information by the other three samples gives the same results on ages; for the three samples, the mean ages were 39.6, 40.2, and 41.4.

4. The pattern was similar across sectors. The highest average was in the production sector (almost 43 years old); the lowest was in modern services (37 years old) and retail and transport (both 39 years old). In general, sectoral information is given here only when sectors diverge significantly or in an interesting way from the overall population numbers.

5. Work experience was calculated as age minus the number of years a person spent in education, which was assumed to be 14 if the person's highest educational level was elementary school, 19 if the person completed some form of secondary education, and 23 if the person completed higher education.

6. This level of experience in the private sector appears to be confirmed by answers to this question, asked in our second Krakow survey, "How much experience do the people in key positions in your company have?" Only 12 percent answered "none"; 19 percent replied either one or two years. Seventy-eight percent said their people had three or more years' experience, and 56 percent indicated over five years' experience.

7. The same declining pattern of responses over time is evident if we look at when people left the state sector rather than when they founded their firm. Interestingly, the highest response rate for founding the firm as a

family tradition is among people who never worked in the state sector—24.4 percent fit this category.

8. Interestingly, the pattern of responses is slightly different if we look at when people left the state sector. There is a much lower positive answer to this question among people who left since 1988—33.3 percent for people in the 1988-to-1989 group and 14.2 percent for people in the 1990-and-after group.

9. A person in a high-level position was the head of a state organization or was in the management level immediately below the top, as the senior manager responsible for production, sales, or economics. This definition was explained to interviewees.

10. Just over 10 percent (89 firms) refused to answer this question. Like the answers to other financial questions, the answers to this question are most likely biased downward, but we expect less bias here than in questions about firms' current financial situation.

11. Valuation for that period is difficult because there was repressed inflation. However, almost all entrepreneurs remember how much they had, valued at the black-market exchange rate.

12. We tried the number of places as well as dummies for more than one place and more than two places. In no case did we find a significant coefficient.

13. We used two dummy variables: one for at least one previous private sector job and the other for at least two previous private sector jobs. The dummies are both significant in the employment regression when included separately. When both are included together, they become insignificant at the 5 percent level but remain separately significant at the 10 percent level, with no change of sign. Not surprisingly, an F-test rejects the null hypothesis that the two dummies are jointly insignificant at the 5 percent level.

14. For more detail on the rules and regulations related to cooperatives, see "The Gdansk Cooperative" in Loveman, Johnson, and Kotchen (1994).

15. For a full series of sales and profit numbers, see "The Gdansk Cooperative" in Loveman, Johnson, and Kotchen (1994).

16. For the details, see "The Gdansk Cooperative" in Loveman, Johnson, and Kotchen (1994). As the company's political activists departed, they withdrew their memberships in the cooperative in order to avoid possible conflicts of interest.

17. For a description of the companies founded by members and financed by the cooperative, see "The Gdansk Cooperative" in Loveman, Johnson, and Kotchen (1994).

18. However, they do not appear to pay higher average wages, and they are more likely to pay low wages to their lowest-paid employees.

19. Note, however, that under the peculiar legal situation in Poland, a person who worked for a cooperative of the form of the Gdansk Cooperative

or Doradca would be strictly correct in saying he or she did *not* work for a private firm. We therefore should treat the numbers from our large samples as lower bounds.

Chapter 6

1. A good translation of the Commercial Code is available: "The Polish Commercial Code. The law as at 15th August 1991," translated by Roman Poplawski and published by the Polish Bar Foundation, Warsaw, 1991.

2. A few spolki existed under the communists, but they had been created before the communists took power, and they were subject to state control.

3. A suspended firm does not have to pay taxes and can be quickly reestablished. In our interviews, entrepreneurs sometimes said that they currently operate one firm but have several more "sleeping." Some sleeping firms can be viewed as a form of tradeable option. For example, in 1991 we were offered the opportunity to buy a sleeping firm that was exempt from taxation because it had been properly registered as a wholesale trader before the end of 1990.

4. De jure, one principal advantage of spolki is that they have limited liability. However, interviews with entrepreneurs suggest that in practice individuals do not face unlimited liability.

5. In 1990–1991, a *spolka z.o.o.* (limited liability company) could be formed in a few weeks, but forming a *spolka akcyjne* (joint stock company) took significantly longer.

6. The actual requirement was that the business had to be new at the address where it was registered. Not surprisingly, there is anecdotal evidence of businesses simply changing their addresses and people active in other sectors—especially retail trade—switching to be registered as wholesale traders.

7. In the trade sector, private sector employment as a percentage of total employment was 72.7 percent in 1989 and reached 90.7 percent in 1992 (Coricelli, Hagemejer, and Rybinski 1993).

8. Most start-up companies fail in any country. Although the evidence is not sufficient to enable us to prove this, our strong impression is that the failure rate in Poland is low relative to that in countries with more established market systems.

9. Many of the workers are skilled; 47 percent of interviewees stated that over half of their employees have had some form of vocational training. Consistent with that finding is the fact that 65 percent of interviewees said that more than half of their employees were skilled. Fifty-nine percent of interviewees said that less than 10 percent of their employees were unskilled.

10. The positive employment effects of the trade boom should not be exaggerated. Table 6 in Coricelli, Hagemejer and Rybinski (1993) shows a fall from 10.0 to 9.7 percent in the share of trade and a fall from 6.3 to 5.4 percent in the share of transport in total employment from 1989 to 1992. At the same time, total employment fell from 17.6 to 15.6 million. Part of the reason for this seemingly strange result is that the private sector already constituted 72.7 percent of total jobs in trade by the end of 1989 (Table 1a, ibid.), if cooperatives are included in the definition of the private sector.

11. Further technical details about heat exchangers are provided in "SeCeS-Pol" in Loveman, Johnson, and Kotchen (1994).

12. For further details on the products developed, see "Profilm" in Loveman, Johnson, and Kotchen (1994).

Chapter 7

1. There is the definite possibility of a simultaneity bias: having a larger firm could plausibly increase the probability that a firm is able to obtain credit. Interestingly, in a profit regression with having obtained credit on the left-hand side, we find the level of current employment in the firm to be negative and significant—that is, the opposite effect to what we expected.

2. For a description of Sopot Bank's commercial activities and 1991 financial results, see "Sopot Bank" in Loveman, Johnson, and Kotchen (1994).

Chapter 8

1. This section draws heavily on Johnson (1994).

2. For a more detailed analysis of spontaneous privatization in the former Soviet Union, see Johnson and Kroll (1991); Johnson, Kroll, and Eder (1994); Johnson and Ustenko (1994). Private sector development is considered by Webster and Charap (1993). Privatization experiences are reviewed by Boycko, Shleifer, and Vishny (1993) and Johnson and Kroll (1994). The emergence of new private banks is treated by Johnson, Kroll, and Horton (1993).

3. There is not a great deal of literature on the private sector in Eastern Europe. An excellent comprehensive survey of the private sector in East Germany and Poland up to the early 1980s is provided by Åslund (1985). Seleny (1991) reviews the development of private business in Hungary, with particular emphasis on the 1980s. A number of papers have been written recently on the general situation of the private sector and the policies needed to stimulate its development, but most of these

papers are rather general and do not contain much concrete detail. Important exceptions include an excellent review of the problems in the Czech and Slovak Federated Republic (CSFR) by Rondinelli (1991) and an interesting survey by Brandsma (1991). Rostowski (1993) is also very useful. Åslund (1992) and Sachs (1993) place privatization and private sector development in its proper macro context. There are also some useful overview papers on the recent development of small business in CSFR (McDermott and Mejstrik 1992; Capek 1990), Hungary (Hare and Grosfeld 1991; Galasi and Sziraczki 1990), Bulgaria (Jones 1993), and Poland (Piasecki 1991; Grabowski 1991; Grabowski and Kulawczuk 1991a; Wyznikiewicz, Pinto, and Grabowski 1993). A recent survey in Poland is reported in Kondratowicz and Maciejewski (1994).

4. Brandsma (1991) estimated that in 1991 the private sector's contribution to GDP was 8.9 percent in Bulgaria, 3.5 percent in former East Germany, 2.5 percent in Romania, and 2.5 percent in the former Soviet Union.

5. Although the small business sector in Western Europe is not directly comparable to Eastern Europe's private sector, we should note that it contributes between 32 percent (in the United Kingdom) and 46 percent (in Germany) to GNP.

6. It is true that agriculture was never successfully collectivized in Poland, but we have not seen evidence that private agriculture was the basis for rapid growth in the urban Polish private sector. In fact, private farmers have been among the most vociferous opponents of the economic program that began in 1990. See Johnson and Kowalska (1994).

7. ART-B might be the only private firm that has benefited from the inefficiency of the Polish banking system. ART-B shifted money rapidly between banks in order to earn interest at several banks simultaneously—this mechanism is referred to in Polish as an *oscylator*. ART-B was also able to obtain a large amount in bank loans that were not properly secured. The owners of this company subsequently escaped the country.

8. Polish entrepreneurs have found numerous ways to reduce their tax liability. One favored route is to have several companies that employ each other as subcontractors and thus reduce their declared profit.

9. For example, a person earning 36 million zloty (about $3000) was exempt from the leveling tax but paid 20 percent income tax and at least 8 percent (2,856,000 zloty, about $260) in annual social insurance contribution, for an effective tax rate of around 28 percent on private entrepreneurs.

10. A notable exception was the package of laws passed in December 1989, which constituted the legal basis of the Balcerowicz Plan. In this case, the legislative process followed a special fast track organized under a special commission of the parliament. This temporary arrangement was possible only with the agreement of all major groups in parliament.

11. This traditional view of U.S. monetary policy has lately come under scrutiny by those who argue that expansionary monetary policy is quickly reflected in higher long-term interest rates, which have contractionary short-term consequences.

12. For a model and detailed explanation of the acceleration of Polish inflation, see Johnson (1991).

13. Strictly speaking, the zloty became convertible for legal persons only on current account. To obtain foreign currency, they had to present a valid invoice from a foreign exporter. However, the zloty was fully convertible for private persons at legal, private exchange offices (*kantors*).

References

Åslund, Anders. 1992. *Post-communist economic revolutions: How big a bang?* Washington, D.C.: Center for Strategic and International Studies.

Åslund, Anders. 1985. *Private enterprise in Eastern Europe.* New York: St. Martin's Press.

Belka, Marek, Stefan Krajewski, and Brian Pinto. 1993. Transforming state enterprises in Poland: Evidence on adjustment by manufacturing firms. In *Brookings Papers on Economic Activity.* Washington, D.C.: The Brookings Institution.

Berg, Andrew. 1993. Radical transformation of a socialist economy–Poland, 1989–1991. Ph.D. diss., Massachusetts Institute of Technology.

Berg, Andrew, and Olivier Jean Blanchard. 1994. "Stabilization and transition: Poland, 1990–91." In *The transition in Eastern Europe.* Vol. 1, *Country studies.* Edited by Olivier Jean Blanchard, Kenneth A. Froot, and Jeffrey D. Sachs. Chicago: University of Chicago Press.

Berg, Andrew, and Jeffrey Sachs. 1992. Structural adjustment and international trade in Eastern Europe: The case of Poland. *Economic Policy* 7, no. 14 (April):117–173.

Blanchard, Olivier, Rudiger Dornbusch, Paul Krugman, Richard Layard, and Lawrence Summers. 1991. *Reform in Eastern Europe.* Cambridge, Mass.: MIT Press.

Blanchard, Olivier, Maxim Boycko, Marek Dabrowski, Rudiger Dornbusch, Richard Layard, and Andrei Shleifer. 1993. *Post-communist reform: Pain and progress.* Cambridge, Mass.: MIT Press.

Bobinski, Christopher. 1992. Restructuring hope for Szczecin yard. *Financial Times* (June 30):15.

Boycko, Maxim, Andrei Shleifer, and Robert W. Vishny. 1993. "Privatizing Russia." In *Brookings Papers on Economic Activity (Macroeconomics):* 139–192. Washington, D.C.: The Brookings Institution.

Brandsma, Judith. 1991. Entrepreneurial development in Czechoslovakia.

245

Paper prepared for the OECD conference on Training for Entrepreneurship, October 10, in Prague.

Capek, Ales. 1990. Small firms in Czechoslovak economy. Institute of Economics, Czechoslovak Academy of Sciences, Prague. Mimeographed.

Carlin, Wendy, John Van Reenen, and Toby Wolfe. 1994. Enterprise restructuring in the transition: An analytical survey of the case study evidence from central and eastern Europe. European Bank for Reconstruction and Development. Working paper no. 14, July.

Chandler, Alfred. 1962. *Strategy and structure: Chapters in the history of the industrial enterprise.* Cambridge, Mass.: MIT Press.

Charap, Joshua. 1992. Entrepreneurship and SMEs in the EBRD's countries of operation. The European Bank for Reconstruction and Development, London. Mimeographed.

Clark, John, and Aaron Wildavsky. 1990. *The moral collapse of communism: Poland as a cautionary tale.* Institute for Contemporary Studies, San Francisco.

Coricelli, Fabrizio, Krzystof Hagemejer, and Krzystof Rybinski. 1993. Poland. Paper prepared for the World Bank Conference on Unemployment, Restructuring and the Labor Market in East Europe and Russia. October 7 and 8, in Washington, D.C.

Dabrowski, Janusz M., Michel Federowicz, and Anthony Levitas. 1991. Przedsiebiorstwa panstwowe w roku 1990—Wyniki badan. (State enterprises in 1990). Tranformacja Gospodarki 11. Institute for Market Economics, Warsaw.

Estrin, Saul, Mark Schaffer, and Inderjit Singh. 1992. Enterprise adjustment in transition economies: Czechoslovakia, Hungary, and Poland. No. EE-RPS 8:2–19. Research paper series, Enterprise Behavior and Economic Reform: A Comparative Study in Central and Eastern Europe and Industrial Reform and Productivity in Chinese Enterprises. Research Projects of the World Bank. Washington, D.C.

Galasi, Peter, and Gyorgy Sziraczki. 1990. Small enterprises and business work partnerships in Hungary. The International Institute for Labor Studies. Discussion Paper 29. Geneva.

Goodman, John, and Gary Loveman. 1991. Does privatization serve the public interest? *Harvard Business Review* (November/December): 26–38.

Grabowski, Maciej H. 1991. Entrepreneurship and the development of small and medium-size enterprises in Poland. Gdansk Institute for Market Economics, September.

Grabowski, Maciej H., and Przemyslaw Kulawczuk. 1991a. Small firms in the last decade and now. *Economic Transformation* 17. Gdansk Institute for Market Economics, July.

Grabowski, Maciej H., and Przemyslaw Kulawczuk. 1991b. Financial study of the private firms in the Gdansk region. *Economic Transformation* 17. Gdansk Institute for Market Economics, July.

Hannon, Michael T., and John Freeman. 1989. *Organizational Ecology*. Cambridge, Mass.: Harvard University Press.

Hare, Paul, and Irena Grosfeld. 1991. Privatization in Hungary, Poland, and Czechoslovakia. Centre for Economic Policy Research. Discussion Paper Series, No. 544.

Johnson, Simon. 1991. Did Socialism fail in Poland? *Comparative Economic Studies* 33, no. 3:127–151.

Johnson, Simon. 1994a. "Private business in Eastern Europe." In *The transition in Eastern Europe*. Vol. 2, *Restructuring*. Edited by Olivier Jean Blanchard, Kenneth A. Froot, and Jeffrey D. Sachs. Chicago: The University of Chicago Press.

Johnson, Simon. 1994b. Employment and unemployment after communism. Prepared for a Hoover Institution book on economic reform in Eastern Europe and the former Soviet Union, edited by Edward Lazear.

Johnson, Simon, and Bakhtior Islamov. 1991. Property rights and economic reform in Uzbekistan. In WIDER Working Papers, 90. Helsinki, Finland.

Johnson, Simon, and Marzena Kowalska. 1994. Poland: The political economy of shock therapy. In *Voting for reform*. Edited by Stephan Haggard, and Steven B. Webb, New York: Oxford University Press.

Johnson, Simon, and Heidi Kroll. 1991. Managerial strategies for spontaneous privatization. *Soviet Economy* 7(4):281–316.

Johnson, Simon, and Heidi Kroll. 1994. Complementarities, managers and mass privatization programs after communism. Revised version of a paper presented at the American Economic Association meeting, Boston.

Johnson, Simon, and Gary Loveman. 1993. The implications of the Polish economic reform for small business: Evidence from Gdansk. In *Small Firms and Entrepreneurship: An East-West Perspective*. Edited by Zoltan Acs and David Audretsch. New York: Cambridge University Press.

Johnson, Simon, and Oleg Ustenko. 1994. Corporate control of enterprises before privatization: The effects of spontaneous privatization. In *Overcoming the Transformation Crisis: Lessons from Eastern Europe*. Edited by Horst Siebert. Germany: Kiel Institute of World Economics.

Johnson, Simon, Heidi Kroll, and Santiago Eder. 1994. Strategy, structure and spontaneous privatization in Russia and Ukraine. In *Changing Political Economies: Privatization in Post-Communist and Reforming Communist States*. Edited by Vedat Milor. Boulder & London: Lynne Rienner Publishers.

Johnson, Simon, Heidi Kroll, and Mark Horton. 1993. New commercial banks in the former Soviet Union. How do they operate? In *Changing the Economic System in Russia*. Edited by Anders Aslund and Richard Layard. London: Pinter Publishers.

Jones, Derek C. 1993. The nature and performance of small firms in Bulgaria. Working Paper no. 93/12. Department of Economics, Hamilton College, New York.

Kondratowicz, Andrzej, and Wojciech Maciejewski. 1994. *Small and medium private enterprises in Poland*. San Francisco: Adam Smith Research Center, Warsaw and International Center for Economic Growth.

Kornai, Janos. 1990. *The road to a free economy*. New York: W.W. Norton & Co.

Kornai, Janos. 1992. *The socialist system: The political economy of communism*. Princeton, N.J.: Princeton University Press.

Lipton, David, and Jeffrey Sachs. 1990. Creating a market economy in Eastern Europe: The case of Poland. *Brookings Papers on Economic Activity* 1:75–147. Washington, D.C.: The Brookings Institution.

Loveman, Gary W., Simon Johnson, and David T. Kotchen. 1994. *Managing business enterprises after communism*. Boston: Harvard Business School Press.

McDermott, Gerald A., and Michal Mejstrik. 1992. The role of small firms in the industrial development and transformation of Czechoslovakia. *Small Business Economics* 4:51–72.

McDonald, K.R. 1993. Why privatization is not enough. *Harvard Business Review* (May):49–59.

McMillan, John, and Barry Naughton. 1992. How to reform a planned economy: Lessons from China. *Oxford Review of Economic Policy* 8, no. 1:130–143.

Milgrom, Paul, and John Roberts. 1990. The economics of modern manufacturing: Technology, strategy and organization. *The American Economic Review* 80 (June):511–528.

Milgrom, Paul, and John Roberts. 1992. *Economics, organization and management*. Englewood Cliffs, New Jersey: Prentice Hall.

Piasecki, Bogdan. 1991. The creation of small business in Poland as a great step towards a market economy. *Economic Transformation* 17. Gdansk Institute for Market Economics, July.

Rondinelli, Dennis A. 1991. Developing private enterprise in the Czech and Slovak Federal Republic: The challenge of economic reform. *The Columbia Journal of World Business* (fall):27–36.

Rostowski, Jacek. 1993. The implications of rapid private sector growth in Poland. School of Slavonic and East European Studies, University of London. Mimeograph.

Rutland, Peter. 1992. The small privatization process. Wesleyan University, Middletown, Connecticut.

Sachs, Jeffrey. 1993. *Poland's jump to the market economy*. Cambridge, Mass.: MIT Press.

Schaffer, Mark. 1993. The enterprise sector and emergence of the Polish fiscal crisis, 1990–91. Policy Research Department, World Bank, WPS 1195 (September).

Seleny, Anna. 1991. Hidden enterprise, property rights reform and political transformation in Hungary. Program on Central and Eastern Europe Working Paper Series 11, June, Harvard University.

Stark, David. 1989. Coexisting organizational forms in Hungary's emerging mixed economy. In *Remaking the Economic Institutions of Socialism: China and Eastern Europe*. Edited by Victor Nee and David Stark. Stanford: Stanford University Press.

Stark, David. 1990. Privatization in Hungary: From plan to market or from plan to clan? *East European Politics and Societies* 4(3):351–392.

Szelenyi, Ivan. 1988. *Socialist entrepreneurs: Embourgeoisement in rural Hungary*. Madison: University of Wisconsin Press.

Webster, Leila. 1992. Private sector manufacturing in Poland: A survey of firms. Industry and Energy Department Working Paper. Industry Series Paper No. 66. World Bank. December.

Webster, Leila. 1993. The emergence of private sector manufacturing in Hungary: A survey of firms. World Bank Technical Paper Number 229.

Webster, Leila, and Dan Swanson. 1993. The emergence of private sector manufacturing in the former Czech and Slovak Federal Republic: A survey of firms. World Bank Technical Paper Number 230.

Webster, Leila, and Joshua Charap. 1993. A survey of private manufacturers in St. Petersburg. Private Sector Development Working Paper, World Bank. May.

Whitlock, Eric. 1990. Notes on privatization in Hungarian industry. Durham, North Carolina: Duke University.

Wyznikiewicz, Bohdan, Brian Pinto, and Maciej Grabowski. 1993. Coping with capitalism: The new Polish entrepreneurs. Discussion paper 18. International Finance Corporation.

Index

251

About the Authors

SIMON JOHNSON is an assistant professor of economics at the Fuqua School of Business, Duke University. He is also director of the Fuqua Center for Manager Development in St. Petersburg, where he manages all aspects of establishing and operating executive education courses for managers from the former Soviet Union. Dr. Johnson's research focuses on post-communist countries, and he has worked extensively in Poland, Russia, and Ukraine over the past five years. His field studies have included an investigation of managerial strategies and changing property rights in Ukraine, an examination of small business networks in Gdansk, Poland, and an analysis of financial market development in Russia. His published work includes articles on banking, spontaneous privatization, and macroeconomic policy. His consulting clients include the United States Department of State, The World Bank, the National Bank of Poland, the Ukrainian government and the Human Development Report of the United Nations Development Programme. Dr. Johnson received a Ph.D. in economics from MIT.

GARY LOVEMAN is an associate professor of business administration at the Harvard Business School. Current research interests include the globalization of labor markets, with a focus on how global service firms provide high-quality service to customers in widely disparate environments. Dr. Loveman has contributed four articles to the *Harvard Business Review*, is the co-editor with Werner Sengenberger of *The Reemergence of Small Enterprises: Industrial Restructuring in Industrialised Countries*, and has developed case studies on a number of service organizations. His consulting clients include American Airlines, Coopers & Lybrand, the Walt Disney Company, and McDonalds. Dr. Loveman received a Ph.D. in economics from MIT.

Simon Johnson and Gary Loveman, along with David T. Kotchen, are authors of a casebook, "Managing Business Enterprises After Communism," which includes seventeen cases for classroom use, some of which are discussed in this book. The casebook and accompanying instructor's guide were published by Harvard Business School Publishing in 1994.